Elvis & Ginger

Most Berkley Books are available at special quantity discounts for bulk purchases for sales promotions, premiums, fund-raising, or educational use. Special books, or book excerpts, can also be created to fit specific needs. For details, write: Special.Markets@us.penguingroup.com.

ELVIS & Ginger

GINGER ALDEN

BERKLEY BOOKS, NEW YORK

THE BERKLEY PUBLISHING GROUP
Published by the Penguin Group
Penguin Group (USA) LLC
375 Hudson Street, New York, New York 10014

USA • Canada • UK • Ireland • Australia • New Zealand • India • South Africa • China

penguin.com

A Penguin Random House Company

This book is an original publication of The Berkley Publishing Group.

Copyright © 2014 by Ginger Alden.
Penguin supports copyright. Copyright fuels creativity, encourages diverse voices, promotes free speech, and creates a vibrant culture. Thank you for buying an authorized edition of this book and for complying with copyright laws by not reproducing, scanning, or distributing any part of it in any form without permission. You are supporting writers and allowing Penguin to continue to publish books for every reader.

BERKLEY® is a registered trademark of Penguin Group (USA) LLC.
The "B" design is a trademark of Penguin Group (USA) LLC.

Library of Congress Cataloging-in-Publication Data

Alden, Ginger.
Elvis and Ginger / Ginger Alden. — First edition.
pages cm
ISBN 978-0-425-26633-5 (hardcover)
1. Presley, Elvis, 1935–1977. 2. Alden, Ginger. 3. Rock musicians—United States—Biography. 4. Actresses—United States—Biography. I. Title.
ML420.P96A64 2014
782.42166092—dc23
[B]
2014009089

FIRST EDITION: September 2014

PRINTED IN THE UNITED STATES OF AMERICA

10 9 8 7 6 5 4

Cover photo courtesy of David Spencer.
Cover design by Jason Gill.
Interior text design by Kristin del Rosario.

The events in this memoir are real events, as experienced and remembered by the author. Most conversations are exact words and a few have been reconstructed from the author's memory and presented in a manner that conveys their spirit and intent, as recalled by the author.

---

*Penguin is committed to publishing works of quality and integrity.
In that spirit, we are proud to offer this book to our readers;
however, the story, the experiences, and the words
are the author's alone.*

To Elvis, for sharing a part of your remarkable life with me and my family. Your love, music, generosity, and many beautiful memories hold a special place in our hearts forever.

To my parents, Jo and Walter, and my siblings, Mike, Rosemary, and Terry, for always being there. To my husband, Ron, and my son, Hunter, whose patience, love, understanding, and support I could not have done this without. I love you all . . .

ACKNOWLEDGMENTS

Thank you to my agent, Frank Weimann, for his initial letter to me, understanding that the true story of Elvis and my relationship had yet to be told. My deepest gratitude to everyone at the Berkley Publishing Group for all of their assistance in bringing my memories to life. A special thank-you to Leslie Gelbman, publisher, and to my editor, Denise Silvestro, for her patience, guidance, and expertise throughout this long, emotional journey. I appreciate all the help from editorial assistant Allison Janice, and a big thank-you to Holly Robinson for our talks and her help in doctoring what needed to be said at various times. To the copy editor, Candace B. Levy, and the book-design department, thank you. To the publicity department, especially Heather Connor and Diana Franco, my sincere thanks.

To Peggy, Teri, Rachael, Jeanine, Cindy, and Louise, your friendships I hold dear, and thank you for your encouragement, support, and always lending an ear over the past years. I love you all . . .

My deep gratitude to my cousin David Spencer, Russ Howe, Shantay Wood, Bob Klein, Keith Alverson, and Ronnie Bell for the use of their photos and for assisting me with others. My deep appreciation to Elvis's fans for your encouragement and support, and thank you for your unending love for Elvis.

"When love beckons to you, follow him,
Though his ways are hard and steep."

"You give but little when you give of your possessions. It is when you give of yourself that you truly give."

—KAHLIL GIBRAN, *THE PROPHET*

AUTHOR'S NOTE

One September afternoon in 2001, I was standing on the side porch of my home in New York. The school year had just begun and I was waiting for the yellow bus that usually came roaring up our street at this time to bring my son, Hunter, home.

When the bus arrived at the end of our driveway, the doors swung open and Hunter jumped out, racing toward me wearing a pair of oversize sunglasses he had taken with him earlier that morning. "Some of the kids on the bus were calling me Elvis!" he exclaimed breathlessly. "Who's Elvis?"

I was surprised that children as young as mine would know who Elvis was. Hunter's question caught me off guard. I wasn't prepared to reveal an extremely special relationship in my life to my son, whose birth seven years earlier had been scheduled for August 16, the same day Elvis died. Hunter arrived four days late, sparing me the irony of having such a happy event coincide with the date of such a tragic event in my life.

That afternoon, I told Hunter the simplest truth. "Elvis was a very famous entertainer," I said. I breathed a sigh of relief when he ran inside, seemingly satisfied with my response.

As the year progressed, however, Hunter occasionally asked me more questions about Elvis: "What kind of hairstyle did he wear?" "What kind of music did he sing?"

I knew these questions had to be prompted by conversations at school. Still, I kept my answers short and simple, knowing one day I'd have to say more.

By the end of that school year, I had decided to tell Hunter a little about Elvis and me. I didn't know quite how to begin. It felt strange to talk with him about a man I'd loved long before meeting his father.

Not knowing what my son's reaction would be, I was a little nervous and felt an involuntary tremble. I hadn't talked about Elvis in a long time. "This person you've been asking about, Elvis, well, Mommy knew him," I said and then paused. I wasn't feeling comfortable enough to tell him that Elvis and I had been engaged, so I simply added, "Elvis was a very nice man I met long ago. He was someone who loved to sing and make people happy."

I waited for any questions, but he just said, "Cool!" and as he went off to play, I began to feel that all of my apprehension about opening up this conversation with him was unnecessary. For him it was simple. For me, it was profoundly complex.

I had written down my memories of Elvis not long after he passed away as a way of holding on to them. I felt I had to grant a few interviews at various times, but I always kept the true, complete story and intimate details of our time together to myself. I went forward with my life, but over time, I was shocked and hurt to see that speculations, exaggerations, and complete untruths regarding Elvis, me, and our relationship were unjustly being told by a few people who had been around Elvis—people I'd barely gotten to know and some I hardly knew at all. Some of their stories were then picked up and spread by other writers for their own Elvis biographies. Many books have sensationalized and even fictionalized Elvis as being depressed and in a downward spiral during his last year of life. However, the Elvis that I knew was not the way he was portrayed in the media. He saw his relationship with me as a new beginning and was excited about both the relationship and what the future would bring for the two of us.

I knew I had a story to tell, but understood that the truth about my relationship with Elvis was one that would require a great deal of time and emotional energy to write.

When I gave birth to my son, I devoted my time to him, as he became my number one priority. I felt I couldn't be there for him as a mother if I chose to write such an intensely personal book. When my son went off to college, I felt the time was finally right, so I began putting together my memoirs. This proved to be an all-encompassing and extremely emotional journey.

Elvis allowed many people in and out of his life, all of whom he developed different relationships with as his needs and desires evolved over the years. I was the last serious love he would let into his heart. Our meeting was a wonderful accident that turned into a life-altering nine months as I got to know a very complicated, intense man. The reasons I fell in love with Elvis don't fit neatly into a tidy, easily categorized list; they were things I felt my heart was telling me: I wanted to marry Elvis and spend my life with him because I loved him for his good heart and generous, kind spirit.

This book is about the steep learning curve of a woman in love with—and loved by—a man who most of the world could experience only from afar. Elvis could be difficult at times, but for me, his goodness and loving spirit greatly outweighed any faults.

I experienced a great deal during my short but jam-packed months with Elvis, and our love story goes beyond any normal description.

Simply put, it's nearly impossible to understand what it's like to be pulled into the orbit of a man as powerfully charismatic as he was. Elvis had his own gravity, and his universe was unlike anything the average person is likely to experience or even come into brief contact with, other than a few select people in history lucky enough to be around supernova personalities or achievers who touch down on our planet from time to time.

When I first met Elvis, I was a young, impressionable woman who had just turned twenty. He was forty-one and wanted to teach me many things. One of the lessons he taught me that proved to be the most valuable during the painful months following his death was this: If something bothers you or if people are saying untrue things about you, "Kill it and get it behind you," Elvis advised me.

He was always quick to point out that it's far healthier to let things go than to dwell on them if they make you angry or unhappy. He would refer to some less annoying things as "pure Mickey Mouse shit," usually adding, "There's a bigger picture out there."

This was powerful advice, coming from a man whose sensitive nature would not always allow him to follow that wisdom. However, although I clung to his rule of "Kill it and get it behind you" as tightly as I could after his death, it would ultimately prove to be impossible for me to remain unscathed by the gossip, rumors, and lies after Elvis was gone.

Some people even dared to dismiss the last year of Elvis's life as a runaway train toward suicide. There is a well-known saying, "If you can't carve your place in history by virtue of your own talent, perhaps you can make it by assassination," and that was the path some people unfortunately chose to take in books and interviews after Elvis passed away.

This mistaken image of Elvis hurt me deeply, as I knew firsthand that his world, during our time together, continued to be mainly filled with love, sensitivity, brilliance, humor, and generosity. I'm not claiming to be an Elvis expert, but I got to know him intimately, in a way that few have.

Elvis, a multifaceted man, with his passion for music; thirst for knowledge; and deep love for family, friends, and fans, was not a depressed, run-down man. Far from it: Elvis was a man who was excited about life and enthusiastically making plans for the future as he endeavored to transform his dreams into a reality—a reality that included marrying me.

Elvis, you and I know the truth about our time together. Unfortunately, you're not here to set the record straight. With this book, I will try to do so. Better late than never.

PROLOGUE

Graceland, August 16, 1977

We all refused to give up hope.

It was after 3 p.m. on Tuesday, August 16, 1977. I was sitting inside Dodger Presley's bedroom at Graceland with members of Elvis's family, including Vernon, his father; Dodger, Vernon's mother; Elvis's daughter, Lisa; and my niece Amber, who had become friendly with Lisa. As the minutes ticked away, I felt my anxiety mounting and was finding it difficult to breathe.

We had been sitting vigil for what seemed like an eternity, silently praying for good news. The tension was unbearable. I suddenly felt like I had to leave the room, as if by doing so, my mind could escape to that precious time a short while ago before I'd made the shocking discovery in the upstairs bathroom.

Of course, I knew that was impossible. The imprint of what I had seen would be forever burned into my memory.

I slowly walked out of Dodger's bedroom door, wishing more than anything that I'd be greeted by Elvis walking downstairs toward me right then, laughing and telling everyone it was all a joke, even as I knew in my heart that this moment, as bad as it was, was very real. Pausing in the foyer, I noticed a few other people praying in the dining room and living room. I said my prayers again as well, feverishly in denial, still wanting to believe that the doctors at the hospital could save Elvis by some miracle, and that he would always be here by my side.

Elvis's aunt Nash saw me standing there. She approached me and gave me a hug. "Everything is going to be all right, Ginger," she said. "He has so much left to do."

I don't know whether it was the fact that she was a relative or an older woman who seemed wise, but I felt a comforting feeling wash over me. I wanted so badly to believe her.

Some of the dark fears haunting me slowly began to ease as I convinced myself that surely Aunt Nash had to be right. It was true! Elvis did have a lot left to do, and so many of his dreams would remain unfulfilled if he left us now!

I returned to Dodger's bedroom after a few minutes, feeling a little more hopeful than when I had left and continued to keep vigil with the others. Lisa was playing by the bed with Amber; as the two of them whispered together, everything seemed almost normal.

The phones throughout the house buzzed intermittently. Somewhere, someone answered them. Each time, with still no word from the hospital, I grew increasingly frightened.

Suddenly a movement in the doorway caught my attention. My breath caught in my throat as I saw Elvis's personal physician, Dr. George Nichopoulos, standing there.

My last flicker of hope faded as I watched Dr. Nichopoulos slowly enter the room, holding a large yellow envelope. Shaking his head at us, he walked over to Vernon and handed him the envelope. "I'm sorry," he said.

I felt like I'd stopped breathing altogether and felt light-headed, my pulse suddenly pounding in my ears. I stared at the envelope. I was unable to look at the doctor's face, much less Vernon's, as I realized that the envelope must contain the jewelry Elvis had been wearing when he was rushed away from Graceland by ambulance. One of those pieces would be a necklace Elvis had purchased while we were together, a gold chain with the Hebrew letter *chai* meaning *life* or *to live*.

I went completely numb, feeling as if not just Elvis but everything around Graceland and within me had died. I felt empty, hollowed out.

Everyone around me was devastated. We cried and hugged one another, searching for comfort in embraces and tears. It was impossible for any of us to grasp that Elvis, a man who seemed larger than life, could be gone from this world.

My head was pounding. I needed to walk a bit. I decided to leave the room, as I experienced an overwhelming need to know if the outside world was aware of what had happened, of what we were suffering.

I left Dodger's room and went to one of the windows in the front living room, where I peeked out through the side of a closed curtain. It immediately became clear that the news of Elvis's passing was spreading fast. Cars were slowing down as they drove past Graceland. Some vehicles had stopped completely, their passengers getting out and standing in the middle of Elvis Presley Boulevard. People had begun gathering by the front gates, too, and along Graceland's stone fence—a fence that had never really been able to separate Elvis from his loyal fans.

This day had begun with excitement and hope for Elvis and me, but ended in heartache and disbelief. At the age of forty-two, my fiancé, Elvis Aaron Presley, was dead. The world around me had crumbled and my heart was broken.

CHAPTER 1

Certain things in life are bound to make you wonder how much of your destiny is due to fate and how much is the product of chance. For my family, the U.S. Army was a catalyst.

In 1943, the world was at war and my father, Walter Alden, was drafted into the army. My mother, Jo Spencer, enlisted in the Women's Army Corps and they were both posted at Fort Stewart, Georgia. Two years after meeting at the base service station one fateful day, they married. Eleven months later, they had my brother, Mike, and five years later my sister Rosemary was born.

My dad decided on a career in the military, and in 1951 they settled in Memphis, Tennessee. Memphis was home to many great musical talents, but in the mid-1950s, Elvis Presley had begun to put our city on the map for millions around the world.

In 1955, the year my sister Terry was born, my family was living in an apartment building on Getwell Road. Unaware that Elvis lived about five blocks away, my brother was riding his bike on Stribling Street one day and recognized Elvis in a flatbed truck as he drove up beside him. Elvis smiled at Mike and slowly passed him. Mike followed him to Dunn Avenue until Elvis made a turn and he lost sight of him. My brother later told my parents, "He probably smiled at me because I was staring at him."

Like my brother, most Memphians felt a sense of pride that Elvis shared their home. I was born on November 13, 1956, at the naval hospital in Millington, Tennessee, and I would grow up feeling that pride even as a small child.

In 1957, my father, now ranked sergeant first class, was in public relations and recruiting for the army. He worked closely with the Memphis draft board, notifying and advising individuals that if they enlisted, they would be able to receive special opportunities. Earlier that year, the board had announced that Elvis would probably be drafted. Every branch of the military began making offers, trying to get him to enlist.

Hoping to speak with Elvis on the army's behalf, my dad made a trip to Graceland, Elvis's recently purchased home, only to be told that Elvis was away. Before my father could return to Graceland, he was informed that Elvis had decided not to enlist and would take his chances with the draft. At the end of the year, Elvis received his notice for induction into the U.S. Army.

On the morning of March 24, 1958, Elvis arrived with his parents, Gladys and Vernon, at the draft board office located inside the M&M Building in downtown Memphis. Elvis and the other recruits being drafted then boarded a bus for physicals at the U.S. Army and Air Force recruiting main station at Kennedy Veterans Hospital. Shortly after arriving, they entered a reception room and sat on chairs lined up in rows behind long tables.

In that room, soon-to-be Private Elvis Presley laid eyes on my father for the first time as my dad walked in and said a few words, giving the new recruits some insight as to what lay ahead. My father had finished speaking and was gathering his things to leave when Elvis approached him.

"Is there someplace inside this building where I could get change?" Elvis asked, explaining that he wanted to use one of the pay phones.

My father reached into his pocket and offered Elvis a dime. Elvis took it and thanked him. Elvis had his physical, and by that afternoon, he was sworn into the U.S. Army.

Due to Elvis's fame, the press covered the event. Photographers took pictures of him with my dad for the newspapers, and whenever I look at those clippings, it still hits me: Here is a young Elvis, and here is my dad. They were worlds apart, yet at that moment they were connected for the first time.

My father came home that evening with two publicity photos of Elvis, one signed, "To Mike," and the other, "To Rosemary." Before going to bed, he wrote inside my sister's small autograph book, "Today I shook the hand of Elvis Presley, March 24, 1958."

Elvis's mother had become ill, and that August, the army granted Elvis an emergency leave so he could return to Memphis to see her. His mother passed away on August 14, 1958, and he was granted an extended stay for her funeral. On March 7, 1960, after twenty-four months of active duty, Elvis returned to Memphis again, this time as a civilian, with four years left in the reserves.

A few nights later, my father decided to stop by Graceland after work, hoping for some follow-up public relations tidbits for an army newsletter. He parked his army sedan near Graceland's driveway and walked toward its closed gates, where some others were milling about. The gates had become a popular place for fans to hang out, chat, and catch a glimpse of Elvis.

My dad saw Elvis and a few others standing in the driveway, talking to a teenager with a bandaged hand. When Elvis noticed my father, still dressed in his army uniform, he yelled, "Let him in," to a guard near the gates.

My father learned that Elvis had assisted the teenager two nights earlier, when he'd been in a motorcycle accident near Graceland, and the teen had returned to thank him. My dad lucked out; he got to see Elvis and now had a story.

My father stopped by Graceland a few more times the following year along with a friend, a reporter for the *Memphis Press-Scimitar*, who was also looking for Elvis-related pieces. They became friendly with a guard at the gates named Travis Smith, who happened to be Elvis's uncle. One evening, Travis invited my dad to bring my mom and join Elvis at a local movie theater called the Memphian, where Elvis often treated others to movie showings—it was the only way he could watch a movie out of the public eye.

As Travis had requested, my parents drove to Graceland and waited in their car by the front gates. Before long, a few other cars emerged from around back of the mansion and, as they exited the driveway, my father eased in behind them and followed.

It was well after midnight when my parents arrived at the theater, its marquee dark, showing it was closed to the public. They saw Elvis and a few others already out of their cars and talking, so they approached them. Recognizing my dad, Elvis shook his hand and my father introduced my mother.

The group soon entered the lobby and Elvis walked over to the food counter while my parents and some other guests made their way inside to get seats. Before long, Elvis came walking down the aisle with popcorn in hand. Upon noticing my father again, he tossed out jokingly, "Hey, Sarge, I'm ready to go back into the army."

My dad replied, "We'll be glad to have you back."

Elvis screened two movies that night, and it wouldn't be until the wee hours of the morning when everyone left the theater.

Not long afterward, Travis invited my parents for a second outing, telling them Elvis was renting the Memphis Fairgrounds Amusement Park, and friends and guests were welcome to bring their children. Travis and his wife were going along this time, and he told my dad when and where to meet them after the park closed to the public.

I was five years old when I rode with my family to the fairgrounds that night. Although I was too young to remember much, that evening became a memorable experience for my entire family. My brother and one of his friends drove separately. A security guard let us into the entrance of the amusement park, where we waited alongside other invited guests.

Travis arrived and introduced his wife, Lorraine, to my parents. Before long, a black car slowly pulled up to the entrance and the security guard waved it inside. The car came to a stop and Elvis stepped out, dressed in a dark shirt with dark pants and wearing a white captain's hat. My most vivid memory is one of seeing Elvis shake hands with people and thinking he must be important, for his face looked just like the ones I'd seen on some record sleeves at home.

My parents greeted Elvis, and as my father introduced each one of us, Elvis shook hands with Mike and Rosemary, then patted Terry and me on our heads. When my mom mentioned that my brother was taking guitar lessons, Elvis joked, "I've got one at home he can have, because I can't play the thing."

Everyone laughed, and then the group continued inside, following Elvis to the park's large wooden roller coaster (a ride that would remain one of his favorites). Elvis climbed into the front car with his date, Bonnie Bunkley, and as the seats began to fill, Travis approached my mom. "Want to ride with me?" he asked.

Never having been on a roller coaster before, she told him yes, as long as he picked a safe and not-too-scary seat. They ended up sitting in the very last car, which unbeknownst to my mom was notorious for being rough.

My father and Lorraine Smith sat in the car in front of them, while my siblings and I stood by to watch. Screams of fright and laughter echoed from the ride as it raced by us multiple times before finally coming to a halt. When everyone got out, my mother, a little rattled but smiling, told Travis, "I think I might just have a heart attack right here."

Elvis continued through the park with his date and some friends while my parents took my sisters and me to the kiddie section. My brother and his friend decided to wander the park alone. A concession stand was open to all of us, and we got to enjoy the rides as many times as we wanted.

Our special night was over too soon. Catching up with Travis and Elvis, my parents thanked them for our amazing evening. Mike and his friend begged my parents to let them stay longer; they didn't return home until nearly sunrise. Later, still excited, Mike told my parents that Elvis and his friends had divided into groups and he got to drive the dodgem cars with them. Then Elvis sent someone across the street to get milkshakes at a place with two large polar bears out front called the Polar Bear Frozen Custard shop.

I didn't know it then, but that night was just a preview of Elvis's giving nature.

CHAPTER 2

By the early 1960s, my family was living in a three-bedroom, one-bathroom house in one of the new suburbs springing up around Memphis. Our home was half a block down the road from a cotton field that a farmer and his mule plowed from time to time, a remnant from the Old South. When the postwar boom hit, part of the field was paved and a gas station was erected there as modernization swept across Memphis, eventually surrounding our home with malls and fast-food restaurants.

My parents were hardworking, everyday people. My father had retired from the army and was managing a local department store. My mother worked up the street from our home, managing a stamp store. My siblings and I were baptized, and our parents did their best to raise us with good morals and values.

During my childhood and early teens, as I was learning to read and write and discovered a love of art, Elvis's celebrity continued to skyrocket. He made music and movies, got married, and had a child. On occasion, when relatives visited us in Memphis, they wanted to see Graceland. We accommodated them and rode along with a security guard in a striped, canopied pink jeep—renowned at the estate—up Graceland's driveway and back. It was a small tour of the estate, usually offered when Elvis was out of town.

Tomboyish, I roller-skated, rode horses, and clambered up trees. I often climbed on my brother's motorcycle, too, pretending to ride it. Though our parents worried, occasionally Mike would take me out for a short spin and I would be thrilled.

My big brother's love for motorcycles quickly became my own obsession. When I was fourteen, I pestered my father to purchase a minibike for me. My parents were apprehensive, having had enough safety concerns with my brother riding motorcycles, but my father gave in and I got my minibike. I continued to love motorcycles, and years later, I would eventually get my own.

Art, however, was my biggest passion. I was constantly drawing and painting, and I revered my brother, Mike, a wonderful artist who had begun taking art classes in college. I had an inspirational art teacher in high school named Mrs. Murphy who usually dressed in purple. She wore purple eyeglasses and carried a purple cane. Even her silvery white hair seemed to have a purple hue. Art was an easy way for me to express myself, and by my teens I was thinking about how to turn my passion into a career.

I also loved to sing. Pretending my hairbrush was a microphone, I'd dress up in one of my mother's old skirts and croon along with various records. This wasn't surprising to anyone because music was central to our home life. My mother was a self-taught musician who could play piano, guitar, and mandolin. Her father had been the minister of a small church in Arkansas, and having been spiritually influenced by both parents, she usually played gospel hymns on our piano.

My mom enjoyed a variety of music, from classical to gospel, and when she was home you'd hear the voices of Dean Martin, Bing Crosby, Engelbert Humperdinck, Tom Jones, and yes, Elvis, resonating from the stereo in our living room. Her love of music rubbed off on us. Terry became interested in the piano and began taking lessons, practicing fervently. At thirteen, I started taking vocal lessons. I could play piano a little bit by ear and occasionally fooled around on a big red guitar I'd been given, but usually when I wanted to sing, I'd pester Terry to accompany me on the piano. Despite the fact that our parents weren't wealthy and had four children to feed and clothe, they had generously found the money for music lessons when we expressed our interest.

Whenever my mother was playing the piano, I'd wander in and stand behind her to sing. My father and sisters would occasionally join in, making those moments some of my fondest memories. When answering machines later came out, my mother, sisters, and I recorded a singing message in harmony on a whim. Friends claimed we sounded just like the Andrews Sisters.

As much as I enjoyed singing, I was too self-conscious and concerned about what others thought to sing in public. I made my family look the other way when I practiced and even asked them not to come to my recitals. I continued voice lessons through high school, then stopped, unable to overcome this great shyness. I decided it would be all right to let this particular passion of mine remain a childhood fantasy, safely tucked away.

Despite my tomboyish inclinations, my sister Terry and I used to cut out pictures of models we liked from *McCall's* magazine and the Sears catalog, using them like paper dolls. As a teenager, I thought, "Wow, being a model sounds so cool."

At sixteen, I finally saw my first live fashion model, and caught a glimpse of the world beyond Memphis when I tagged along with Rosemary and her girlfriend to Lowenstein Department Store downtown to watch auditions for a pageant called "Model of the Year." The pageant was put on by Stewart Cowley, the owner of a New York modeling agency.

As I stood among the crowd gathered to view the entrants, I became fascinated by the sight of a female model seated beside Mr. Cowley, helping him interview contestants. This girl was rail thin and she'd cut her black hair very short. In my mind, she represented everything I thought a New York City model must be.

Looking about the room, Mr. Cowley stood up at one point and walked our way. He approached me and asked, "Why aren't you in the contest?" Offering me an entry form, he returned to his table.

I began filling out the form, but my hand was shaking. I was excited but unprepared for this. Rosemary pressed me to personally hand the form back to Mr. Cowley and said, "Make sure you smile." She had more confidence in me than I did. I returned the form but, upon seeing my age, Mr. Cowley asked me to come back in a few years, for eighteen was the eligible age to enter.

A few weeks later, through friends, I modeled some clothing alongside two other girls during a brief segment of the show *Talent Party*, which showcased bands. My interest in modeling had outweighed any fears. Someone saw me on the show, and not long afterward, I was contacted and hired to work in a hometown television commercial. I also held two part-time jobs after school, working at a restaurant on weekends and decorating the windows of a dress shop. I viewed the latter as an apprenticeship and a stepping-stone in the artistic field.

My interest in art continued throughout high school, and I began entering my paintings into local art competitions, even winning some awards. I graduated in the spring of 1974 with scholarship money to put toward a college that fall. I chose the Memphis Academy of Art, a small private college of art and design. As I started classes, I gave up my job at the restaurant but continued working part-time at the dress shop.

I was one of the younger students in my classes; between my drawing, sculpting, and pottery courses, I felt out of my depth and slightly overwhelmed. Although my teachers, friends, and family told me I had talent and I believed it on some level, the academy's curriculum proved to be too intense for me. Wanting to slow down and figure out my future one step at a time, I decided to take a sabbatical from the art academy after my first year. I hoped to find a different path that could lead to a future art-related career.

In the spring of 1975, Terry saw an ad for the Miss Memphis pageant. Pageants were prominent events in the South, and she decided to enter, winning first runner-up. Finding it challenging and fun, by the end of that year she began encouraging me to enter the Miss Tennessee Universe pageant. I wasn't a competitive person, but I could definitely see how competing could help me overcome my shyness. So, with nothing to lose, in the beginning of 1976 I took the plunge. The title went to the sister of the pageant's executive director and I placed first runner-up.

In February 1976, my family moved into a larger home on a nice corner lot in east Memphis. My father still managed a local department store and my mother had been working for the Internal Revenue Service. My brother, now a firefighter, lived close by with his wife and two daughters, while my sisters and I still lived at home. Rosemary worked in sales, Terry attended Memphis State University, and I did extra work at the dress shop while tending to the store's windows.

My parents' relationship had not been at its best the past few years. My mother had applied for a divorce twice in 1974, but dismissed it both times, hoping to work things out. When my parents purchased our new home, my siblings and I wanted to believe it was the beginning of a brighter future for them.

In the spring, Terry entered Miss Memphis again and won. This led her to the Miss Tennessee pageant in June, and our family proudly watched as she was crowned Miss Tennessee of 1976. The pageants had been exciting, and with my sisters encouraging me, I entered a few more local ones around the same time, winning Miss Traffic Safety and Duchess in our annual Cotton Carnival Ball.

As Miss Tennessee, Terry was invited that summer to a country club in Memphis, where she got free tickets to see Elvis perform at our local Mid-South Coliseum on July 5. Due to official obligations elsewhere, she was unable to go to the concert, so she gave the tickets to my mother, Rosemary, and me. Little did my family or I know that, in the very near future, Terry's title would open the door to Graceland, leading me straight into Elvis's life.

When July 5 rolled around, I was thrilled to see Elvis perform for the first time. I didn't personally own any Elvis albums, but my mother had his gospel and Christmas ones, and my brother, Mike, owned a few of Elvis's Sun label 45s. I enjoyed a variety of music, from classical to rock 'n' roll, and some of my favorite bands at the time were Fleetwood Mac and Led Zeppelin, and the singer Elton John.

Our seats weren't too close to the stage, but as Elvis entered and the cameras began flashing, I was completely spellbound. The man whose voice I'd grown up hearing all my life was suddenly right there in front of me, flesh-and-blood and very real! It was wonderful to hear him sing the songs that I'd heard before only on television and the radio.

His hair was longer and he looked a little heavier than in his earlier years, but I was captivated by the way Elvis strutted onto the stage dressed in a white jumpsuit with an Egyptian bird design, blue silk puff sleeves, and a matching belt with chains hanging from his waist.

That summer night in 1976, the crowd was a mix of middle-aged adults, teens, and children. Elvis put on a great show and at one point that night, he told the audience, "The first record that I did here in Memphis, ya know, was 'That's All Right (Mama),' and so forth and they . . . had a couple of people say well you can't do that anymore. You, by God, watch me!"

He went full force into the song then and proved them wrong. My mother, sister, and I were three out of thousands that night, captivated by a show that unfortunately would turn out to be Elvis's last hometown performance.

CHAPTER 3

In early September 1976, Terry went to Atlantic City, New Jersey, to represent the state of Tennessee in the Miss America pageant. I was able to work around my job at the dress shop and go with my family to New Jersey to support her.

Terry was an extremely gifted pianist whose many hours of disciplined practice had gotten her far. On one of the preliminary nights, she won all three honors in the swimsuit, talent, and evening gown competition. Although the Miss America crown wouldn't be hers that year, she was always a winner in my eyes.

Before going to New Jersey, I had entered and won Miss Mid-South Fair, a huge two-week event that I looked forward to every year, when it came to Memphis at the end of September.

A little over a week after returning from New Jersey, the Mid-South Fair began and I attended it each day as the official hostess. As usual, it was a lot of fun, but before I knew it, the fair was over and so was the month of October.

A typical weekend night in Memphis usually found my sisters and me out to dinner, the movies, or socializing with friends. On the evening of Friday, November 19, 1976, however, all three of us were at home. We were sitting in the den with Larry, a young man I'd been seeing, when the phone rang. Our mother answered it in the kitchen, then entered the den to say that George Klein was calling for Terry.

My sisters and I exchanged curious looks. George was a well-known local disc jockey and television personality. Last, but certainly not least, he was also a longtime friend of Elvis Presley's.

Terry picked up the receiver in the kitchen. Meanwhile, our mother, looking slightly stunned, reported that George had told her Elvis had been dating around and would like to meet the new Miss Tennessee. He was inviting Terry to Graceland!

It certainly wasn't your everyday phone call. Having seen Graceland only from the outside made it all the more surreal. Rosemary and I scurried into the kitchen to unashamedly eavesdrop on Terry's conversation.

Terry may have been Miss Tennessee, but the idea of a "date" with Elvis was unimaginable to my sisters and me. That only happened in the movies! Terry had also been dating someone since high school, so upon hearing her accept the invitation, we knew she had done so for the same reason we would have: She was eager to meet Elvis in person and get a peek inside Graceland.

The three of us were very close, and knowing Terry would feel uneasy about going alone, Rosemary brought up the possibility of the two of us accompanying her. As exciting as it sounded, I didn't feel comfortable with this idea because we hadn't been invited.

Before I could protest, however, Rosemary quickly approached Terry while she was still on the phone and whispered, "Ask George if Ginger and I can come!"

Terry paused for a second—she knew this wasn't proper, but she was our sister, and we always looked out for each other, so she went ahead and asked. Then, lowering the receiver from her ear, she told us George had sounded a bit hesitant and put her on hold while he checked. Now we were embarrassed.

When George came back on the line, however, much to our relief, Terry nodded yes and Rosemary and I went to tell our mother and Larry. Larry wasn't too keen about me going to Graceland, but seeing how excited we all were, he said, "I don't blame you for wanting to go," and left.

When Terry finally hung up the phone and joined us back in the den, she said Elvis had wanted to send a car for us, but she'd told him she would drive. George had asked what car we would be in so he could tell the guard at the front gates to watch for us.

Our appointed time to be at Graceland was 11 P.M. We began getting ready, feeling enthusiastic but nervous. Meeting Elvis plus touring the inside of Graceland meant we were in for a double treat!

As we chatted and touched up our makeup, Terry said, "I'm glad you and Rosemary are going." A few moments later, she reflected on George's hesitancy and having to check about it. "I really hope it's all right you're coming with me."

Feeling uneasy about it myself and not wanting Terry to feel worried, I walked away and stopped getting ready. Rosemary soon noticed and told me, "George said it was fine." Then, half-joking, she added, "The worst Elvis can do is ask us to leave."

She was right, so I finished getting dressed. By 10:30 we were saying good-bye to our parents and excitedly heading out the door.

Graceland was a little less than half an hour from our home. We were so keyed up, we chatted all the way over. What once had been a section of Highway 51 South was now Elvis Presley Boulevard; as we turned onto it, the three of us grew quieter. The fieldstone wall surrounding Graceland soon came into view and, as we entered the turning lane, blinker flashing, the wrought-iron gates with the image of Elvis holding a guitar slowly began to open. It was an incredible feeling, knowing this was happening just for us!

Terry gave her name at the guardhouse. The gates swung closed behind us as we started up the long driveway, eventually stopping just shy of Graceland's lit front porch. We sat in the car for a few moments, unsure of what to do next. Would someone come out to get us? Should we park here or around back?

A security guard soon emerged from the darkness and approached the driver's side of the car. Terry lowered her window and asked, "What should we do?"

Smiling, the guard replied, "Try knocking on the front door."

My sisters and I climbed out of the car, laughing at ourselves and the guard's comment as our nerves got the better of us. Passing between two huge lion statues, we jokingly chanted, "Lions and tigers and bears, oh my!" in an effort to relax.

We walked up the stone steps to the front porch where Rosemary, always the bravest among us, pressed the doorbell beside the green wrought-iron front door. Expecting Elvis to appear at any moment, my earlier concerns about showing up uninvited resurfaced. I grew increasingly anxious, wondering, "What if Elvis really doesn't want Rosemary and me here?"

I hung back, letting Rosemary and Terry wait at the door. When it opened, George Klein greeted us, which surprised me. Naive as this may seem, because this was Elvis's house, I expected him to answer the door.

George was the same age as Elvis, forty-one, and a friendly guy with black hair. It had been his *Talent Party* show that I once briefly modeled on. I didn't say anything about this, because I didn't think he would remember.

He introduced himself and then beckoned for us to follow him.

Feeling like Alice stepping through the looking glass, I took a deep breath and entered Graceland for the first time.

My feet sank into thick, red shag carpet, which extended into the foyer and up a staircase with a gold-and-white banister and railings. George invited us into the dining room. Passing beneath an enormous, ornate crystal chandelier, I glanced to the right and saw a room decorated all in red with French provincial furniture. Peacock stained-glass windows were on either side of the entrance to a music room dominated by a black baby grand piano. Many people have referred to this red décor as gaudy and it would eventually be changed. But, gaudy or not, it impressed me at the time, and it's still one of my most lasting memories of Graceland.

To my left, I heard voices. I turned and saw some people seated in red, silver-studded, high-backed chairs around a mirrored dining table. Cigar smoke curled into the air as we approached. Staring at the chair at the end of the table, its back facing us, I excitedly thought, *This has to be Elvis!* and slowed my steps, almost holding my breath.

I was wrong. George introduced the chair's occupant as GeeGee Gambill. His wife, Elvis's cousin Patsy Presley, was there, too, along with another cousin, Billy Smith, and Billy's wife, Jo. They were playing cards, the men smoking cigars, all of them casually dressed in jeans and T-shirts or blouses.

Everyone greeted us cordially. I couldn't tell by their reaction whether they had been expecting us or knew who we were, but I did get the sense that they were sizing us up as they gave us quick, up-and-down appraising looks. The three of us had dressed nicely to meet Elvis, but hadn't put a lot of thought into overly trying to impress anyone.

George then led us through the kitchen. Its floor was covered in wall-to-wall carpet in a multicolor patchwork design. I had never seen carpeting in a kitchen, but this was Elvis's home, so I figured there would be much I had never seen before. The room looked warm, with dark brown cabinets and stained-glass lamps hanging from the ceiling. The kitchen had a breakfast nook and opened into a den.

"This is the Jungle Room," George announced, gesturing around the den as he paused to answer a green phone buzzing on a nearby table. As I watched George listen to someone on the phone, I heard laughter echoing from the dining room and it struck me how comfortable everyone was in Elvis's home.

I began to relax a little and gazed around the room. The Jungle Room was far from your typical den. I noticed water trickling down the face of a stone-covered back wall, and the furniture featured carved animal heads and engravings.

George hung up the phone. "Can you please wait right here?" he asked. "Elvis isn't ready yet. He's practicing karate." Then he walked away, leaving the three of us alone in the room.

It seemed a little odd that Elvis would invite us here at a certain time and not be ready. Still, I wasn't complaining. I was excited just to be seeing inside Graceland.

I sat on a faux-fur chair with wooden arms carved to look like Asian dragon heads. Rosemary and Terry chose a matching couch. In front of it was a huge coffee table made of lacquered wood. Statues of jungle animals were placed randomly about the room; a large mirror framed with feathers was hanging on a side wall; and the green carpet was, surprisingly, on parts of the ceiling as well as the floor.

After a few minutes, a maid entered and offered us a drink. We asked for sodas and, when she left, eased our tension by taking our mirrored compacts out from our purses, opening them, and jokingly pretending to primp.

Suddenly, I noticed cameras mounted on the walls near the ceiling. The cameras seemed to be aimed our way! I quickly closed my compact and pointed them out to my sisters. Mortified, I wondered if we were being watched.

The maid returned with our drinks and we sat quietly, now cautious of every move we made.

Considering the late hour, I was surprised that Graceland was so active. Phones periodically buzzed (they did not ring) and various people came and went. At one point, a young man in his twenties, with long blond hair, stepped into the Jungle Room and casually introduced himself as Elvis's brother, Ricky Stanley.

Brother? I was puzzled. I didn't know Elvis had any siblings. Later, I learned that Ricky was Elvis's stepbrother; his mother, Dee, had married Elvis's father, Vernon, after Gladys Presley died. We introduced ourselves and found out that Ricky worked as an aide to Elvis.

Not long afterward, a short, dark-haired man in his forties appeared and introduced himself as Charlie Hodge. With a drink in one hand and a cigarette in the other, he began telling off-color jokes, all the while leaning as if balancing on the deck of a heeling ship. If Elvis was considered the King of Rock and Roll, I thought Charlie would certainly qualify as his court jester. I wondered if he'd been sent expressly to entertain us. As I discovered after I started seeing Elvis, Charlie sang harmony with Elvis and assisted him onstage during his shows.

George finally returned. "Elvis is still practicing karate," he said. "Would you like to see downstairs?"

Thinking we were downstairs, I was surprised to follow him down a staircase at the back of the den. We entered a colorful room with vibrantly patterned fabric in blue, red, and yellow lining its walls and ceiling. Pieces of furniture were upholstered in matching material. An electric organ stood against one wall, and a billiard table sat in the middle of the room beneath two large Tiffany-style lamps suspended from the ceiling.

George then took us into another room he called the TV Room. I felt immediately disoriented as we entered this room, because it was filled with mirrors: Mirrors covered the ceiling, framed the fireplace, and covered a square coffee table. What looked to be small mirrors were shining in the embroidered fabric of yellow-and-white pillows scattered across a large navy sectional sofa. Yellow leather stools were pulled up to the bar, and three television sets had been built into a side wall.

A huge white lightning bolt inside navy and yellow clouds had been painted above the couch. George explained that Elvis had a motto, *TCB*, which stood for *taking care of business*. The lightning bolt was a symbol for *taking care of business lightning fast*.

A phone began to buzz in the room. George answered it, listened, then hung up, saying we were going upstairs next, to Elvis's daughter's room.

Upstairs? I couldn't believe it! Our tour had helped me calm down, but now my nerves began to hum again. I knew Elvis had to be on the top floor because we'd pretty much covered the entire downstairs. The time had come, I thought: We were finally going to meet him!

Elvis's relatives were still playing cards in the dining room as we passed by them again, this time headed for the foyer. When George started up the staircase, my heart began to beat even faster. At the top, we followed him down a hall and into Lisa's bedroom.

This room was decorated mainly in yellow and white. A black leather sofa was against the wall to the right, and the center of the room was dominated by a large round bed blanketed in white faux fur with matching canopy. My sisters and I sat on the couch and George turned on a nearby television set.

George leaned back against Lisa's bed and continued visiting with us. Ricky and Billy Smith both entered, leaning against the bed and joining the conversation.

I hadn't paid any attention to the time and glanced at my watch. It was now approaching 1 A.M.

Two hours had passed since our arrival. Although it hadn't really felt like that much time had gone by, the more Ricky, George, and Billy continued to talk, the more I began to wonder whether they were covering for Elvis. Had he changed his mind about meeting us? Now that we'd been entertained with a tour, would we be asked to leave without meeting him?

Another man's figure appeared in the doorway of Lisa's room. I turned to look, prepared to greet another relative or friend, but it was Elvis entering the room. I was caught off guard. I had halfway been expecting to hear trumpets sound at his entrance.

Elvis's jet-black hair was casually styled. There was no pompadour or glitzy outfit, just Elvis, dressed in a dark blue karate top, black pants, and black boots. I was immediately attracted to him. His hair looked soft and shiny; his skin was clean-shaven and smooth. Thinking he was gorgeous, my shyness flew right out the window.

"Hi, Elvis!" I blurted, as if I'd known him for years.

"Hi," Elvis said and shook our hands, correctly acknowledging my sisters and me by name, one by one. Someone had obviously informed him who was who.

Then, crossing the room in front of us, Elvis sat in a large dark chair to our right and put a cigar to his lips. Billy quickly leaned over and lit it for him. Elvis settled farther back in the chair and apologized for keeping us waiting.

Billy then left the room while Elvis proceeded to ask Terry about herself. She talked about her music and the various titles she had won.

"How about you?" Elvis asked me. "Have you won any titles?"

I told him a little about myself. When Elvis got to Rosemary, she mentioned she had never entered any pageants outside of high school. He smiled and said, "Well, you should have, but for now you'll just have to be Miss . . . Miss . . . Miss . . . Understood."

We all laughed. The more Elvis joked around with us, the more I noticed how similar his humor was to ours. I'd had this feeling of a powerful presence and energy the minute Elvis entered the room, and he continued to hold my focus completely throughout the night. At the same time, I was taken by how down-to-earth he was, and by his sexy smile and laugh.

We continued to talk, with Ricky and George chiming in periodically. Elvis told us what an honor it was to have the street name changed to Elvis Presley Boulevard and mentioned he sometimes joked, "Get off my street!" to other motorists while driving down it. He talked about karate, too, letting us know he was a ninth-degree black belt.

"It's a beautiful art form," I told him, adding that I'd wanted to take lessons when I was sixteen, but my parents thought I was too young.

Elvis disagreed, saying it was never too young to start. Terry talked about the classical piano music she enjoyed. I brought up my love for art, but didn't dare mention my singing. Rosemary, the most comical of the three of us, often had him laughing.

Elvis was polite and easy to talk with, which was putting me at ease until he tilted his head to one side, looked toward the floor and said, "Ginger, you're burning a hole right through me." His intense blue eyes slowly drifted back up to my face.

"Who, me?" I asked.

"Yes, you," he replied.

I didn't know what he meant, as I didn't feel I'd been staring at him. We were just talking. I was embarrassed and felt a flash of heat warm my face.

We talked a little more, then Elvis asked, "Would you like to see the rest of the upstairs?"

Thrilled, we said, "Sure!"

Along with Ricky and George, we followed Elvis out into the hall. I was still holding my unfinished glass of soda. Elvis reached for it, took a sip, and handed it back to me. This distracted me so much that I made a wrong turn and headed toward the front stairs. I then felt Elvis's hands on my shoulders, gently turning me and guiding me back through a set of double doors.

Everyone followed Elvis and me as we cut through an office and then another set of double doors into his master bedroom. The first thing that struck me was that the matching couch and chairs looked identical to the furniture we had in our den at home. What were the odds of that?

Otherwise, the room décor here was very different from anything I'd ever seen before. A shiny, black, Naugahyde headboard crowned the massive bed, which Elvis proudly told us was nine feet by nine feet. Reading lamps were attached to the wall on either side of it. The same red shag carpet covered the floor, with black and gold wallpaper lining one wall and padding on the other. The bedroom doors and ceiling were also padded and, much to my surprise, there were two television sets embedded in the ceiling. Elvis explained the padding by saying he didn't care for outside noise when he slept.

Ricky left as my sisters and I followed Elvis, along with George, into his office. It was decorated in masculine tans and browns. On my left was a glass case filled with rifles and handguns; in the center of the room, two couches faced each other, a coffee table between them. Near the back of the room was a large desk with a chair, and behind it, two bookcases stood against the wall.

Elvis walked over to an electric organ near a closed accordion-style door and sat down on the bench. I stood behind him with George and my sisters gathered around. Something about this felt comfortably familiar because I'd so often stood and sung behind my mom while she played piano.

Placing his fingers on the keyboard, Elvis began to sing "You'll Never Walk Alone." If I'd ever felt like I was dreaming, it was now!

At various times during the song, Elvis looked up from the organ, smiling at Rosemary and Terry or glancing over his shoulder to smile at me. At one point, I looked into the mirror above the organ and noticed George yawning. That made me wonder whether he'd seen Elvis do this sort of thing many times before or if he was just tired because it was so late.

Elvis finished and we applauded. Standing up, he said, "I'd like to show you my dressing area."

I was surprised by this; I'd always thought of people's closets as personal. On the other hand, seeing Elvis's dressing room would be an added bonus because I was enjoying being with him and thrilled by the idea of seeing one of his inner sanctums.

We followed Elvis back through his bedroom and into his bathroom, which was carpeted in the same royal red shag carpet. On my left stood a black commode with a telephone attached to the wall nearby. A black vanity was covered with toiletries on the right. Above it, the mirrored wall was outlined with makeup lights.

Beyond an enormous, curved shower with multicolored tiles, we entered Elvis's dressing area. It was filled with racks of clothing surrounding a bed covered in a faux fur similar to the one in Lisa's room. A bust of the Greek god Apollo sat on a pedestal beside an open doorway leading out to the hall. (Later, Elvis would tell me he thought the bust resembled him. I thought it did, too.)

Pointing out a few stage jumpsuits, Elvis said he was proud of the workmanship that went into making them. He told us they were made of material that didn't let any air in or out. Then he began showing us his boots and casual clothes.

"Casual" for Elvis appeared to be coats with fur collars; brightly colored, high-collared satin shirts; flared pants; and hats that looked like they could have been worn on the set of the movie *Shaft*.

I could understand Elvis wanting to show us his costumes, but again I was surprised that he'd be willing to show us his more personal clothes. Was this an extension of his persona? Was this something he felt he needed to do with us?

When Elvis was finished giving us a tour of his dressing area, he excused himself and, as he walked toward the front of the bathroom, called out for George to follow him.

My sisters and I now found ourselves in the extraordinary position of standing alone in Elvis Presley's closet, trying to process what had started out as an innocent evening at home. Elvis had been captivating, entertaining, funny, and gracious. We talked quietly, assuming the show was over and we'd be asked to leave when George reappeared.

To my surprise, George came back and said, "Ginger, Elvis would like to see you for a minute."

What did Elvis want with me? I glanced uncertainly at Terry and Rosemary.

"He's waiting for you," George urged, motioning me toward the front of the bathroom.

Taking a few steps forward, I turned back to see George guiding my sisters out through the door by the dressing area. My anxiety roared back. My sisters and I had acted as a safety net for each other, but now I was on my own.

When I stepped past the doorway of his bathroom, I saw Elvis seated on the side of his bed. He smiled and patted the red bedspread, motioning me to sit down next to him. Unsure of what he wanted, I nervously walked in and complied.

"Did you notice I was paying more attention to you than to your sisters?" he asked with a faint smile.

I briefly looked away.

My heart began to pound. Was Elvis actually *hitting* on me? It went far beyond my wildest imaginings that he would single me out. I felt he had treated the three of us fairly equally, but when I thought back, I remembered his comment about me "burning a hole" through him, how he'd taken a sip from my glass of soda, and the way he'd placed his hands on my shoulders in the hallway. Was that what he meant?

Not quite sure, I looked up at him and answered, "Yes."

He nodded. "When I like someone, I really like them a lot," he said. "It's not just a fling. I don't like one-night stands."

"I don't like one-night stands, either," I replied, wanting him to be sure I wasn't that kind of woman.

Elvis regarded me silently for a moment, then gestured toward the window. "I'm not that street out there," he said. "If you cut me, I bleed."

I couldn't believe that Elvis, a charismatic, handsome superstar, was talking to me in this intimate way. The only thing I could think to say was, "I understand."

"Good," he replied. He leaned over then and picked up a book lying with some others on the floor beside his bed. It was the *Book of Numbers* by Cheiro, the world-famous seer.

"When's your birthday?" Elvis asked, opening the book.

"November thirteenth," I replied.

"You're a number four," he said, and began explaining that he reached the number by adding the one and three together. Picking up a pair of glasses from his night table, he put them on and began reading to me about the number four. He told me that fours are sensitive and had their feelings hurt easily. Fours were likely to feel lonely and isolated, with few real friends, but to the few friends they did have, they are very loyal.

Elvis had my attention. I didn't feel lonely, but I was shy, sensitive, and loyal to my friends. Elvis obviously was passionate about the subject of numerology and I found myself being drawn into it. Telling me January 8 was his birthday, which made him a number eight, he read on regarding that number. He said these people were often misunderstood and for this reason felt lonely. They usually "play some important role on life's stage, but usually one which is fatalistic, or as the instrument of Fate for others." He also said that eight people are either very successful or complete failures. They feel different from others and "seldom reap the reward for the good they may do while they are living." It is only after their death that they are praised and honored.

My first thought was, *Wow!* Some of the characteristics really seemed to fit him, but Elvis *lonely*? That was difficult for me to believe, given the number of people gathered downstairs on this night.

Elvis stayed on the topic of numerology for a while, then lifted another, larger book off the floor and began leafing through it. "This is supposed to be an illustration of God," he said, stopping on a certain page and showing it to me.

It was a drawing of a man with a long white beard seated on a throne with symbols of fire, ice, rain, and wind at his sides. The book reminded me of a large illustrated Bible my mother had that she often read to my siblings and me when we were younger. Still holding the big book in his hands, Elvis settled farther back on the bed and motioned me up beside him.

By now, I was feeling more comfortable and decided it was a harmless enough request; Elvis seemed absorbed by the book. I scooted up to sit right next to him with my back against a pillow. He then surprised me again by handing me the book and asking me to read aloud. I did, feeling shy about it. I didn't want to make a mistake because I could feel him watching me closely.

The subject matter in this book was different. I was again drawn into it while Elvis observed, periodically sipping ice water from a large glass jar sitting on his night table. Cool air was blowing from an air conditioner unit situated inside the bedroom's front window. I was chilled, but Elvis seemed fine and I didn't feel right asking him to turn it down.

We took turns reading and talking into the early morning. At one point, Elvis went into the bathroom, leaving me to think that it had been an unforgettable night. I was going to have quite a story to tell my friends.

Having been up almost twenty-four hours by now, however, I was starting to feel overwhelmed by fatigue. I hated it but could tell that I wasn't going to be able to concentrate well anymore. Now that Elvis was out of the room, I also became aware that a lot of time had gone by and our parents still hadn't heard from us. I was worried, too, about Terry and Rosemary having to wait for me.

When Elvis returned from the bathroom, I politely said, "Elvis, I should find my sisters and probably leave. It's really late."

He sat back down on the bed. "They've already gone," he said casually. "Your sisters went home earlier."

I was stunned. They'd already *left*? I'd been at Graceland all this time without them? Puzzled, I wondered how he knew. Had Elvis arranged all this earlier with George?

"Someone will take you home when you're ready," Elvis added, watching the confused expressions flit across my face.

I decided that Elvis was probably tired, too. Thinking it was proper for me to go, I thanked him on behalf of my sisters and myself for the night. He moved to the edge of the bed and I inched my way beside him as he picked up a telephone receiver from his night table and asked someone to give me a ride home.

To my shock, he added, "Please be sure and get her number," before hanging up. Then he turned to me and said, "You should always politely ask someone to do something for you. Never tell a person what to do."

As I nodded, still dumbstruck, Elvis took a pen and a matchbook from the night table drawer, opened the matchbook, and asked, "What's your phone number?"

This can't be happening! My thoughts suddenly flashed on Larry, who hadn't wanted me to come to Graceland tonight. Despite feeling conflicted, I gave Elvis my number. He wrote it down.

As I looked at him, Elvis suddenly leaned in toward me, catching me totally off guard. He kept his hands on the bed and gave me a quick, light kiss on the lips. It was so quick I barely had time to register what had just happened, but I was stunned and excited.

Afterward, I walked out of Graceland in a trance. As I rode home with an employee named Steve Smith, I went over the kiss again in my mind. I certainly didn't want Elvis to get the wrong impression of me. I wasn't a seasoned pro when it came to sex or relationships. On the other hand, I hoped he had liked kissing me.

Even though it was nearly sunrise, the lights were on inside my house when we pulled up to the curb. Before getting out, Steve asked me for my phone number. Giving it a second time, I quickly ran inside.

My mother and sisters were sitting on the couch in our den. I figured my father must be in bed because he sometimes worked on weekends. Our parents had been excited when we were invited to Graceland, but my mother admitted now that they'd started worrying when so much time went by without any word from us.

"I felt bad about leaving you there," Terry said, explaining that George had taken them outside to a racquetball court behind the house, where Charlie and Ricky joined them for a tour of the court.

George then told Terry and Rosemary that Elvis wanted to spend more time with me, and that they were welcome to wait if they wanted or, as it was so late, to leave. He had assured them that Elvis would see I got home safely.

Exhausted, but still running on nerves, I filled them in on what had happened, leaving out the kiss. We weren't a kiss-and-tell sort of family. Some things were personal, and we were private with each other when it came to that sort of thing.

Now that I was home, the whole night seemed unreal. Elvis was different from anyone I'd ever met. Here was this rock-'n'-roll superstar singing to my sisters and me, showing us his closet, and then inviting me to join him on his bed, where he'd been a gentleman. He'd read religious books with me and shared his thoughts and feelings.

Elvis had been polite and funny, too, which I related to. He'd demonstrated a sincere desire for me to understand what he was about in a short amount of time, and in the hours we'd spent together, I'd felt an intense attraction between us.

I had enjoyed the night; it was magical and unique, and from what Elvis had said and how he had acted, I thought he had enjoyed spending time with me, too.

When I was finally alone in my bed that morning, none of that seemed real or even possible. I was in turmoil. Would Elvis call me? And, if he did, would I agree to see him again, knowing it would hurt Larry, the nice guy I'd been dating? I honestly didn't know if I was more afraid of Elvis being attracted to me because of this or more afraid that I'd find myself feeling let down if he didn't call me.

I rolled over in bed, searching for sleep. Before long, I had to admit to myself that if he didn't call, I'd be disappointed, and so I decided if Elvis wanted to see me again, I would say yes.

CHAPTER 4

I woke late that Saturday afternoon and began thinking about the evening again. I had, of course, been enthralled with meeting Elvis, that was to be expected: This was Elvis, after all. However, he had been trying to connect with me, and after I saw how open and approachable he was, he had succeeded. Our age difference didn't even enter my mind, and I hoped I'd get the chance to try to get to know him better.

Gathering with my sisters in the den, we talked about the evening's events. I ended our conversation, musing, "If I don't hear from Elvis, I'll write last night off as the most amazing night of my life so far."

Around 8 p.m., the phone rang. My mother answered it in the kitchen, and I heard her say hi to George. I walked in and she handed me the phone.

"Elvis would like you to come over," George said. "I'll drive by and pick you up."

"All right," I said and rushed to get ready. I wondered why Elvis hadn't called me himself, but it made me feel great that he'd actually been thinking about me and wanted to see me again so soon.

George and I made small talk on the ride over to Graceland, where he led me straight upstairs to the master bedroom and left. I was just as nervous as the night before and could feel my heart racing.

Elvis was sitting on his bed, watching television. He wore a loose-fitting navy jumpsuit and a black rhinestone belt with chains. As he greeted me with a smile, I relaxed a little and thought with relief, *So last night was real.*

Elvis got up and walked past the foot of his bed to turn off the TV, looking over his shoulder at me. "You know, television destroys the art of conversation," he said.

This was an interesting observation, coming from a man who had at least one television set in just about every room. Returning to his bed, he asked me to sit beside him. I did as he requested, trusting him to be as gentlemanly as he'd been the night before.

We talked a little about music. When I told Elvis that my mother often played hymns, and that "In the Garden" and "How Great Thou Art" had always been two of my favorites, he asked me to follow him into his office. I was touched when he started playing the organ and sang "In the Garden" just for me.

I had always admired Elvis's voice, which was so uniquely his—it could be soulful, tender, or powerful as he chose. Now, as Elvis sang softly to me, I felt calmed by the same peaceful, comforting feeling I'd had back home when listening to his gospel albums. Elvis knew how to reach inside you and touch your soul with his voice.

Afterward, I followed Elvis back to his bedroom, where he began talking about a car he owned, a Ferrari that he'd nicknamed the Black Mamba. "I named it after the fastest snake in the world," he said enthusiastically and then went into more detail about the car.

I had never even sat in a Ferrari, much less ridden in one. When he brought up his car, I thought he wanted me to see it. "Can we go for a ride in your Ferrari?" I asked.

"Not now," Elvis said. "I'll decide when we take a ride in it. That car is too fast for you."

Ha! I thought. Little did he know how much I loved to speed down the highway on a motorcycle. I felt a little awkward at that moment, wondering if this was Elvis's way of letting me know he liked to be in control.

A few books still lay on the floor beside his bed. Elvis reached for Cheiro's *Book of Numbers* and seemed eager to pick up where we had left off reading the previous night. Going through books again wasn't what I had expected, but I thought it was interesting that he wanted to read together on a date.

I felt a little less tense this time as we read to one another, and I found the subject of numerology intriguing. It wasn't something I thought anyone could understand right off the bat, but I was open to it. Elvis seemed to enjoy teaching, and I listened closely, trying to grasp the material.

After we'd discussed the book a little while, Elvis changed the subject, bringing up another of his cars, a Stutz Blackhawk. He mentioned taking me for a ride in it over to Memphis Aero to see an airplane he owned. (Memphis Aero was a part of Memphis International Airport for private planes.)

I grew excited as Elvis made a few phone calls, setting his plans in motion. He even invited some cousins along, which made me wonder whether Elvis, like me, sometimes needed a safety net, just like I relied on my sisters.

When Elvis went into his bathroom, leaving me seated on his bed, I glanced about the room and observed more details than I'd taken in during my first visit. Antihistamine bottles, a box of tissues, and two telephones crowded his night table. A closed-circuit television monitor, its power off, was close by. I wondered again if Elvis had been watching my sisters and me the night before. (I never would see it turned on though.)

A television set with a Betamax tape player on top of it stood against the wall opposite the foot of the bed. To the left of that, a bookcase held a record player, radio, and some Betamax tapes. On top of the bookcase were a couple of framed photos of a woman I had seen in some movie magazines. I remembered now that her name was Linda Thompson.

At that point in my life, I knew very little about Elvis's personal relationships, other than these facts: that he'd been married to and divorced from a woman named Priscilla; had one daughter, Lisa, from that marriage; and had dated various girls, Linda among them. Now I wondered why Linda's photos were still in Elvis's room.

I didn't have time to wonder long. Elvis stepped out of his bathroom, now dressed in a coat, and said, "You know, last night while I was practicing karate, George came up to me and said, 'Terry is very nice and Rosemary is very nice, but Ginger . . .'" He paused, shaking his head. "Then Ricky came in later, saying, 'Man, I think you're gonna like Ginger.'"

Elvis's voice was tinged with sarcasm as he went on. "I told Ricky that I'd had a lot of girls brought up to Graceland in the past few weeks, and yeah, I'm sure I'm gonna find someone I really like in Memphis on a Friday night." He then added that his cousin Billy's wife, Jo, had told him, "There's someone down here you are going to like."

I was flattered by the attention, but slightly uncomfortable. I realized that my initial instinct about my sisters and me being scrutinized the night before had been right on target.

It was after midnight by the time we went downstairs. A few people were waiting in the foyer, including two bodyguards and GeeGee and his wife, Patsy. We walked out onto the front porch, and I suppressed a gasp when I saw a car like none other I'd ever seen before.

It was Elvis's Stutz Blackhawk, glistening in the soft glow from the overhead light. The car was black with chrome trim, exhaust side pipes, and wire wheels. It was so beautiful that I found myself wondering whether this was why Elvis hadn't wanted me to ride in his Ferrari first.

Elvis opened the passenger door for me, pointing out that the trim on the dash and throughout the car was plated in eighteen-karat gold. Patsy and GeeGee climbed into the backseat and I slid into the red leather passenger bucket seat. Elvis got behind the wheel, started up the engine, and we proceeded down the driveway with his bodyguards following in a car close behind.

The streets were quiet as we rode toward the airport. It was about fifteen minutes away, and as we neared it, Patsy suddenly suggested we take a tour over Memphis in Elvis's plane.

"Let's fly over Nashville," Elvis quickly countered.

I didn't say a thing. Taking a short flight in his private plane would be an extraordinary experience for me, not only because it was with Elvis, but because I had only flown commercial one other time at the age of thirteen.

At Memphis Aero, Elvis's Lockheed JetStar stood alone on the tarmac. Its interior lights were aglow, the door was open, and the steps were down, awaiting our arrival. I followed Elvis into the plane, where he introduced me to a pilot with the fitting name of Milo High and his copilot, George.

As Patsy and GeeGee took a seat on a lime-colored couch, I followed Elvis down the plane's small aisle past yellow chairs facing each other, with small tables between them. Patterned fabric lined the walls near each window.

I chose a lime-colored chair in the back and Elvis's bodyguards sat nearby. I expected Elvis to sit down near me, but instead he turned around, walked to the front of the plane, and began speaking with Milo.

After a few moments, he looked back at me and said, "I forgot something."

Elvis headed out the door with his bodyguards in close pursuit; I suspected he had gone back to Graceland. Patsy and GeeGee remained seated and I stayed in my chair, the three of us making small talk. By the way they were acting, like this was any other ordinary night, I got the feeling that this sort of impulsive outing with Elvis wasn't unusual for them.

When Elvis and his bodyguards returned, he walked down the aisle with a mischievous grin on his face and sat down in the chair opposite mine. The plane's door closed and the engines fired up. As we began to taxi, Elvis announced that he had gone to get pajamas for everyone and we were all going to Las Vegas.

Las Vegas! Pajamas! The thought of flying over Memphis or Nashville was one thing, but I had never been out west. Nor had I ever spontaneously left with anyone on a trip—never mind a man I'd just met! How long would it take us to get there? How long would we be gone? Where would I sleep?

I was twenty years old but suddenly felt like I was about ten. I wanted to call home to let my family know what was happening. When Elvis asked me if this plan was all right, what could I say? "No"? "Maybe"? "It's too far"? "Stop the plane, I want to get off!"

Seeing Elvis's enthusiasm, I made an effort to hide my concerns. I simply smiled, answered yes, and allowed myself to be swept away to Las Vegas.

I was silent as we took off, and gazed out my window into the night, my mind racing. Out of the corner of my eye, I could see that Elvis was watching me. I glanced at him and he quickly turned his head, looking out his window as if not wanting me to know he had been staring at me. The cabin remained fairly quiet until a while into the flight, when Elvis looked over his shoulder toward Patsy and GeeGee and said, "You know, I would like to see Ginger in new clothes and jewelry."

Elvis stood up and took a few steps to the rear of the plane. He returned carrying a small, worn black square case by its handle. Placing the case on the table between us, he sat down, opened it, and took out a long necklace made of black plastic beads with a cross at the center.

"Lean forward, Ginger," he said, and gently placed the necklace over my head.

"Thank you," I said.

"Hold out your wrist and close your eyes," he said then.

I felt something slip over my hand. Opening my eyes, I was shocked to see a gold identification bracelet on my arm with "Elvis" written in sparkling diamonds.

"That's better," he said. "Now everyone will know you belong to me."

As I thanked Elvis for these pieces, I felt stunned that he would give me gifts so early in our relationship and unsettled that everything seemed to move so fast with him. I wondered if Elvis did this sort of thing with women on a regular basis, or whether he was serious about wanting me to belong to him.

For my part, I felt suddenly special despite my anxiety. I was more excited than apprehensive though and falling "in like" with Elvis.

Later, when I took the bracelet off, I noticed a date inscribed on the back and saw that he'd been given the bracelet in 1963. It wasn't until after Elvis passed away that I discovered he had worn this bracelet onstage and in private for many years before generously gracing me with it as a token of his affection.

Sandwiches were passed around, but I was too overwhelmed to eat. Shortly, the lights inside the plane were dimmed so everyone could rest, but I was keyed up emotionally and couldn't sleep. So I sat, eyes closed, wondering what lay in store for me. My concerns eventually gave way to excitement, however, the more I thought about seeing Las Vegas.

As we neared the end of the flight, Elvis asked me to follow him to the cockpit. I did, and as I stood next to him behind the pilots, looking through the windshield at the lights below, I suddenly felt his arm slip around my waist.

"Isn't it beautiful?" Elvis whispered in my ear.

In the distance, what looked like an island of tiny shimmering diamonds surrounded by a sea of black velvet slowly began to appear as we approached Las Vegas.

"Yes," I replied, as it was truly breathtaking.

We landed at the Hughes Air Terminal. As we descended the stairs from the plane, a dark-haired man in his late thirties greeted us. Elvis introduced him as Dr. Elias Ghanem, his friend and personal physician. The two of us joined Dr. Ghanem in his car while Elvis's cousins and bodyguards followed in another.

Riding through the streets of downtown Las Vegas, I felt like I was moving through a dream world. I was mesmerized by the city's endless, brilliant display of lights. I couldn't believe I was really there.

We drove around to the back of the Hilton International Hotel, entered the building, and took an elevator up to one of the rooms. Elvis's bodyguards brought in a suitcase and, after making sure things were secure, they left.

I sat next to Elvis on the bed as he began chatting with his cousins and Dr. Ghanem. I would later learn that Elvis and Patsy were double first cousins. Her father, Vester, who worked as a guard at Graceland's gates, was Elvis's dad's brother and Patsy's mother, Clette Smith, was Elvis's mom's sister.

After a while, Patsy and GeeGee left, and Elvis continued talking with Dr. Ghanem. Their conversation eventually turned to vitamins. Elvis mentioned that he got vitamin B_{12} shots regularly. Understanding they were supposed to help give energy, I told him that my mother, on occasion, had gotten them from a nurse who used to be our neighbor.

Dr. Ghanem offered to give each of us a shot of B_{12}. I'd never had one and was hesitant, but since he was Elvis's doctor, I trusted him. Not knowing what lay ahead and with no sleep to fuel me, I decided a little energy boost couldn't hurt. Elvis and I each got a shot in the arm.

When Dr. Ghanem finally left, I was expecting that Elvis and I would venture outside, but Elvis turned on the TV and settled down on the bed. "What about television destroying the art of conversation?" I nearly said, but I held back.

I quickly learned that Elvis liked to joke around and talk about things on television. He had a quick wit, and we were having such fun that I didn't mind staying in the room after all. At one point, Elvis went into the bathroom and returned wearing blue pajamas.

Just as I got my mind around the fact that Elvis was in pajamas, I realized that he held a matching pair in his hand. I hesitated as he held them out to me. The thrill of being in Las Vegas had taken my mind off some of my initial reservations about being in Elvis's hotel room, but now they quickly resurfaced. Shouldn't I be in a room of my own? I didn't want him to think I was as easy as that.

Elvis handed me the pajamas and said, "Go ahead. Put these on. You can change in the restroom."

I was shy about wearing pajamas in front of a man I didn't know, and worried about how to handle what might be a too-soon sexual situation for me. Now that he'd given me the bracelet, would Elvis expect me to become intimate with him? I sensed Elvis was a good man, but I wasn't ready to be with him in that way. Putting on pajamas would definitely send the wrong signal.

But what else could I do? I was alone with Elvis in a hotel room. I had to follow my instincts and trust him.

Taking the pajamas, I walked into the bathroom and slowly began to undress, my fingers trembling a little. I had lost all track of time, and knowing my parents thought I was still in Memphis, I felt I should at least tell them where I was. I walked out and sat on the bed. "Is it all right if I call home?" I asked. "I need to let my parents know where I am."

Elvis understood. I phoned our house, waking my mother. When I told her where I was, she was shocked, to say the least! I was filling her in on how the trip came about when Elvis suddenly motioned for me to hand him the phone.

Confused—why would Elvis want to talk to my mother?—I complied and gave him the receiver. Elvis began speaking with my mother, often calling her "ma'am," which I found endearing. He seemed a bit nervous, actually stuttering a little as he assured her that he would take good care of me and see I got home soon.

Handing me back the phone, Elvis settled under the covers and continued to watch television while I finished saying good-bye. When I hung up, he took my hand and again I felt uneasy. Although I wasn't a virgin, I certainly wasn't about to leap into bed with anyone right away, even Elvis. My mind began to race for something to say, a way to explain my hesitation.

But Elvis didn't make a move beyond holding my hand. I gradually relaxed and lay back beside him, watching television. He went to sleep holding my hand. By then daylight was visible along the edges of the closed curtains in the room. Exhausted, I finally fell asleep beside him.

Upon waking, Elvis ordered room service. GeeGee brought in the food, laying a towel in front of us on the bed and placing trays with our food on top. Elvis sat cross-legged and I followed suit as we ate, talked, and watched television.

When I finished eating, I walked over to the curtains and pulled them aside to peek at the view. The lights of Las Vegas were shining brightly. Anticipating the prospect of experiencing the city, I went into the bathroom and changed back into my clothes. When I came out, Elvis was on the telephone and I heard him arranging our return to Memphis.

Had I done something wrong? I thought it would be rude to ask if we were going sightseeing, but to fly all the way here without seeing Las Vegas seemed odd. I tried making sense of it. Maybe he had to get back for work? Or maybe Elvis just did this at times, flying someplace because he relaxed better with a change of scenery?

I may not have understood Elvis in those moments, but I consoled myself with the thought that at least I'd gotten a chance to spend more time with him. I'd flown on his plane and received beautiful gifts, and all the while Elvis had remained a gentleman. Reflecting on this, my disappointment about not seeing Las Vegas began to evaporate.

We reconnected with his cousins in our room, and what had started as a Saturday night "date" for me lasted until our return to Memphis in the early hours of Monday, November 22. We drove back from the airport to Graceland, where Elvis asked me to stay for a while. I followed him up to his bedroom, where he sat on the bed, turned on the television, and began flipping through channels with a remote control.

He stopped when a newscaster reminded us it was the anniversary of John F. Kennedy's death. Elvis talked briefly about Kennedy's assassination, thinking many were involved rather than there being a single shooter, and then he moved on to talk about self-defense.

At one point during this conversation, Elvis leaned over the side of his bed and sat back up with a gun in his hand. It startled me; I hadn't noticed it on the floor before. My father owned a revolver and rifle at home, but I wasn't used to seeing a gun up close and out in the open like this. Elvis said it was a Colt .45 and proudly showed me its turquoise handle with the initial E on one side and P on the other.

"It's for protection," he explained, and told me about a threatening letter he had received once while getting ready to perform in Las Vegas. "My daddy came to me one night with tears in his eyes, asking me not to go on," he said. "I told my daddy, as a performer, the show *must* go on, so they tightened the security and I took the risk. Luckily, the letter turned out to be a fluke."

Speaking of yet another incident during a Vegas show, Elvis told me about three thugs approaching him onstage and how he'd defended himself using karate. He laid the gun back on the floor and I could only imagine how many other frightening experiences he'd had to deal with in the past. I appreciated him sharing these stories, and was newly aware of the fear he obviously lived with on a daily basis. I understood how that fear could bring him to a point where he felt in need of constant protection.

The buttons atop a phone on his bedside table lit up then and Elvis answered, listening with a concerned look. When he hung up, he told me the guard at the front gates, his cousin Harold Lloyd, said that the entertainer, Jerry Lee Lewis, had arrived in his car and wanted to see him.

Jerry Lee Lewis? I was amazed. Much to my surprise, though, Elvis told me he didn't want to see Jerry Lee.

"He's a great piano player and performer, but I just think he's crazy," Elvis said. Getting the guard back on the phone, Elvis instructed him to tell Jerry Lee he was unavailable.

I didn't get to meet Mr. Lewis in those early morning hours, but it had been one heck of a date. By now I was exhausted. When I told Elvis I thought it was time for me to leave, he surprised me again, asking, "Would you like to go on tour with me sometime?"

I'd barely had the chance to absorb what I'd already experienced over the weekend, but I was thrilled by the offer and curious about what other new worlds I might experience with Elvis. "Yes," I said at once.

Elvis had singled me out, pursued me, and said things that made me feel special. Yet a small part of me still wasn't fully sure how he felt about me, because we were just getting to know one another. There had been no passionate kisses or heavy petting, and the fact that he'd been such a gentleman fueled my attraction to him even more. I thought Elvis was a fascinating man, and I definitely wanted to learn more about him.

Before I left, Elvis kissed me lightly for the second time, another gentlemanly peck. I found it hard to say good-bye because the word sounded final. Instead of saying good-bye, I chose to say, "I'll see you later," hoping, in some strange way, that this magic phrase might guarantee I'd see him again.

And, for the rest of my time with Elvis, I never would say good-bye when leaving Graceland because I always wanted to come back to him.

CHAPTER 5

After that first exhilarating, overwhelming trip to Las Vegas with Elvis, I tried to resume my normal life. I slept briefly and went right back to work at the dress shop for a couple of hours that Monday afternoon and didn't tell anyone there about my weekend.

After work, my friend Teri stopped by my house and we went for a drive in her car. By then I was about ready to burst; I couldn't resist telling her about my adventures. "You'll never guess who I met over the weekend," I said, deliberately trying to sound casual.

"Who?"

"Elvis."

Teri slammed on the brakes, pulled over to the side of the road, and refused to drive until I'd recounted how my sisters and I had met Elvis. Needless to say, she was blown away. I didn't blame her. I still had a hard time believing any of it was real myself. I then went on and told her about our Las Vegas trip.

I didn't hear from Elvis Monday night. By early Tuesday morning, it was all over the news that Jerry Lee had been arrested outside of Graceland. He had returned in the early morning hours and nudged the front gates with his Lincoln, demanding to see Elvis with a Derringer .38 pistol in his possession. As I listened to the news, I remembered Elvis's comments regarding Jerry; maybe Elvis had been right not to have seen him that night. I wondered what Elvis had been thinking when Jerry returned.

Wednesday evening rolled around without any word from Elvis. It had only been a few days, but I wondered why he hadn't called. He had seemed to want to see me again after our time together in Las Vegas, and he'd certainly acted like I was special to him, with all of the things he had said and done.

From his affectionate behavior toward me, I would have thought Elvis might have at least called to say hello. After all, I was the proud owner of a bracelet with his name on it, and he had declared, "Now everyone will know you belong to me."

My doubts began to swirl, as I wondered whether he'd really meant the things he'd said to me. Was it possible that maybe I was placing more value on our time together than he did? I hoped not.

When Larry, the man I'd been seeing for a few months, telephoned me at home that night, I was thrown into another emotional tailspin. Whether it was my doing or not, things had changed for me. The past weekend had been completely mind-blowing, and I hadn't gone one day without thinking about Elvis.

I needed to be honest and up-front with Larry, so I asked him to come over that night. I knew that telling him about Elvis and my sudden change of heart would catch him as off guard as it had me, and I felt bad about that. I didn't know if Elvis would even call me again, but I was willing to wait and see.

Larry and I talked for a while. Afterward, he still wasn't ready to accept that I wanted to end things, and he left expressing the hope that we could sort things through.

I had gone about my normal schedule, worked at the dress shop and otherwise spent time with my family, but I hadn't gone out in the evenings, wondering if Elvis would call. My family had been stunned by the bracelet Elvis had given me. I was so afraid of having it fall off my wrist that I didn't wear it often; I only looked at it in my bedroom, still surprised that Elvis had given it to me. It seemed to have been something special to him and yet I hadn't heard from him.

When Thanksgiving came and went, and all day Friday, too, without a call from Elvis, I truly felt that something wasn't right. I must have misinterpreted what had happened between Elvis and me. I was just going to have to wake up and return to my real life.

On the Saturday after Thanksgiving, a man called our home. He said he was Elvis's road manager, Joe Esposito, and asked to speak with me. My mood immediately lifted as Joe told me Elvis was on tour, would be in San Francisco, and wanted me to fly there and see his show.

My initial reaction was one of enormous relief. *That's why I haven't heard anything,* I thought. *He's been on tour!* I even rationalized that maybe this road trip was the reason why we had left Las Vegas so soon.

In the middle of arranging things with Joe, I suddenly heard Elvis's voice come on the line. "I need you out here with me, Ginger," he said, and added with a chuckle, "Get your ass out here!"

I was so glad to hear his voice that I simply said, "Okay," even though "Get your ass out here!" wasn't exactly the way I thought I'd be invited. It wasn't the sort of language I was used to hearing. I was momentarily taken aback, but my excitement kicked in, and I decided to overlook it. Elvis wanted me to join him on tour!

Elvis then asked if he could speak with my mother. "I want to ease any worries she might have about you traveling to see me," he said.

My mother and Elvis spoke for a few moments, then Elvis put Joe back on the line to finish discussing travel arrangements. Joe told me to be at Memphis Aero at 10:30 that very night.

Tonight? Panicked, I hung up and quickly began to pack. I had no clue what to wear and felt nothing in my wardrobe was right. Thankfully, Terry came to my rescue and generously loaned me a couple of nice outfits she'd received from her pageants.

It was a brutally cold, snowy night in Memphis, and my parents were worried about me traveling in those weather conditions. Just as I finished packing, Milo High, Elvis's personal pilot, called to say that the door to the JetStar was frozen shut. "We're not sure we can open it," he admitted.

He also told me they had to wait for the runways to be cleared and the plane to be deiced. After the anticipation of seeing Elvis and all of my rushing around, I sat in our den and anxiously wondered if I'd even be making the trip at all.

A few hours later, Milo finally called back. "We're ready for you, Ginger," he said.

My mother asked me to call when I arrived in San Francisco as I left with my father for the airport. The JetStar was waiting for me on the edge of the runway; I said good-bye to my dad and hurriedly boarded the plane, already feeling the bitter wind seeping through my coat.

It was so cold inside the plane, I could see my own breath. Milo and George greeted me when I boarded and handed me a blanket. As we took off and began our journey west, I reflected on how, once again, I was experiencing things with Elvis that I'd never done before in my life: leaving Memphis alone for the first time and going to another city I'd never seen before, to be with a man I hardly knew.

I felt a shadow of trepidation creep over me. I suddenly wished my sisters or a friend could have accompanied me, so I wouldn't feel quite as alone. I lay across the couch, pulled the blanket up around me, and tried to sleep, knowing I'd need my energy for whatever adventures lay ahead.

We landed in San Francisco a few hours past midnight on what was now Sunday, November 28. I rode with Milo and George to a Hilton Hotel, where they helped with my suitcase and escorted me to my room.

The first thing I did was place a collect call to my parents to let them know I was okay. Then I started unpacking. I didn't know if Elvis would have a show that afternoon or evening, but because he had arranged my travel, he must have surely known of my arrival. I was certain I'd get a knock on my door or a phone call shortly. I was really looking forward to seeing him.

The minutes ticked by. I began to feel tired from the thrill of the trip, the anticipation of seeing Elvis again, and being awake for so long, especially since I was still running two hours later on Memphis time. I tried to fight sleep by watching television.

A couple of hours went slowly by. It was getting closer to dawn, but still feeling like I was on call, I was reluctant to wash my face, put on pajamas, and crawl into bed only to have Elvis knock at my door. So I stayed up, letting a few more hours pass.

Finally, feeling silly, I decided Elvis was asleep and I should get some rest. I gave up and went to bed.

I woke that afternoon around 3 P.M., feeling better but still a bit jet-lagged. Positive that I'd hear from Elvis any minute now or at least from someone who'd give me information about his show, I took a quick shower and hurriedly got dressed.

I hurried for nothing, as it turned out. More time passed. Even if Elvis had performed last night and had not gotten to sleep until early morning, he must have been up for a while now because it was after four. Why hadn't I heard from him?

Again, I tried to rationalize what was going on. Since I'd arrived so late, maybe Elvis was letting me sleep, I thought. I hadn't eaten since leaving Memphis and began to feel hungry. Suddenly I realized that, in all of my excitement and rushing around, I hadn't brought any money with me. I'd never been in a situation like this.

I didn't feel right taking advantage of Elvis by calling room service. I wondered if I should leave the room and try to find a member of his staff, but I was afraid to leave for fear of missing Elvis or a phone call from one of his employees.

Feeling more awkward by the minute, I continued to watch television as the hours marched by. It was bizarre, being whisked out of Memphis and then having to wait around like this without a word from anyone.

I didn't really feel angry at Elvis because he clearly had wanted me to see his show enough to bring me here. I was happy that he'd asked and excited about seeing him. But, as day turned into night, I was starting to feel abandoned and confused. Where was Elvis?

The phone finally rang around 6 p.m. I leaped to answer it, excited that someone had finally remembered I was here.

It was one of Elvis's employees, asking if I needed anything. When I told him I was hungry, he said, "Order anything and charge it to the room." Then he hung up with no mention of Elvis or where he was.

Was Elvis's location a secret? I felt completely baffled. I still had no idea what was going on. At that point, though, I was just relieved to know I could be eating soon, and so I ordered room service—another new experience for me.

It wasn't until late that night, after eleven, that there was finally a knock on my door. I figured it had to be someone associated with Elvis, or maybe even Elvis himself, so it would be safe to open the door.

A man in his early thirties stood there. He had mid-length, dark shaggy hair and introduced himself as Jerry Schilling.

"You're going to be moving to a different room," Jerry announced, then quickly walked away.

I closed the door, more bewildered than ever. *A different room? Why?*

Things had happened slowly up to now, so I figured I had plenty of time to pack. I sat back down to watch more television.

A few minutes later, however, another sharp rap sounded at my door. *Already?* I opened it and Jerry was back, this time accompanied by Joe Esposito, Elvis's road manager. Joe was shorter than Jerry, in his late thirties, with a compact build and a dark receding hairline.

While the two men waited in the hallway, I quickly threw things into my suitcase. Joe and Jerry then led me on a long walk to another section of the hotel. When we reached what I thought was my new room, Jerry opened the door and gestured for me to enter. I was surprised to see Elvis inside, sitting on a couch in the center of a suite and dressed in a hooded blue terry-cloth robe. He was surrounded by men.

Our eyes locked and my heart did a little skip. All of the hours of waiting and uncertainty were worth it. I was thrilled to see him.

At the same time, I felt uncomfortable walking into this room full of men. I'd always been shy with men, and even though I knew I'd been inspected during my first time inside Graceland, the scrutiny was even more intense when I entered this room.

Elvis seemed at ease. He stood up with a smile and walked over to give me a hug, then turned to the group of strangers and began introductions. The men in the room included Larry Geller, his hairdresser, a lean man in his late thirties; Billy Stanley, Elvis's stepbrother, in his twenties and an aide; Ed Parker, a strongly built Hawaiian man in his mid-forties with thick silver hair who had trained Elvis in karate; Dr. George Nichopoulos, late forties, Elvis's silver-haired physician; Dean Nichopoulos, the doctor's son; and Al Strada. Dean and Al were both in their twenties and working as Elvis's aides along with Billy.

Finally, I was introduced to an overweight man in his early forties with salt-and-pepper hair named Lamar Fike. No job was mentioned for him at the time, so I was left to wonder if he was employed by Elvis, too, or simply visiting.

Elvis took my hand and led me into the suite's adjoining bedroom. He didn't explain why I hadn't heard anything or seen him until now, but I didn't care anymore. My feelings of confusion and abandonment had vanished the minute I saw him.

Books were scattered everywhere, on top of his bed, on the floor, and spilling out of the suitcases. A few looked familiar; they dealt with the same topics I remembered seeing in his bedroom at Graceland, including religious philosophy and numerology.

Seeing that most of the books had to do with spirituality, I realized for the first time that Elvis truly was on a serious personal quest. We sat on his bed and talked for a little while about my trip, what he'd been reading, and this and that. He told me that he had a show the following night, and I wondered if he'd had one tonight.

Elvis wasn't interested in talking about his shows, however. He wanted to look through some of his books. As we continued to sit together, Elvis began reading to me, pointing out phrases he had underlined on well-worn pages, some of which had loosened and were falling out of the bindings. Seeing that he had even written notes inside some of the margins, I understood this wasn't just casual reading for Elvis. He was studying these books in detail. I admired the fact that he was hungry for knowledge.

Elvis had left the bedroom door slightly ajar. After a time, I noticed some of the men I'd met earlier still seated in the living room. Could these be normal hours for all of them, Elvis included? It was now well after one in the morning.

The past times I'd been with Elvis, I had thought he was staying up late only because he was off work and enjoying himself. I began wondering if maybe the late night hours provided the only time Elvis could truly feel relaxed and find some peace because the rest of the world was asleep.

We talked until the early morning hours. When the two of us were both exhausted, Elvis told me I had a separate room adjoining the living room suite. Still the gentleman, he escorted me across the now-empty living room and said he would see me later that afternoon. With another light kiss, he headed back toward his own bedroom.

I entered my new, larger room and saw that my suitcase had been placed inside. I opened it, took out pajamas, and walked into a generous bathroom wallpapered in a paisley print, noticing a telephone attached on the wall above the toilet. The phone wouldn't have meant much to some, but this was my first time in such a lavish hotel suite and I was tickled by this small touch of luxury.

I soon settled in bed, marveling at how my life could change so quickly. Between the trip and the anxiety that had mounted while I was waiting to hear from Elvis, I was bone-tired. My head had barely hit the pillow when I fell into a sound sleep.

I was jolted awake at 4 P.M. by a loud knock on my door and a voice announcing, "Breakfast!" A little late for breakfast, I mused, but then again, I was in Elvis's world and living in the Elvis time zone now.

I jumped up, quickly dressed, put on some makeup, and entered the suite's living room. Elvis's bedroom door opened and he joined me, still wearing pajamas and a blue hooded robe. For the first time, we actually sat together on a couch instead of a bed.

One of Elvis's aides spread a towel across the coffee table and placed two plates of southwestern omelets, bacon, coffee, and juice in front of us. The television was turned on, and Elvis and I chatted as we ate.

Shortly, some of the men I'd met the night before began filtering into the room. Given the fact that every man there wore the same gold necklace with the TCB lightning bolt emblem, I guessed they had to be part of a special group associated with Elvis.

I hadn't spent much time alone with Elvis, but now I had the opportunity to witness more of his sharp sense of humor as he lit up a cigar and began joking around with the guys. He found some of the things on television amusing and made funny comments as he surfed through various channels.

As the other men laughed along with him and the conversation became increasingly animated, Elvis's conversation was peppered with curse words. I thought this must be his way of talking around the guys since, except for an occasional foul word here and there, I hadn't noticed him speak this way before. Later, as our relationship grew, I learned to overlook the choice words Elvis used at times, although I'd never be 100 percent comfortable with them.

Elvis and the men continued to pal around with one another while I ate quietly. When I finished, I stood to go to the bathroom.

Elvis grabbed hold of my hand, startling me. "Where are you going?" he asked.

"Just to wash my hands," I replied.

"Oh. Okay. Hurry back," he said.

I was pleased and flattered. Elvis had been so engaged in conversation with his entourage, I'd thought he wouldn't even notice if I slipped out of the room for a few minutes. Apparently, though, he was still focused on me, and my presence was important to him.

As the time for Elvis's show drew near, he went into his bedroom to get ready while I dressed in mine. By the time I returned to the living room, there was a buzz of activity. Various aides, along with Elvis's hairdresser, physician, road manager, and bodyguards, were all rushing in and out of his bedroom.

Before long, Elvis stepped out of his room wearing a white jumpsuit with varying shades of blue in a rainbow pattern swirled across the front of his suit and down the sides of both pant legs. His hair was styled to perfection. He wore a matching belt with chains around his waist, and his feet were clad in white leather boots. Seeing him dressed in one of his stage suits up close like this, he looked so handsome, it took my breath away.

While some people gathered around to finish preparing him to go onstage, Elvis glanced over at me with a faint smile, placing his hands on his belt and shifting it up a bit. He raised an eyebrow at me and gave me a slightly worried look.

I couldn't believe Elvis was showing a hint of anxiety before a performance after so many years! That endeared him to me even more. I mouthed the words "very nice" to him from across the room, wanting him to know that I thought he looked great.

Surrounded by Elvis's entourage, we finally left the room and walked down the hotel corridor. Elvis grew quiet. I could tell he was focused on his upcoming show.

We took the elevator down to the hotel's ground floor. Outside, a couple of cars and a limousine were waiting for us with a police escort. I had never been in a limo, so climbing into one of these cars was yet another novelty for me.

I scooted into the center of the backseat. Elvis sat beside me. Some of the other men crowded in with us, while others piled into the second car. I sensed that Elvis was still anxious about his performance. He stared pensively out of the window during the short ride, occasionally making small talk or kidding someone, but speaking softly. He explained this by whispering to me, "I'm protecting my voice."

Upon our arrival at the Cow Palace arena, a huge indoor arena in Daly City, everything warped into hyperspeed. We immediately exited the car, and Elvis was rushed into a dressing room. I was escorted past backstage hands onto the floor of the arena and told to wait by the stage.

The arena looked full and there was a comic named Jackie Kahane already performing onstage. I would later learn that he had been Elvis's opening act for the past six years or so. I stood alone and felt extremely excited but a little scared, too, as I waited for someone to tell me what to do or where to go.

Reflecting on the only other Elvis concert I'd seen, back in July with my mom and sister, I thought about how lucky I was to be here right now, about to watch his show from the perspective of a guest instead of one more ticket holder.

Eventually, Dean Nichopoulos approached and handed me a soft drink, then brought over a steel chair, explaining it was for me. Elvis wanted the chair placed right onstage behind his soundmen! It felt great that he wanted me this close to him!

"Just make sure you head for the limo at the start of his closing song, 'Can't Help Falling in Love,'" he warned. "Otherwise, it might be tough to get you out of here when the fans rush the stage at the end of the show."

My heart beat faster as I was assisted onto the stage. There I met soundmen Felton Jarvis and Bruce Jackson as I sat down.

Jackie Kahane did a great job of warming up the crowd. As Jackie's routine wound down, a thrill of anticipation began to ripple through the audience. I was feeling this excitement, too, but on a much more intense, personal level. I wasn't just going to watch Elvis the performer tonight, but a man who made me feel special and was beginning to stir feelings in me. I really wanted to see Elvis do well.

Finally, the lights slowly dimmed as musicians and singers walked onto the stage and took their places. Screams erupted from the audience as the orchestra began playing "Also Sprach Zarathustra," better known as the theme music from the motion picture *2001: A Space Odyssey*.

Elvis's onstage entrance was greeted by thousands of flashing camera bulbs. The flashes blinded me momentarily and gave the arena's interior an eerie strobe light effect. Like a magnet, Elvis drew all eyes to him as he assertively strode back and forth across the stage to grant everyone the best chance to see him and take photographs.

Elvis then approached Charlie Hodge, who helped place the strap to a guitar across his shoulder, and moved to the center stage microphone. There he began playing his guitar, belting out "C.C. Rider" with great passion, volume, and timbre. His iconic voice boomed out over the arena, immediately bringing many in the audience to their feet.

Throughout the concert, Elvis genuinely seemed to be having fun. He joked with the crowd, his musicians, and the background singers. Charlie sang harmony, played rhythm guitar, occasionally handed Elvis a glass of water, and was quick to place a fresh scarf around Elvis's neck after one went soaring from his hand out into the audience. Sitting onstage so close to him, I found it alarming to watch how the fans tumbled and climbed over one another in a heated competition to grab a scarf. I was afraid one of them might get hurt.

As I watched Elvis perform, real time seemed suspended. He'd been onstage for well over an hour when the band started to play "Can't Help Falling in Love." With a start, I suddenly remembered Dean's warning about being in the limo before the song ended.

I stood up and prepared to leave. Suddenly, the word "Stay!" resounded through the speakers.

I glanced over my shoulder and saw Elvis momentarily point at me while continuing to sing. I couldn't believe that he was immediately aware that I was leaving!

I sat back in my chair, embarrassed, wondering if anyone else had picked up on this. I could only hope the dim lighting in my corner of the stage had made it impossible for anyone in the audience to notice me.

I grew increasingly nervous as the seconds ticked by, worried about how I'd make it to the car in time. Finally, when I saw Elvis walking to the opposite side of the stage, I jumped up and ran off, still a little fearful that he'd notice I was gone. The last thing I wanted him to think was that I didn't want to hear his closing number or appreciate the effort he'd gone to in order to bring me here.

The limousine was waiting at the end of an underground ramp, its engine running, its doors open. Someone led me there, and not a moment too soon, for suddenly Elvis came rushing toward the limo, surrounded by members of his entourage.

He hurriedly climbed into the car, drenched in sweat, with a towel draped around his neck. His bodyguards, Dr. Nichopoulos, Joe Esposito, and a few others quickly joined us.

"Good show, good show," Joe congratulated him as Elvis leaned back in the seat, wiping his face with the towel.

Others began complimenting Elvis as well. I finally jumped in. "You were wonderful," I said.

As the limousine slowly began moving forward, Elvis leaned toward me and softly asked, "Did you see the very end of the show?"

"No," I admitted. "I was told to be in the car before the last song finished."

I saw a flash of annoyance darken his face. "Be sure Ginger remains seated until the very end of the next show," he announced to everyone in the limo.

I felt a smile tug at the corners of my mouth. I was going to see another one of his shows!

Fans mobbed the limo as our car emerged from the building. It was a scary feeling to be surrounded like that, with some fans even trying to climb on top of the limo.

I took hold of Elvis's hand. Elvis, however, seemed calm. He was clearly accustomed to this sort of thing. He waved to his fans and joked with me about buying a plastic arm with a hand attached so it would look like he was still waving, while resting his own.

I couldn't help but think about the early Beatles movie *A Hard Day's Night* and the shots in that film of their fans chasing after them. Wait a minute, I thought. Elvis must have experienced that long before they did! I didn't see how anyone could ever completely get used to this kind of attention.

Back at the hotel, Elvis went into his bedroom with his aides and Dr. Nichopoulos. I went into mine. After the men left, Elvis asked for me and ordered room service.

I walked into Elvis's bedroom and was surprised to see him already dressed in pajamas and a robe. I couldn't blame him for wanting to get out of his stage suit and into more comfortable clothing, but I was still surprised by the pajamas. It wasn't that late at night.

Various other members of his staff entered the room and our food was soon brought to us. While we ate, Elvis began scrutinizing his performance. I saw how important a top-quality show was to him as he went over everything: the band, the lighting, the sound, and the audience experience. He didn't want to disappoint his fans in any way.

As we sat there and talked about the show, it dawned on me that I had entered Elvis's suite at around the same time the previous night. Elvis had been dressed in his robe then, too, and surrounded by these men. Had he finished a show last night? And, if so, why wasn't I invited?

(It wouldn't be until after Elvis's death that I would learn the real reason I had been left sitting in my hotel room for a day: Linda Thompson had been in the hotel and Elvis was ushering her out with one hand and me in with the other. What Elvis wanted, Elvis got. For many around him, this was "taking care of business.")

After the guys left, Elvis told me that his tour would finish the following evening in Anaheim, California. "You'll stay, won't you?" he asked.

"Of course," I said, thrilled by the invitation to see another of his performances.

Once we'd settled that, Elvis picked out a book to read. After entertaining thousands of his fans, he seemed to need a way to focus his thoughts and turn everything off—a feat I imagined couldn't be easy, especially for a man who loved performing as much as Elvis did.

We read together for a long time. Elvis always put intense philosophical thought into interpreting what he felt various authors were trying to say in their books. This exercise was helpful to me because the books themselves weren't easy to understand right away. I felt like I was in the presence of an interesting teacher.

I began to get sleepy after a time, but I did my best to stay focused, feeling it was important to Elvis. Around dawn, an aide brought in a small yellow packet and left it on the night table. Elvis swallowed its contents with water from a nearby ice-filled jug.

I was instantly alert and curious. "What's that for?"

"Something to help me sleep," Elvis said.

He had been deeply absorbed, even energized by the different books we'd been looking over, so I didn't think twice about him needing to take something to help him sleep. Although it was morning by now, I told him good night. Once again, he walked me to my room like a gentleman.

For some reason, I didn't sleep long—probably because of the combination of jet lag and the strange reverse schedule Elvis kept, turning day into night and night into day. When I got up around 1 P.M., it was quiet in the rest of the suite.

I figured Elvis was still asleep because we'd been up so late. I hadn't really eaten much dinner and now I was hungry. I felt more comfortable about ordering room service, so I did, eating alone in my room as I contemplated this intriguing new world I was inhabiting. There was Elvis's lifestyle and dynamic personality to think about, along with his music, his religious studies, and the many people who seemed to surround him 24/7.

It was intense, exhilarating, and exhausting as I tried to process everything and understand where I was in all of this. I didn't yet think of myself as "the one," though Elvis seemed to be doing his best to make me feel like I was special to him. If he wanted our relationship to go further, I decided I was ready.

Finally, around 4 P.M., someone knocked on my bedroom door. I opened it to find Elvis standing there in his pajamas and robe—a sight I was beginning to think of as normal. "I'm going to order us food," he said. When I confessed that I'd already eaten, it seemed to bother him. "From now on, I'd like us to eat together," he said.

"I'm sorry," I apologized. I had no idea Elvis would be sensitive about that. At the same time, I was pleased that he'd said "from now on," which indicated he was certainly seeing a future for our relationship. I wanted to fit in however I could.

On tour with him later, whenever I happened to be in my room when breakfast was brought in, Elvis would knock on my door, take my hand, and lead me to the coffee table or his bed so we could eat together.

Before long, Elvis's food was brought up to him and we sat together in the living room while he ate. He told me he was going to perform in Las Vegas right after this tour and asked if I would like to go with him. "I'll be there for ten days," he said.

I loved watching his shows and was excited by the prospect of spending more time with him. I was concerned, though. I'd only brought enough clothes for what I thought would be a short visit. Could I really go from California to Las Vegas with him? And what about my job? How could I just not show up for ten days?

As I was thinking about the logistics, the men in Elvis's entourage began showing up one by one. What was quickly becoming a familiar scenario ensued: Elvis joked around and smoked while everyone laughed along with him. After Elvis's death, I would learn more of the personal history Elvis had with some of these men, who unbeknownst to me at the time, had been dubbed the "Memphis Mafia" by the media.

I left the living room to place a call to Memphis, letting my parents know I wouldn't be coming home for a while. It was unusual for me to be away from home for so long, and it felt good to hear their familiar voices.

At the end of our conversation, my mother mentioned that she had spoken to her father, my grandfather, whom I was close to, about me traveling with Elvis. Being eighty-five and old-fashioned, my grandfather had expressed concern as to whether this was proper. "Tell Elvis she's my girl," my grandfather had said.

I understood how someone from his generation might have concerns about what I was doing. I figured my parents did as well because I seemed to be moving headlong into an uncertain future. I had my own fears; I didn't want to fall in love only to get my heart broken. On the other hand, Elvis's magnetism was pulling me closer and closer to him by the day.

I asked my mother to call the shop where I worked. "Please explain what's happening," I told her, wondering whether I'd still have a job when I came back from Las Vegas.

I couldn't worry about that right then, though. My focus now was on being with Elvis. I wanted to do that more than anything in the world. The rest of my life could wait.

As we prepared to leave for Anaheim, I began to pack. I knew I was totally unprepared for Las Vegas, but what could I do?

I closed my suitcase and walked into the living room, thinking I'd just have to manage with the clothes I had. Elvis soon joined me, having changed into his casual navy blue jumpsuit.

During the ride to the airport, Elvis fell into what I was starting to see was one of his frequent habits: He propped his right foot on top of his left knee and began to nervously shake it. I was tickled to notice he hadn't really changed clothes at all, for the edge of his pajama bottom was sticking out from beneath the pant leg of his jumpsuit.

A huge passenger jet waited for us at the airport. Until then, I'd had no idea Elvis owned another plane. His daughter's name, Lisa Marie, was written in blue on the upper front of the aircraft. High upon the tail was a picture of the American flag, and below that appeared the letters *TCB* in gold above a gold lightning bolt.

As we walked up the stairway to the door of the plane, Elvis told me he had picked out the color scheme himself. "The first time I showed it to my daughter, Lisa, she just yawned," he said with a grin.

A flight attendant greeted us. I also met the rest of the crew and the pilot, Captain Elwood David. I thought the captain's name was a cool coincidence, since my father's middle name was Elwood and this was the only other time I had heard it.

The JetStar had certainly impressed me, but the *Lisa Marie* was magnificent. The main compartment of the plane was furnished like a living room, with two suede couches—one green, one brown—leather chairs, leather-topped tables, and even television sets. As I followed Elvis deeper into the plane, we passed a large conference table surrounded by tan leather chairs and entered a sitting room furnished with blue suede chairs.

Finally, we entered a bedroom. Decorated in blue, it had everything you could want: a queen-size bed, a reading chair, and even a dressing area with a half bath and blue washbasin. I stayed in the bedroom with Elvis while the others took seats up front. During the short flight, Elvis proudly continued telling me about the plane's various special features.

After landing, some employees began entering the bedroom to help Elvis prepare for his show, so I moved up front. When Elvis finally walked out, he was dressed in a beautiful jumpsuit with an ornate Native American feather design. We were soon off to the Anaheim Convention Center, where, once again, I found myself seated onstage behind the soundmen to watch the show.

This time I was mindful about remaining in my chair a bit longer. It was fantastic to be so close to Elvis when he performed. Sitting onstage really pulled me into his show. I felt lucky to be so completely in the moment with him, following his every gesture, comment, joke, and glance.

As the song "Can't Help Falling in Love" drew to a close, the band's drummer kicked in and Elvis began doing impressive karate moves, which ended with him crouched in a long low stance, one leg bent and the other extended. He looked quickly over at me and smiled.

I smiled back, realizing this was what he'd wanted me to see. Having been a fan of karate as a child, I loved seeing it on television and in films. I could tell Elvis must have studied it for years to be this proficient. I wouldn't have traded being where I was that minute to be anywhere else—or with anyone else.

When the show was over, I hurried to catch the limousine, almost bumping into Elvis as we exited the theater. Safely inside the car, he said he was happy I'd seen his finale.

"Good show, good show," Joe declared once again as our car sped away from the building.

Back aboard the *Lisa Marie*, Dr. Nichopoulos and some aides walked to the back of the plane with Elvis and closed the bedroom door. As I followed behind them, I noticed that many of the same people were on the plane with us, along with some new faces.

Al Strada walked out of the bedroom, carrying Elvis's boots and stage suit. He'd left the door partially open. Through the crack, I could see Elvis, half clad in his casual navy jumpsuit, standing with his arms in the air and out to his sides. I was amused to see Dean scrambling around him, zipping up his suit and putting socks on his feet.

Elvis saw me watching and motioned for me to enter the bedroom as Dean and Dr. Nichopoulos left. Walking toward him, I noticed the zipper tag to his suit was flipped upward. Deciding to place the finishing touch on his change of clothes, I quickly flicked the zipper down with my finger.

I was stunned when Elvis reached out and grabbed my wrist. "Don't do that again," he said. "I've been trained to guard against sudden moves."

I believed him for a second. Then Elvis broke into a smile and I saw he was joking. Still, after seeing his karate moves onstage, I believed Elvis would have been perfectly capable of taking someone down if the need arose.

Elvis sat on the edge of his bed and I took the chair beside it. As the *Lisa Marie* took off, Elvis opened a suitcase and removed Cheiro's *Book of Numbers* again. By then I understood enough from our readings to know that the point of this numerology book was to help people use the power of numbers to predict the future using things like birth dates.

Now Elvis turned to a page I hadn't seen yet. On this page, Cheiro described how people should wear certain colors and carry lucky stones according to their numbers. As we talked about colors and their meanings, Elvis was reminded of a story his father had told him about the day he and his twin brother were born in Tupelo, Mississippi.

"While my momma was in labor," Elvis said, "my daddy went outside our home to get water from the well. When Daddy turned around, he noticed a blue light above our house. Daddy rushed back in and found out my brother Jesse was stillborn. Then I was born."

Elvis spoke with reverence, as if the blue light represented God's relationship to him and his own understanding of the path his life had taken. Vernon's story initially sounded far-fetched to me, but still, it gave me chills. I wondered if Elvis really believed the story and decided from his tone that he most likely did. Reflecting on where Elvis had come from and who he had become made me wonder if he really had been chosen by God.

Since I had been brought up in a Christian family, I believed the miracles described in the Bible to be true. I felt Elvis was a strong Christian because of his love of gospel, and if he didn't see a conflict with this way of thinking, I felt there wouldn't be a conflict in my beliefs as well. I was determined to keep an open mind, feeling that maybe God does touch each of us in different ways. "I do believe certain things like that can happen," I told Elvis now, speaking as solemnly to him as he had to me.

At that moment, Elvis pulled off one of his socks to show me his right foot. His second and third toes were joined together at the bottom, a physical attribute he called "twin toes."

"I think being a twin was the cause of it," he joked.

When I laughed, Elvis gave me a long look and said softly, "You know, Ginger, I feel like I've known you for a long time. When I first saw you it was like a siren went off inside me saying, 'Back . . . whoa. Back, boy! Find out what she's like.'"

As Elvis told me this, he placed one hand over his heart and raised the other in the air as if trying to halt something. "Seeing you was like seeing someone I've always known and yet never known," he went on. "I kind of see my mother when I look at you."

Too surprised to speak, I wondered if he was talking about how I looked or how I acted. Either way, I was deeply touched and took this as a compliment. Elvis turned his attention back to Cheiro's book without waiting for a reply. He'd made these strong statements so casually, yet so sincerely. I couldn't help but ask myself whether I felt the same way: As if I'd known him for a lot longer than the few days we'd spent together.

The answer had to be yes. When I met Elvis that first night at Graceland, in Lisa's bedroom, I was the one who had greeted him first. Something deep inside had made me feel instinctively comfortable enough to do so.

After a short while, Elvis mentioned he needed to talk some business and called a few others to the back. I left the room to give them privacy and waited just outside the bedroom door.

The other passengers on the *Lisa Marie* were conversing with one another. Several were playing cards or other games. I definitely felt like the new girl in town.

I squared my shoulders, took a deep breath, and deliberately walked up front to introduce myself, then tried to join the conversations. Charlie Hodge weaved in and out of the main room with a cocktail, telling jokes. Dean shouted, "I'm the king!" after making a good move in backgammon, a game I had never heard of before.

There were a few other women on the plane as well. Some of them wore gold necklaces with the letters *TLC*, similar to the TCB necklaces a lot of the men had. Soon I would learn that *TLC* stood for *tender loving care*. These necklaces were gifts from Elvis, given to his family, friends, and a few select others.

I had introduced myself to a couple of people, trying to make headway, when someone approached to say Elvis was asking for me to return to his room. I did so, hoping that at least I'd made the first step in trying to get to know the insular group surrounding Elvis.

CHAPTER 6

After landing in Las Vegas, we climbed into a waiting limousine and were escorted by police to the Hilton International Hotel. As we passed by a large, glitzy marquee displaying Elvis's name, I mused on the fact that I'd never been to Las Vegas before in my life, and now I'd been here twice in a short time.

Once again, we entered the hotel through the back door, but this time rode the elevator to the thirtieth floor. I followed Elvis down a hallway toward a security guard sitting in a chair beside some double doors. One of the doors was opened; we walked through it and down a few steps into the living room of a penthouse.

It was a sumptuous suite decorated with gold carpeting and drapes. Black pillows accented the gold sofa and chairs furnishing the living room. There was a dining room and kitchen, too.

I'm sure I must have looked as awed as I felt, as I gaped at our new surroundings, because Elvis was watching my reaction and smiling. From the main part of the enormous suite, he walked me down a short hallway and into a master bedroom. There were his and her bathrooms, a sitting area, and a king-size bed on a raised platform. The mirrored ceiling above the bed reflected our movements.

An aide entered the bedroom, opened a suitcase containing books, and laid a few on the floor beside the bed. Another aide placed a water container on the night table, along with a box of Roi Tan cigars, the brand Elvis had occasionally smoked in front of me. The aide also left a schedule on the nightstand listing which employees were on duty and at what time, along with their room numbers. By now I had observed that the aides seemed to have various assignments. Some helped with wardrobe, while others served as extra hands during concerts or brought food and packets of medication to Elvis.

Once they'd made sure everything was to Elvis's liking, the aides evaporated. No sooner had they left when Elvis pressed a button by the bed. The drapes against one wall slowly began to open, revealing windows and a spectacular view of Las Vegas spread below our penthouse.

Elvis gave me a tour of the other rooms connected to the suite and mentioned that his father was coming and would be staying in one. I wondered which bedroom would be mine, after noticing Joe Esposito in one of them.

Telling me that his dad, Vernon, had suffered a heart attack the year before, Elvis said he was glad Vernon was able to come to his shows again. We returned to the living room and Elvis walked over to a record player. The song he chose to play was Charles Boyer singing "Once Upon a Time."

As the song echoed throughout the suite, Elvis closed his eyes and began to speak the lyrics, Boyer-style. He continued to do the same with the song, "Softly I Must Leave You." The words were beautiful and I sat, enchanted, as Elvis delivered them with great passion.

When the album ended, Elvis told me that "Softly I Must Leave You" was written by a man in a hospital who began to feel like he was dying after his wife lay beside him and fell asleep. Not wanting to wake her, the man wrote the words to the song in a letter to his wife. I knew this song had touched Elvis deeply, as I recalled him singing and talking about it onstage, the first time I saw him perform back in July. Elvis would play this album many more times for me while we were in Las Vegas.

With no show until the next evening, Elvis had time to relax. I followed him into the bedroom, thinking we might rest, but he stayed up as various employees popped in and out, some going over business and others just checking to see if he needed anything.

Dr. Ghanem stopped by to say hello, making me wonder what had happened to Dr. Nichopoulos. When Elvis wanted to speak to one of his staff privately, he'd sometimes gesture to the bathroom door and jokingly say, "Step into my office." I decided it made sense; the bathroom was private and more convenient for him than going to an outer room or asking others to leave.

When things quieted down and we were finally relaxing in bed, Elvis picked up a book. This time it was *The Prophet* by Kahlil Gibran, the Lebanese philosopher and artist. I didn't know it yet, but during the intimate months we would spend together, Elvis would refer to this book many times. It was an important philosophical touchstone for him.

Elvis turned the book over and showed me the author's photo on the back cover. "Doesn't he have a knowing look?" he asked.

I took in what seemed to me to be a pensive Gibran and answered yes.

The Prophet spoke of a person named Almustafa who was waiting to return home after living twelve years in the city of Orphalese. With sadness, he answers questions from the people of the isle before he departs.

Elvis singled out some quotes and read them to me. One of them came from a section where Almustafa is asked to speak of love:

When love beckons to you, follow him, Though his ways are hard and steep. And when his wings enfold you yield to him, Though the sword hidden among his pinions may wound you. And when he speaks to you believe in him, Though his voice may shatter your dreams as the north wind lays waste the garden. For even as love crowns you so shall he crucify you. Even as he is for your growth so is he for your pruning.

Elvis read the words with great passion and power. I could sense that he really wanted to grasp what the author knew or how Gibran had been feeling in order to write this way. For my part, I listened to the words and felt my own inexperience in relationships. At age twenty, I had yet to know a truly great love. Would Elvis be my first?

After sharing these passages with me, Elvis explained, "I don't think a person can control love. When it happens, you just go along with it and try your best to be prepared for the good and bad."

And, when Almustafa is asked what of marriage, Gibran wrote these words:

You were born together, and together you shall be forevermore.
You shall be together when the white wings of death scatter your days.
Ay, you shall be together even in the silent memory of God.
But let there be spaces in your togetherness,
And let the winds of the heavens dance between you.

At one point during this reading, Elvis paused to smile and say, "I think I could be engaged to you," then returned his attention to the book.

I was no longer concentrating on the book. I was too flabbergasted. *Engaged?* Had I heard Elvis right?

I decided he was joking, saying this just because we happened to be reading together and enjoying ourselves. We'd only been together, in all, about a week.

Still, his statement hung over me as Elvis continued to read, emphasizing certain words and shaking his head in amazement at their power.

I thought the writing was wonderful, too, and found myself going over quotes and asking questions while Elvis analyzed different passages from the book. Even in such a short time, I could feel that reading with him was helping me learn and grow.

A little while later, Elvis paused again and shut his eyes. "You know, when I close my eyes, I can envision you in a long white gown," he said. Then he slowly opened his eyes, cocked his head to one side, and raised an eyebrow at me, gauging my reaction.

"Oh," I said, struggling to think of some reply. "That's nice," I added and smiled. *A long white gown? Engaged? Is it possible he means what I think he means? This can't be right,* I thought. *Not after such a short time.*

On the other hand, I'd already seen how spontaneous and decisive Elvis could be about certain things. I had certainly felt a strong attraction between us from the first day we met, but the idea of us already discussing marriage was nearly impossible for me to grasp. I was just two years out of high school and we couldn't have been at more different places in our lives. Yet, these potential obstacles seemed to be rapidly fading. Also, it was no small thing that this was Elvis, a man who seemed to live in a world of his own making.

Without remarking on my shocked expression, which I'm sure must have mirrored my thoughts, Elvis simply smiled and went back to reading. Meanwhile, my mind continued spinning out of control. How could Elvis feel so strongly about us already?

As dawn broke, Elvis went into his bathroom and changed into pajamas with no mention of a separate room for me. Realizing there would be little to no privacy now, I decided to just go with the flow and went into the designated ladies' bathroom to change for bed. Not only did I still have to work on feeling comfortable wearing pajamas around Elvis, I now had to be okay being dressed in them, chances were, in front of his entire clan of male pals and support staff.

I came out of the bathroom and sat beside Elvis on the bed. I had been trying hard all evening to understand and accept the ideas and information he'd been sharing with me. Now he sprang something new yet again.

"Come on, let's meditate together," he said. "It's calming and a way of being in touch with one's higher self."

I had never meditated and had no clue what he meant by a "higher self." Still, I was willing to try it. I sat beside him and crossed my legs, imitating his position.

"Pyramids possess a special energy which help give strength to an individual," Elvis explained as he showed me how to form a pyramid shape with my index fingers and thumbs. Then he placed his hands up to his forehead and told me, "Pray to the third eye and say, 'Christ light, Christ love, Christ peace.'"

After I'd repeated these words, Elvis explained that the third eye was an energy center that related to being able to evaluate our past experiences and life patterns, so we could put them into perspective through the wisdom of the third chakra, which was located between the eyes. If this chakra malfunctioned, the symptoms might be a headache and eye tension.

We sat in this position and I tried to focus on blocking out everything else as I repeated these words with Elvis. To my surprise, after a while I felt a peaceful feeling wash over me. I could definitely understand how someone like Elvis, with so many demands on his time and energy, could benefit from meditation.

Elvis looked relaxed when we'd finished meditating. He told me that when his ex-wife, Priscilla, was speaking with him on the phone once and telling him that she didn't know how to handle Lisa, he'd said, "Get a pen and a piece of paper and write down this word . . . *meditate*."

He had yet to make any physical advances toward me, other than the light kisses I'd received. I wasn't really surprised by this, given his schedule. But now here we were, in another hotel room, and he wasn't exhausted from a show tonight. Would he make a move? And what would I do if he did?

There was no need for concern. Elvis took two cotton balls and put them in his mouth to wet them, then placed a cotton ball in each ear. "This helps to block the outside noise," he explained. He was clearly preparing for bed.

It seemed that Elvis was as eager to respect me as I was to be respected. He purposely kept his distance from me and I got the feeling that he was saving our physical encounter for a time when it would be right for both of us.

We started watching television and, after what had been a long, exhilarating night, we both soon fell asleep.

When we woke again, an aide brought in a packet for Elvis and left. Elvis told me it was a mixture of vitamins, medication, sinus pills, and aspirin. I figured this was a combination designed to give him the energy and clear head he needed to perform.

We then went into the living room and ate, visiting with some of his entourage. When his karate instructor, Ed Parker, appeared, Elvis referred to him as his high priest. Elvis had explained to me earlier that Ed was a martial arts expert. Ed had trained many stuntmen and celebrities, and Elvis had hired him to help with security.

"My previous bodyguards kept getting into trouble and causing problems for me," Elvis said, "so they had to be fired."

This was the first time I'd heard Elvis talk about karate with Ed, and Ed's knowledge was extremely impressive. Now I learned that it was Ed who had promoted Elvis to a ninth-degree black belt. Elvis told me he didn't want the rank of tenth degree, because "there was nowhere to go after that." He wanted something to aspire to in karate.

Early in the evening, Elvis asked me to go shopping. "I want you to look special for my shows," he explained.

He asked a bodyguard to accompany me. I understood that Elvis felt responsible for my safety, but I felt a little uncomfortable shopping with a strange man and having Elvis buy me clothes. On the other hand, I was sure that appearances had to be important to Elvis, and I didn't want to disappoint him.

The Hilton had some beautiful shops downstairs. I browsed inside a few stores while the bodyguard waited just outside them. We were going to be in Las Vegas quite a while and I didn't know what to buy.

Conscious of not spending too much, but wanting to get something that pleased Elvis, I finally decided on a pair of silver and rhinestone evening shoes, a smoky gray cocktail dress, a peach gown, and another white evening dress with long sashes. The bodyguard paid for everything and we returned upstairs.

Elvis was in the master bedroom when I returned, sitting on the bed and still in his pajamas. "Let's see what you got," he said. "Try them on for me."

Feeling shy again, I ducked into the bathroom and slipped into the white dress. I paused for a minute in front of the mirror, hoping Elvis would be pleased.

When I walked out, a big smile flashed across his face and I felt a mixture of pride and relief. "I love it!" Elvis said. "You look like a Greek goddess."

Feeling more confident now, I quickly tried on the other dresses and he complimented those as well. I sensed the white one had been his favorite, though, and decided to choose that one to wear for his opening show.

I put my new clothes away and, since Elvis was in pajamas, changed back into mine as well. I might as well get used to wearing them, I decided, since he appeared to live in his.

Elvis handed me one of his robes and picked up Cheiro's *Book of Numbers*. I followed him into the living room, taking a seat beside him on the sofa.

Elvis had earlier told me that his number was eight. Now he pointed out passages about certain colors of stones that, according to Cheiro, were lucky for those who were a number eight to wear. One of these stones was a black diamond, so he'd had that stone placed in a few of his rings.

"I lost one of the rings and another got broken when I slammed my fist on the floor during a show," he said.

Listening to him talk about lucky numbers and stones, I sensed that Elvis felt a strong desire to feel protected both on- and offstage—not just physically, but psychologically and spiritually as well.

Elvis stood up and went back into the bedroom, then returned with a magnificent ring I'd seen him wear during his performances. Proudly rotating the ring in his hand to catch the light, he told me it was custom made of gold with black onyx. The center stone was an eleven-carat diamond. Below it, the letters *TCB* were in diamonds surrounded by diamond lightning bolts.

"I wear Band-Aids on my fingers while performing to guard against cuts," he said, "and so no one can pull my rings off." Then he asked, "Did you notice how, onstage, I keep a side stance when I bend over to accept a gift or give a kiss?"

"Yes," I said. "Why is that?"

"So nobody in the audience can pull me off the stage."

As Elvis began talking about his upcoming shows, he seemed a little more nervous about these than he had about the previous ones I'd seen.

"I'm not being judged by just the general audience here," he pointed out, "but by my peers as well."

At one point, Larry Geller walked into the suite. He hesitated, silently signaling to Elvis, "Should I stay or go?" Larry wanted to color Elvis's hair—a fact that shocked me. I had no idea that Elvis's hair color wasn't natural. Looking slightly annoyed, Elvis dismissed Larry and asked him to come back the next day.

The interruption made Elvis change the subject. Now he brought up the theory of soul mates. He believed two people could be fated to be soul mates and play certain roles in one another's lives.

"They're meant to meet and be part of a larger, inevitable picture," he told me.

This was the first time I'd ever heard of this concept. I was intrigued, but I wondered why Elvis was mentioning it to me.

I thought back to his earlier comments about being engaged, envisioning me in a white gown, and me being like someone he'd known and yet never known. Was Elvis thinking that we could be soul mates?

Again, I experienced conflicted emotions, wanting to believe Elvis thought I was special in his life, while at the same time trying to protect myself against being hurt.

Our conversation continued, alternating between numerology and delving deeper into Elvis's thoughts about soul mates. I learned as we talked that Larry was the one who'd given him most of the books we'd been reading.

Deciding he wanted to learn more about soul mates now prompted Elvis to ask an aide to contact Larry, hoping he might have some books on it. Larry reappeared almost immediately, eager to speak with Elvis. However, seeing that Larry didn't have a book with him, Elvis spoke to him briefly and Larry left.

We continued talking through the night, with the notion of soul mates and a possible future with Elvis swirling through my mind. Near dawn, Elvis took the contents of a yellow packet that, once again, had been left on his night table. I noticed the word *sleep* written on the outside of it. This was only the second time I became aware of Elvis needing help to get to sleep; I hadn't noticed any packet the previous morning, and assumed he'd gone to bed without any medicine.

After taking the sleep medication, his speech began to slow down as it took effect. I hadn't noticed this before. Shortly, Elvis lay back in bed and I helped pull the covers up around him. I rested my head on the pillow beside him and reflected on the things we'd read and talked about for the past several hours. His powerful belief in certain things like numerology and fated soul mates was persuading me to broaden my horizons beyond the traditional Christian beliefs of my childhood. Our dialogue had also shed more light on how Elvis saw the two of us through the filter of what he was studying. That he saw us as possible soul mates was a profound thing.

That next afternoon, I met Elvis's father, Vernon Presley, for the first time. Vernon was sixty-one years old and close to Elvis's height (five feet, eleven inches according to army records), but Vernon was thin and frail looking. His hair and mustache were both silver, but I could see the strong resemblance between Elvis and his father.

Vernon entered the suite with an attractive blonde in her thirties. I learned that Vernon and Elvis's stepmother were no longer together as Vernon introduced the woman as his fiancée, Sandy Miller. (Vernon and Dee Presley had been separated since 1974; Sandy was a divorced lab technician and nurse from Colorado.)

Elvis spoke with Vernon about how things were going, and I could tell that Elvis took his father's opinions and thoughts to heart. Vernon was pleasant to me, but he didn't say much, understandably focusing his attention on his son.

After Vernon and Sandy left, Elvis asked Larry to come in and color his hair. Closer to showtime, Elvis invited Joe into our room and wanted to speak with him in private. I stepped into the living room to give them time alone.

After a few minutes, Joe reappeared and left the suite. I thought Elvis would ask for me, but instead Joe returned, went back into Elvis's bedroom, and hastily exited the suite again. Joe did this a few more times.

When Elvis did finally call for me, no sooner had I sat down beside him on the bed, when Elvis got up and walked into the living room. I was completely mystified.

Then Elvis returned to the bedroom once more, sat across from me on the bed, and asked me to close my eyes and hold out my right hand. I did as he asked, trembling a little with nerves by this time, and felt him slip a ring onto my finger.

Opening my eyes, I saw that he'd given me a gorgeous gold and diamond cluster ring. I was trying to wrap my mind around this generous gift when Elvis asked me to hold out my other hand. This time he placed a ring of sapphires and diamonds onto my left ring finger.

"Here," he said cheerfully. "You have to have backups." Bringing one hand from around his back, he proceeded to give me two more rings! One of them was set in rubies and diamonds, and the other was a second diamond cluster ring.

"Man, this one reminds me of my birthday," Elvis said, pointing to the free-form diamonds on the ring. "They're set in the shape of the number eight."

Any one of these rings was more than I'd ever been given. I was speechless and overwhelmed. I felt that all of Joe's comings and goings must have had something to do with Elvis putting him in charge of securing the rings.

It was all too much and I felt slightly awkward. I didn't want Elvis to feel like he had to do this. Hesitantly, I tried to explain this to him.

"Elvis, these rings are beautiful, but I've never really been a jewelry person."

Undaunted, he said, "This is only the beginning! You'll learn to like it."

"Okay," I agreed. "I guess I will."

CHAPTER 7

While Elvis got ready to go onstage that night, I went into the bathroom and made my own transformation. I changed into my new white gown and buckled the straps on my rhinestone shoes. I placed my new rings on four of my fingers, still amazed that Elvis had thought to buy them and managed to pull off such a huge surprise with everything else on his mind.

Finally, feeling much like Cinderella after her fairy godmother has waved her magic wand, I walked into the living room and discovered a few other women waiting there. They were dressed more casually than I was, and I worried that I had overdressed. I was afraid this would alienate them, and I really wanted to fit in.

You're wearing what Elvis likes, I reminded myself. I had to admit, I liked it, too.

A thin young woman with short blond hair introduced herself as Shirley Dieu, Joe Esposito's girlfriend. I didn't get a chance to speak with the other women there, however, as one of the aides appeared and quickly led me downstairs to the Hilton showroom.

Once again, I was awed by the splendor of my surroundings. The showroom was absolutely beautiful, with chandeliers, a large stage, and stylishly dressed men and women in the audience, some of them sitting in curved red booths. I was escorted to a center booth, where I took a seat beside Vernon and Sandy.

As the opening act concluded and the lights dimmed, I was shocked when someone approached our booth, stuck out a piece of paper and pen toward me for an autograph, and said, "Priscilla?"

How odd. Did I look like Elvis's ex-wife in the dark, I wondered?

Vernon immediately shooed the fan away with his hand. The Joe Guercio Orchestra began to play, and Elvis walked onstage wearing a King of Spades jumpsuit. Right off the bat, he had the audience captive in the palm of his hand. This was a much smaller venue than I'd ever seen him perform in before and the show felt more intimate and personal. Elvis joked around with the audience, and they felt comfortable enough to yell back at him, making comments and requesting songs.

Elvis was clearly enjoying the interplay with the audience and seemed to be in great spirits. At one point, he introduced the actress Vikki Carr, singer Glen Campbell, and Vernon. When he sang "Softly I Must Leave You," I remembered the story he'd told me about the dying man lying next to his wife and got chills.

Despite the smaller, lush setting and designer clothing and expensive hairstyles, these fans were only slightly less exuberant than the fans at the Cow Palace. They seemed to have the same uncontrollable need to make physical contact with Elvis. At various times, women in elegant gowns actually lifted their dresses and began climbing over tabletops, hoping to get close enough for a kiss or one of Elvis's scarves, but they were stopped by security. Children were thrust onto the stage, too, and Elvis never failed to notice, immediately connecting with them. He had a big soft spot for kids.

When the show ended, Vernon, Sandy, and I were ushered into a backstage dressing room while Elvis changed in an adjoining room. I sat quietly on a couch while Vernon and Sandy greeted people. I didn't think I'd see Elvis until he'd finished visiting with everyone, but after a few minutes an aide made his way through the crowded room, leaned over, and told me that Elvis wanted me with him. Once again, I felt a thrill at being singled out.

As I followed the aide into the adjacent room, I saw Elvis seated and in deep conversation with the singer Glen Campbell and his wife, Sarah.

After being introduced to Glen and Sarah, they continued the conversation they'd been having about the science of numbers and various other topics. I listened carefully and was able to reflect on what Elvis had discussed with me over the last few nights. I was actually surprised that what was brand-new to me seemed to already be something of real interest to another person in the entertainment field.

Thinking and talking about these alternative beliefs didn't feel threatening to me. Elvis was just deeply curious about life in general, and wondering why his own life had turned out the way it had. Spending time with Elvis often felt like taking a philosophy course, making me open up and consider new ideas.

Despite my interest in the conversation, at one point my thoughts momentarily drifted to the people waiting to see Elvis in the next room. He'd been talking with Glen for quite a while. I wondered if any of the other people would get tired of waiting and leave.

When Elvis and Glen finished visiting and we stepped into the outer room again, however, it was still crowded. Elvis took time to greet all of those waiting for him—he was generous that way—and then we finally returned to the suite, where at last I got a chance to tell Elvis how much I had enjoyed his show.

Elvis ordered room service while his father and Sandy came in to visit. Vernon gave a curt, candid appraisal of the show. I would later feel that, when it came to his performances, Elvis seemed to value his father's judgment above that of all the other men around him.

At one point, Elvis mentioned to Vernon, "You know, Daddy, Lisa's comin' in." As Vernon smiled, Elvis proudly added, "And, Ginger, I want you to meet her."

"I'd love to," I said, looking forward to it.

Once Vernon and Sandy had gone, an aide appeared, laid a towel on the bed, and placed a tinfoil pan full of lasagna in front of Elvis. It was a large amount, not portioned out. I wondered if he was intending to eat the whole thing as Elvis sprinkled it with salt.

Ed Parker and a few other members of Elvis's entourage came and went. As the men were talking, I sat quietly and noticed Elvis salt the lasagna again. Caught up in visiting, he didn't take a bite, but ended up salting the food several more times.

When he finally took a bit of lasagna, of course it was cold. Elvis sent it back to be reheated. When the food was brought back, I knew it had to be extremely salty and worried about how that might affect Elvis's health. Luckily, he didn't eat much of it.

Late into the night, we were finally alone. As Elvis picked out a book to read and we settled back against the headboard of his bed, he asked, "Do you know what a Ferrari looks like?"

"No, I'm not exactly sure," I admitted, thinking he must not remember telling me about his Black Mamba.

"If you were me and you were going to buy a new car, what kind would you get?" he asked.

I was flattered he wanted my opinion, but had no idea what kind of car he might like to drive and didn't dare guess. "Well, it depends what you want," I hedged.

He pondered this thought for a few seconds, then said, "I don't know. I need your help."

I took a deep breath, considering. "A Cadillac or Continental would be nice," I ventured.

"What color?" he asked at once.

"Blue or white would be pretty," I said.

A hint of a smile passed over his face. "Thanks, Ginger. I've just been thinking about getting a new car lately." Then we went back to reading.

I continued to be impressed by Elvis's zealous spiritual appetite. Despite the long day and the energy he'd expended onstage, followed by talking with people for hours, Elvis was still on a spiritual high. He got energized as he read. Whenever he came across a new idea or had a fresh thought about something we'd found in a book, he would discuss his thoughts and ideas with me even at the expense of going to sleep at a normal hour.

"Aren't you tired?" I asked at one point.

He shook his head. "It's much better to think at night, when the air is still and others are sleeping," he said. "Most writers and geniuses work best at night."

I didn't know any writers or geniuses, but this certainly seemed to be true for the man I was starting to have strong feelings for, so I continued to read with him.

As dawn approached, an aide brought in a yellow packet and placed it on the night table. These packets were routine, I realized, delivered in the same casual manner as the jug of water at Elvis's bedside. He placed a cotton ball inside each ear again, took the packet of medication, and went to sleep.

I fell asleep beside him. A few hours later, I felt movement. Elvis was awake. "Who's on duty?" he asked. "Can you call whoever it is for me?"

I could tell by his voice and the way he was moving that Elvis was still groggy from whatever sleep medication he'd taken. I quickly looked at his employee contact list sheet and called the room number of the person on duty.

An aide entered, assisted Elvis to the bathroom and back as he was a little unstable on his feet, then left. This was unsettling for me to witness, yet the aide had treated it as completely normal.

Elvis went back to sleep almost immediately, but I lay awake, wondering how long he'd been taking this medication and why he needed it. Because it was delivered in little yellow packets, I had no idea what he was taking, but it seemed quite strong.

I thought, too, about Elvis's padded bedroom doors and covered windows at Graceland. I felt a sharp pang of sympathy for him. Elvis seemed to have everything, except the ability to do what most of us take for granted: just close his eyes and peacefully fall asleep.

Elvis wanted me by his side nearly every minute. I was his primary focus, and he was mine. Still, I often felt like I'd been transported to a foreign country where I had yet to understand the language or customs.

Getting to know the average person is one thing, but trying to understand Elvis, his job, and the many different people who surrounded and supported him was a steep learning curve. The best analogy I can come up with is that Elvis at work was like a champion athlete competing in an event each day, with trainers, doctors, and staff keeping him in performance-ready shape.

I would often feel tired from not getting a full "night" of sleep, but gradually I was starting to adjust to his schedule and to being surrounded by other people. Most of the people working for Elvis were friendly to me, but a little distant. They were doing their jobs rather than just visiting.

It was now Friday, December 3, and I discovered that Elvis would have two shows on weekends: one at 9 P.M. and the other at 1 A.M. It said something about his stamina, I thought, that he had the energy to do both.

We woke around four in the afternoon, as usual, and ate in the living room while members of his entourage visited off and on. A little while later, Elvis was in his bathroom and I was sitting on the bed when the phone on the night table rang. I waited to see if anyone might answer it from an outer room, but the ringing continued.

Finally, I picked up the receiver. "Hello?"

"Is Elvis there?" a woman asked.

"Yes, but he's busy right now," I said.

The woman then inquired, "Is this Ginger?"

"Yes," I replied, my curiosity aroused. "Who is this?"

"This is Linda Thompson. Do you mind if I wait?"

I was shocked. *Linda Thompson?* Why was she calling him now? And how did she know my name?

"No, it's fine," I said, and put down the receiver.

Dr. Ghanem walked into the room just then, and I told him Linda was on the phone. He went to the bathroom door, knocked on it, and stepped inside.

Elvis emerged from his bathroom, looking none too pleased. Feeling ill at ease, I left the bedroom to give him some privacy and walked into the now-empty living room, my thoughts whirling. I began to wonder if Elvis had seen Linda recently. I hoped not; I didn't want to be in the middle of anything.

Dr. Ghanem walked out and Elvis called my name from the bedroom. When I entered, he looked bothered and said, "Sorry about that call," then asked me to sit beside him on the bed. "Linda and me . . . that relationship's been over, you understand? We're friends," he said.

In recent years, I'd seen some magazines with photos of Elvis with various women and accompanying stories that he was dating them, so I thought he was being honest and hadn't gone out with Linda in a while. If he had, maybe it was just as friends. Still, I couldn't help but remember Linda's pictures in his bedroom at Graceland.

"Okay," I said, but my guard was up.

Elvis must have read the closed expression on my face. "You know, my bodyguard, Sam, is Linda's brother," he said. "I don't want you to feel uncomfortable with that, okay?"

I hadn't known. But that explained how Linda knew my name. Outwardly I agreed, but I knew this would be awkward, not only for me but for Sam. Accepting the situation would be more easily said than done.

Showtime was nearly here. The bedroom was abuzz with members of Elvis's staff helping him prepare. Once he was dressed, he saw me watching him use eyedrops. "They help keep the glare down from the stage lights," he explained.

I sat with Vernon and Sandy to watch his first show, unable to fully enjoy myself because I was still feeling emotionally unsettled by Linda's call. When Elvis sang a song called "Trying to Get to You," I focused on the lyrics, one line in particular: "There were many miles between us, But it didn't mean a thing." In a way, I thought, that song related to the two of us, with the miles being our age difference of nearly twenty-two years. We were trying to get to know each other, Elvis and I, and our age difference "didn't mean a thing." I relaxed and listened to him sing this song, which quickly became one of my favorites.

Between the hot stage lights and his jumpsuit, Elvis perspired a lot when performing. During this show, the sweat constantly dripping from his brow irritated his eyes. Afterward, he quickly visited with a few people backstage and then hurried to our suite, where he lay on the bed.

"Will you help me, Ginger?" he asked. He wanted me to dampen a washcloth so he could place it over his eyes.

I did so, sitting beside him and gently laying the washcloth across his brow. I was happy to feel needed and useful even in this small way. From then on, after some performances, we had a ritual of me sitting on the bed and putting a warm, wet washcloth over his eyes to give him comfort.

Elvis rested for a while, then ate something before returning downstairs for the second show.

When Elvis's performance ended, I was escorted backstage, but instead of going to his dressing room, Elvis asked me to follow him. I did—my curiosity on fire—along with a few people from his entourage.

We followed Elvis out of one of the hotel's back doors. There, gleaming beneath nearby lights, was a brand-new white Lincoln Continental Mark V with white leather seats and a burgundy dashboard. Elvis walked toward the car and everyone gathered around it.

I was still confused about why this car was here or what we were doing. Then Elvis looked at me and nonchalantly said, "It's yours, Ginger."

To say I was overwhelmed doesn't even begin to describe the enormity of my emotional reaction. I had never even owned a car before, and now I had a Lincoln Mark V?

I hugged Elvis hard, my heart brimming with gratitude as I suddenly realized that our conversation the night before had absolutely nothing to do with him wanting to buy a car for himself.

"There weren't any white Lincoln Continentals in Las Vegas," Elvis told me proudly, "so we located one in California and had it driven to us."

Stunned, speechless, awed: There weren't enough words in the world to tell Elvis how I felt. All I could say was, "Thank you."

I was excited to test-drive my new car, but Elvis turned to go back inside. I didn't know Las Vegas, understood he must be tired, and was okay with following him back up to the penthouse. I was still reeling with excitement.

Once we were back in the suite and seated in bed, Elvis asked me, "Have you ever been married before?"

"No," I said, a little surprised by his question.

"Were you seeing anyone before we met?" he pressed.

I answered, "Yes," momentarily thinking about Linda's phone call. I wondered if that was what had prompted this conversation.

Elvis thought about this for a few moments, then said, "Well, I would like it if you wouldn't see anyone else."

He was seriously asking for a commitment!

"I won't," I said, certain that Elvis meant he wouldn't see anyone else, either.

It felt good knowing that we were now taking this to a different level.

Elvis surprised me again by picking up the phone receiver and handing it to me. "I want you to call whoever you've been seeing and end your relationship with him."

I knew the object of my affection now was Elvis, but this put me in an awkward position. Although I had spoken to Larry about Elvis, he had still held out hope that we'd get back together, and I knew finalizing our breakup over the phone would hurt him. This would be insensitive and I didn't want to hurt someone who had been nothing but nice to me. I owed it to Larry to do this in person.

"Elvis, I can't do that right now," I said.

I started to explain this when suddenly, Elvis's mood changed. For the first time, I saw that he had a hair-trigger temper as Elvis picked up a full bottle of Gatorade from his night table and stormed out of his bedroom and into the middle of the suite.

I followed him, completely stunned, into his road manager's room. In front of Joe and his girlfriend, Elvis took the Gatorade container and threw it against the wall. Its contents splashed all over.

Shocked and embarrassed, I again tried to explain my feelings. None of this made any sense! I had never meant to anger him.

Joe and his girlfriend didn't have a clue about what was going on. I wasn't sure, either.

I realized for the first time, that if Elvis and I continued our relationship, it would most likely be played out in front of his entourage and, at times, in the public eye. I was also going to have to come to terms with the fact that others might speculate about me, and about my relationship with Elvis, without fully understanding what was going on with us in private. Could I live with that?

I had to, if I wanted to be with Elvis.

Joe said a few words to Elvis and, between the two of us, we managed to calm Elvis down after a few minutes. I followed Elvis back into the master bedroom, where he shut the door and remained silent as he got into bed. I tentatively sat down beside him, wondering why he'd gotten so angry. Had this been a big misunderstanding? Had he misinterpreted me saying, "I can't do this right now," to mean I wasn't going to commit to him? Was it simply because I hadn't done what he wanted when he asked?

It troubled me that Elvis had flown off the handle like that and I was still reeling a little with embarrassment. As odd as this sounds, it also made me feel good to think that Elvis was really that serious about us. But how could I be sure?

What Elvis did next made me believe he felt as deeply about me as I did about him. Without saying a word, Elvis suddenly leaned in and kissed me on the mouth, but not a light kiss like before. Then he slowly began removing my bathrobe.

I felt chills as he touched me. Was this it? Were we finally going to make love? I was aroused but anxious, barely able to breathe.

I had been afraid of letting go of my feelings, terrified of being hurt by sleeping with Elvis and then have him move on to someone else, but at this moment, I wanted to make love with him. I stayed completely still, letting Elvis open my robe and begin touching me.

"I don't believe people should be completely undressed until they're married," Elvis said softly, kissing me again.

Then, still partially dressed in our sleepwear, Elvis and I made love for the first time. This crazy tension and our heightened emotions made our intimacy all the more intense. Elvis's lips were soft and his kisses were filled with passion. He was gentle, yet I felt his determination to prove that he should be the only man in my life.

He succeeded. I was experiencing emotions and physical sensations that were completely out of control, and, in keeping with Elvis's TCB motto, it was all happening lightning fast.

There was no doubt about it. I was falling in love with Elvis.

CHAPTER 8

Making love with Elvis helped forge an even deeper emotional bond between us. I felt like I was completely his, in every way possible. I no longer had any control over my feelings for him. In our brief time together, Elvis had already turned my sleeping and eating patterns upside down, and almost everything else in my life as well. Now things were rapidly moving beyond any normal frame of reference for me, and all my intuitive guideposts were falling by the wayside. The new normal for me was that there was no normal.

The very next afternoon, Elvis and I eagerly awaited his daughter's arrival. Now eight years old, Lisa had been living in Los Angeles with her mother since her parents divorced in 1973. Having the two of us meet, I felt, was one more way for Elvis to bring me into his life.

I was sitting beside Elvis on the sofa in the living room when the door to the suite opened and a petite blond-haired girl came in, followed by a nanny. Lisa's resemblance to Elvis was uncanny.

Elvis and I stood up as Lisa ran toward him and they hugged. He introduced me to her and we sat back down. Lisa was seated between us, but she remained completely focused on her dad. It was clear that she adored him. At one point, Lisa accidentally rested her hand on my knee and glanced my way, but was quick to turn her attention back to her father.

I enjoyed watching Elvis with her. His face really lit up around Lisa, and I sensed he was a caring, proud dad. At one point, Elvis looked at me over Lisa's head and said, "When Lisa was born, I heard my mother's voice say, 'She's beautiful, son.'"

I loved children as well and had been an aunt since I was ten years old, so I was happy to have Lisa with us.

When it was time for Elvis to prepare for his first show, Lisa and her nanny went off to her room and I left for my bathroom to get ready. In the middle of applying my makeup, I looked in the mirror and was startled to see Lisa's reflection. She had been standing behind me and silently watching.

"Hi," I said, and turned around to smile at her.

"Hi," Lisa said, then sat down and began trying on some of my shoes.

I didn't mind. I was glad that she seemed to be so comfortable with me. Then she surprised me again.

"I thought you were Linda," Lisa said, glancing up at me.

It was an innocent remark on her part, yet I was suddenly aware that Lisa may have gotten close to some of Elvis's former girlfriends. I was a new face in Lisa's life, and we both needed time to get used to each other.

"Well, I'm not Linda," I said gently, and went back to the business of putting on my makeup, chatting with her a bit as she continued playing.

I may not have gotten a tour of glittering Las Vegas yet, but that didn't stop Elvis from bringing more sparkle to me. Disregarding what I'd told him about not really being a jewelry person, he surprised me with a beautiful diamond and emerald necklace before his next show. That was followed shortly by the gift of another diamond necklace and a diamond watch. When I told him, "This is really too much," he shook his head.

"People love to see beautiful things when they wake up," he said.

I felt this was an insight into Elvis's thinking. He saw himself as someone who was in a position to enhance other people's lives by bringing beauty into it, because he thought that would make them happy. He was not only a generous man but he had a fundamentally generous and kind spirit; he wanted to make life better for those he touched in all ways that he could both through music and in his everyday life. He was a giver in the most decent way, not a taker, and this was one of the things that drew me to him.

Elvis wanted me to wear all of my jewelry at the same time for his shows. Although I did feel regal, I also felt overdressed. I wasn't used to this. I reminded myself that I was with Elvis, and needed to dress in a way that complemented his style.

In the showroom, Lisa sat with Vernon, Sandy, and me. Elvis came onstage dressed in a beautiful Inca Gold Leaf jumpsuit, and I wondered what was going through Lisa's young mind as she listened to her father sing. She must be so proud, I thought.

Fans yelled out various requests during that show, as they so often did, and Elvis did his best to give them what they wanted.

Elvis's audience may have begun to age, but they wanted him to remain timeless and perform the moves that had made them fall in love with him. As a showman, he was a perfectionist with a keen ear. Any time he heard the smallest thing that didn't sound quite right—feedback from a microphone, a strange noise, an off note—Elvis would stop, apologize to his audience, and usually start over.

That night, Elvis introduced Lisa and his dad to the audience, prompting a large stage light to sweep across the room and settle on the two of them. Smiling, Lisa stood up and Vernon waved.

The singers Roy Orbison and Engelbert Humperdinck were there, and Elvis acknowledged their presence as well. He was in a jovial mood, joking with his band and trying on various hats handed to him by members of the audience. I sat in wonder, struck by what a charismatic performer he was. One moment, Elvis would be delivering an electric musical performance. The next, he was playful and flip, using humor to segue from one song to another.

Charlie, always ready with lyric sheets, handed one to Elvis before he sang "Bridge over Troubled Water" that night. It was a lengthy song, but Elvis only read a line or two and then discarded the sheets, giving me the sense that he really knew the song, but wanted to make sure he didn't risk missing a single word.

Back in the dressing room after the show, I sat on the couch near Lisa, Vernon, and Sandy, quietly watching people mingle. Roy Orbison and his wife, Barbara, entered the room. I was thrilled to see Roy, since I'd been a fan of his music. He was easy to spot, dressed in all black, with pale skin and his trademark sunglasses.

By then, Elvis had finished changing out of his jumpsuit. He entered the room, greeted his daughter, dad, and a few others. Then he sat down beside me, and the Orbisons came over to sit across from us and talk. The room was so noisy that Elvis had to lean forward to hear them. I continued to sit quietly beside him and watch everyone.

Suddenly, Elvis looked over his shoulder at me. "Would you put your hand on my back and calm me down?" he asked.

I hesitated a moment. My family was close, but we rarely displayed any public affection. Even though Elvis and I had been intimate, I felt shy about casually massaging his back in public, let alone in front of a celebrity like Roy Orbison.

I lightly placed my hand on his back and gently began to rub it.

Elvis looked over his shoulder at me again and smiled. I was glad that the touch of my hand did seem to calm him. I wanted to please him and seeing that small gestures like this did, was helping me learn to be more openly affectionate in public.

After the Orbisons left, I caught a glimpse of how truly appreciative Elvis was of his fans. He greeted three ladies who'd been waiting to present him with handmade figures of the three wise men. Each figure was beautifully crafted, and Elvis spoke with the ladies for a while, admiring the detail and workmanship that had gone into making them. These gifts would be brought up to the suite and eventually taken back to Graceland.

When his second show was over and we were finally alone in the suite, Elvis was served a late meal. As he grabbed the salt shaker and began sprinkling it over his food, once again I thought this couldn't be healthy. This was confirmed when, shortly after finishing his meal, he held up his left hand. "I can't believe how bloated I get," he said with a discouraged look. He then tried bending his fingers to show me how swollen they were from fluid retention.

"The doctors have me take water pills before I go onstage," he continued, sounding aggravated, explaining that the pills were meant to help remove fluid from his system. "I hate to do this, because those pills make me feel weak and zap some of my strength."

Our relationship was still so new that it was difficult for me to feel comfortable telling him what he should or shouldn't eat. "I heard too much salt can cause fluid retention," I told him and left it at that, hoping that over time I might be able to guide him to take a healthier approach to food.

We went to bed around dawn, as we usually did. The next afternoon I woke up early and walked out onto the rooftop terrace to admire the view.

I stood outside for a few minutes, feeling like a tourist, amazed by the sheer fact that I was here right now, experiencing so many new things with Elvis. Just as I was finally turning to go back inside, I was startled to see Lisa starting to climb onto a ledge behind me. She must have entered the suite and followed me outside.

"Lisa, don't do that," I said as calmly as I could. As I walked her back inside, I gently explained how dangerous it could have been for her to climb on that ledge. I couldn't even imagine what Elvis would do if something happened to his only daughter.

Lisa scampered off to her room. I returned to the bedroom and, seeing Elvis still asleep, decided to keep the incident from him. He had enough concerns at the time. Lisa was okay and, after our talk, I was sure she wouldn't do it again.

Later that afternoon, a stout, balding man with a large cigar clenched between his teeth entered our suite. Elvis introduced him to me as his manager, Colonel Tom Parker. Elvis told me that they needed to talk some business and asked if I'd mind leaving the room.

Other than a casual hello, I wouldn't see or speak much with Colonel Parker in Las Vegas. He never stayed long when he came to the suite, and he and Elvis always met in private to discuss business.

That evening, Elvis injured his ankle. I was in my bathroom when it happened, but he later told me he had stepped off the platform in the bedroom and twisted it. To ease the pain and protect it, he had his ankle wrapped. He told his audience about it that night during the show.

He chatted about a few other things onstage as well, including his birthday, numerology, and the significance of black diamonds. "They don't shine," he said of the diamonds. "They don't do nothin'. They're just there . . . they're like Charlie," he joked.

Uncomfortable, and not wanting to injure his ankle further, he sometimes sat on a stool while performing, but still put his best effort into putting on a good show.

In the suite afterward, Elvis began experiencing pain in his upper leg as well. He told me he thought he had a pinched nerve and felt that he might have pulled a hamstring muscle during a previous show.

My heart went out to him. Elvis called for Dr. Ghanem and Larry Geller. I could understand why Elvis wanted to see his doctor, but I was mystified about why he'd requested his hairdresser.

When the two men appeared, Elvis put Larry to use by having him massage his leg. Dr. Ghanem administered a shot of cortisone into the injured muscle so that Elvis would be able to perform.

When we were alone again, Elvis started talking about the dry desert air. He had already mentioned it during a few shows and was worried about getting a sore throat. "I don't see how some singers can actually live and perform full-time in Las Vegas," he said. "It's essential to always protect the voice. That's why I don't usually talk loud. You should never shout or talk loud over a television so you can preserve your vocal cords as well."

Elvis deeply appreciated the vocal talent of other performers, especially the beautiful voices of his backup singers, Sherrill Nielsen and Kathy Westmoreland. That night, suddenly in the mood to visit with one of them, he called Sherrill and asked him to come to our room.

Elvis teased Sherrill onstage but truly admired him, telling me, "His voice never seems to falter or crack." I could appreciate what Elvis meant. Sherrill really did shine as he played guitar and sang for us while we sat in bed.

Elvis also enjoyed having conversations with his bass singer, J. D. Sumner. He invited J. D. to our room occasionally, and asked him to hit some of his famous low notes for me.

These special moments would continue on future tours with Elvis, and I treasured them all. They were like having mini concerts right in the privacy of our own bedroom.

Before going to sleep that morning, I learned that Elvis sometimes liked to be coddled. He asked me to wet a pair of cotton balls in my mouth and place one inside each of his ears. Seeing this as a little boy side to Elvis, I didn't mind doing it. This became one of the small things I was happy to do for him, like rubbing his back or soothing his eyes with a washcloth.

This Las Vegas engagement was letting me get to know two different men. The first was Elvis the entertainer, who gave me a rare inside look at the intense nature of his preparation for shows, his joy and strain during performances, and what it took for him to wind down and sleep after being onstage in front of so many adoring fans.

The other man was the private Elvis, with his love, passions, concerns, hurts, likes, and dislikes. He was very observant and had some pet peeves that I never would have guessed. He would get annoyed, for instance, if a person didn't look directly at him while he was talking. It also bothered Elvis whenever he noticed someone yawning while he was speaking. "It's the sign of a short attention span," he told me.

After that, whenever I was tired from trying to keep up with his schedule, I made sure to stifle my yawns whenever I was around him.

Elvis had given me a little spending money. While Lisa was visiting, I asked if I could take her shopping, since I hadn't really had a chance to be alone with her, and he said yes.

Waking early, I got Lisa and took her downstairs. She had shown a genuine fondness for shoes and later, if mine went missing, I would find her wearing them. I decided a shoe store would be a treat for her.

We entered a shoe store in the hotel and, in the midst of me trying on a pair of pumps, I looked over and saw Lisa seated on the floor. She was surrounded by shoes she had removed from various display racks.

As Lisa began trying some of them on, I walked over to her. "Lisa, these are ladies' shoes and too big for you," I said.

She looked up at me and said, "That's okay. I'll grow into them."

I had to laugh, because she was right.

We continued on, visiting other stores in the hotel. A couple passing by stopped us at one point. "Is that Elvis's daughter?" they asked.

"Yes," I said, startled. Although Lisa resembled her dad, it hadn't even entered my mind that someone could possibly recognize her, especially if she was with me. I had underestimated the keen interest of Elvis's fans.

We ran into the pilot Milo soon after that, and he kindly offered to drive Lisa and me in my Continental to do some shopping outside the hotel. I knew our time was limited before Elvis woke, but I thought it would be fun to go around Las Vegas for the first time, especially in my new car.

Lisa and I made our way to the Hilton entrance and in a few minutes, Milo pulled up in the Continental. Lisa climbed into the middle of the front seat. I got in beside her and shut the door, still in disbelief that this gorgeous car was actually mine!

Milo drove us to the MGM Grand Hotel and waited while Lisa and I browsed inside. Carefully keeping track of time, I ended our shopping at a store that had large barrels of candy and let Lisa fill small bags with some goodies.

It was nice spending time with Lisa. She was a sweet little girl, close to my niece's age, and I hoped we would become friends.

Upon our return to the Hilton, Elvis was awake and, much to my surprise, displeased that we'd gone out. He didn't recall telling me that I could take Lisa. "You should never have gone out without a bodyguard," he reprimanded.

I was a little hurt. I explained that I would never have taken her without his permission. This new world I'd entered into was something I definitely wasn't used to navigating.

Sensing my feelings, Elvis delicately repeated, "Just next time, make sure you take a bodyguard."

It dawned on me then that one of the daily fears Elvis lived with was that someone might kidnap his daughter. "I will," I said.

Lisa visited off and on in the suite as often as she could in between Elvis's schedule. She stayed only a few more days, but when she flew back to Los Angeles, I was sure a large piece of Elvis's heart went right along with her.

CHAPTER 9

Elvis liked having me with him anytime he wasn't performing or discussing business. This fact, along with my shy nature, meant that other than a casual hello, I didn't talk much with the many other people who were always swirling around him.

On occasion, I'd see a few women chatting together out in the living room of Elvis's suite close to showtime, but they kept their distance. In part, I think this was because I was identified as "Elvis's girl," but I was also younger than most of them and inclined to keep to myself. I'm sure the other women were trying to figure out what to make of me.

One of them, a friendly Hawaiian who accompanied Charlie, made an effort to speak with me. I thought she resembled Elvis's ex-wife, Priscilla; others must have thought the same thing, because one night someone mistook this woman for Priscilla as I was accompanying her from the showroom to the ladies' room. I thought this was ironic because a fan had mistaken me for Priscilla, too, and this woman and I didn't really look alike.

Overall, though, I was left pretty much on my own. I was acutely aware of having this incredible experience, but with no one around who I really knew or felt comfortable enough to share it with, I sometimes wished one of my close friends were with me. I had checked in once with my family early on but it was impossible to describe over the phone just what I was experiencing.

Elvis managed to perform his next show despite still experiencing enough pain in his leg that he even mentioned it to the audience while he was onstage. The pain was definitely starting to interfere with his singing; at one point, he asked a couple of his backup singers to perform without him so he could rest.

Back inside the penthouse that night, he summoned Larry and Charlie to our bedroom. When they arrived, Elvis told me he wanted Larry to perform a "healing" on his leg.

I had no idea what this meant, but from that moment on, I was soon plunged into the literature and practice of both psychic healing and self-healing. Larry and Elvis were firm believers in this. I was open-minded, but my only experience had been with traditional medicine. However, being with Elvis, I would soon witness some things happen around him, and start wondering if perhaps he was right, and that maybe God did instill in us the ability to heal ourselves, if we could concentrate hard enough.

That night, as Elvis and Larry explained how psychic healing worked and what they were about to do, I understood why Elvis had asked for Larry's presence the previous night. As Larry explained, if a person was in pain and concentrated on a healing color in the area where the pain was, they or others could help heal the injured area or, at the very least, make the pain subside.

Elvis and Larry went on to explain the correlation between colors and spiritual healing. Green was the healing color; yellow, the Christ color; purple, the God color; and so on. As bizarre as this all sounded to me that night, I was curious to see what would happen next. So far, with Elvis almost anything seemed possible. Why not this, too?

Charlie closed the bedroom door and Larry began lighting candles, placing them in various areas around us. He then turned off the lights.

In the dimly lit room, Elvis lay down on his stomach across the bed while Charlie and I stood to one side and watched. It was exceptionally quiet. Then Larry asked each of us to imagine a golden light over Elvis's leg, and to channel all of our thoughts and energy into that visualization. I understood the golden color to be a Christ color, but figured it must also be for healing. I also guessed that Larry wanted Charlie and me to be there because the more energy that was focused on healing, the better it might work.

As Larry began to alternately massage or hold his hand over the muscle in the back of Elvis's leg, I focused intensely on that area. I wasn't aware of how much time passed, but whether it was just the effect of the candles or an actual phenomenon, I thought I saw a soft golden glow radiate from beneath Larry's hand.

When Larry had finished, he turned the lights back on and blew out the candles. Elvis stood up, took a tentative step and said his leg felt better.

Had I just witnessed a true psychic healing? Clearly, Elvis and Larry believed so. Did I?

Common sense made me question this. Yet, another part of me had always believed in the power of faith. I had just witnessed Elvis have pain and now I'd heard him say, "I feel better."

As unbelievable as this seemed, if this mystical type of healing had indeed given Elvis some relief, that's what mattered most to me.

After Larry and Charlie left, Elvis began telling me about a breathing technique he had learned while studying martial arts. Elvis believed that, if done correctly, this technique would enable an individual to move objects without touching them, using mental energy alone.

"Show me," I said.

Elvis walked over to a section of the bedroom curtains and placed his palm a couple of inches away from them. He took a few deep breaths, focused on his hand, and said, "Watch."

I stared at the curtains and tried to keep an open mind. Suddenly, I thought I noticed a hint of movement. I blinked. Was I really seeing the curtains move because of Elvis, or was it the result of circulating air?

Elvis gave me a little smile. His knowing expression helped support my growing belief that, with Elvis, things I'd once thought were impossible might not be so far-fetched after all.

A little while later, as Elvis and I were talking, he began quoting from one of his books. We had gone over them so often that I'd memorized some of the lines. Now, when he forgot part of a sentence, I was able to jump in and finish it for him. He liked that, telling me that I was a quick learner, which made me feel good.

At one point, I suddenly began to feel a little queasy. Elvis noticed my discomfort and asked me to lie back on the bed. When I did, he placed his hand lightly over my abdomen and held it there, asking me to focus on the color green so he could heal me.

I forced myself to lie quietly and concentrate on the color green. After a few minutes, Elvis suddenly whipped his hand high into the air, as if pulling an illness right out of my body.

Miraculously, I felt less nauseous. Could Elvis really heal me? And could he teach me to heal myself?

I was a bit shaken by the experience. I felt that, in order for this kind of thing to work, one had to believe in it. Maybe I was becoming a believer. Elvis had, once again, challenged me to experience something new.

As the night went on, the teacher in Elvis continued to emerge. At one point, I was reading to myself with my head tilted forward off my pillow, and Elvis looked over at me. "Lift your chin and sit up straight," he suggested. "You're not getting enough oxygen."

I took his advice and sat up in bed.

Later, Elvis said, "You should avoid wrinkling your forehead and you should drink lots of water because it'll help prevent dark circles under your eyes."

Figuring that Elvis didn't want me to look like an eighty-year-old raccoon, and always open to beauty suggestions, I was glad to follow his advice.

Despite Larry's massages and ministrations, Elvis's leg continued to bother him. During his December 7 show, he talked about his pinched nerve and apologized to the audience, saying he would do his best to give a good performance.

Later in the show, Elvis announced that he wanted to do something he hadn't done before and sing a couple of spiritual songs that weren't normally included in his set list. With all of the reading Elvis had been doing on Eastern religions, I had yet to ask him how he felt about Jesus, or what he believed about God. But, when a member of the audience shouted to Elvis, "You're the king!" his answer told me a great deal.

"Thank you, sir," Elvis said. "I'm fixin' to sing about Him." He was making it clear that, for him, there was only one King.

I hadn't spoken to my family since my earlier call. Once we returned to the suite after that particular show, I felt like checking in with them. I called home and my mother answered. She sounded sleepy, and I felt bad, realizing I'd forgotten about the time difference. Even worse, my mother told me that my grandfather, Alonzo Spencer, had been taken ill a few days earlier in his nursing home in Arkansas.

I loved Alonzo and had always felt close to him. He was my sole surviving grandparent. My mother was never one to worry others, but I knew her well enough to detect an uneasiness in her voice.

After I hung up, I sat there, staring at the phone and worrying. Did I need to go see my grandfather? I felt torn. I didn't want to leave Elvis, but what if I didn't go, and something happened to Alonzo?

I went back to the bedroom and told Elvis about the phone call and how I was feeling.

"Did your mother say anything that alarmed you?" he asked.

"No, not really," I said. "I just heard something in her voice."

Elvis reassured me that my grandfather would be all right, which was comforting, and said he would like me to stay. I knew he was probably right—after all, my mother hadn't said anything about me needing to see my grandfather—so I agreed.

Meanwhile, Elvis said he was still feeling some pain in his leg and wanted to see Dr. Ghanem. Instead of having the doctor come to the Hilton, Elvis arranged to go see him this time.

I figured he probably wanted to get out for a change and I accompanied him. Once we were in the car, however, my concern about my grandfather's health returned and gnawed away at me. I must have been extra quiet, because Elvis asked what was bothering me.

"I'm thinking about my grandfather," I said.

Elvis again tried to calm my worries. When we arrived at the physician's office, Dr. Ghanem offered me a seat in the chair behind his desk while he and Elvis went into another room. I waited, hoping that Dr. Ghanem could help him with his pain.

After a few minutes, Dr. Ghanem returned and walked up to me. "Ginger, can't you see Elvis needs you?" he asked. This surprised me. I'd been concerned about my grandfather but hadn't said I was leaving.

I realized with a start that Elvis must have discussed this possibility with Dr. Ghanem. Before I could reply, Elvis joined us.

"I want to get a top doctor to help your grandfather," he told me. "I'll see to it that everything possible will be done, if need be, to help him."

Elvis then asked for the phone number of the nursing home. I was taken aback despite deeply appreciating his offer. It was hard to fathom that Elvis had a need for me that was so great that, even with my grandfather's health issue, he didn't want me to leave.

Dr. Ghanem left the room to give us some privacy while I called my mom. She had no idea how alarmed I had become, and she gave me the number of the nursing home. As Elvis began dialing it, I wondered if whoever answered at the nursing home would really believe it was him. I was unaware at the time that the press knew of my existence and stories about me and Elvis were circulating. Word was already spreading rapidly about a possible marriage between Elvis and me. My aunts, for instance, had heard radio personality Paul Harvey announce my engagement to Elvis. The nursing home employees seemed to know about it as well. They put Elvis straight through to the head nurse administrator.

Elvis talked to the administrator for a few minutes about my grandfather's care. When he hung up, he told me my grandfather had the beginning of what could be pneumonia, but they were watching him closely and he was in very good hands.

"Thank you," I said, and immediately felt better.

Just when I thought Elvis couldn't possibly be any kinder or bighearted, he asked me to get my mother back on the telephone. "I'd like to fly your family in to give them a break, to meet me and see my shows," he said.

Stunned, I redialed my home number and handed Elvis the receiver. As he spoke with my mother, Elvis told her about calling the nursing home, then said, "I'd like to see to it that your father has the best possible care, with the best doctor, should he suddenly take a turn for the worse."

Looking down, he listened silently for a few minutes. I knew my mother must be thanking him.

Then Elvis interrupted her. "Mrs. Alden, I'm in love with your daughter and I want to marry her," he said.

A shock rippled through my body. I straightened beside him as Elvis looked directly into my eyes, and I had to force myself to breathe. Could this really be happening?

I figured someone back home at that moment must be picking my mother right up off the floor, as Elvis casually proceeded to invite my family to Las Vegas for the weekend. Then he hung up the phone with a look of total satisfaction.

For my part, I was having trouble finding any words at all. Elvis may have made a remark about us being engaged earlier, but this declaration completely blew me away! Now I looked back on everything Elvis had said to me about soul mates and wondered if I'd found mine.

Many of Elvis's words and his behavior had certainly intimated he had been thinking a great deal about how I might fit into his life. Now he'd mentioned marriage to my mother as if he had come to a conclusion, formulated a plan, and just wanted me to know so he could carry it out. Elvis was someone I certainly thought I could marry, but everything was happening too fast for me to process it all at once. Our time together had been so intense that I felt like I needed to slow down and catch my breath. But all I could think to do at the moment was thank him again for his kindness and generosity toward me and my family.

After we'd returned to our suite from the doctor's office, Elvis began flipping through the pages of Cheiro's *Book of Numbers*. Stopping on some passages dealing with our respective numbers of four and eight, he began examining their qualities and analyzing how they affected one another. I wondered if he knew how stunned I was feeling and was trying to prove to me that we were compatible. Or was he looking for a numerological validation of his feelings? My mind was on overdrive as he talked. How could Elvis know with such certainty, after so short a time, that I was the one for him?

The next time I called home, my mother mentioned Elvis's declaration that he wanted to marry me. I could only say that I'd been as surprised as she was and that Elvis sure looked serious. "You know as much as I do," I said.

Meanwhile, my mother had spoken with doctors at the nursing home and been told that my grandfather was doing okay and that he wasn't any worse. "They say it's all right for us to come see you," she said.

Delighted, I relayed the news to Elvis, who immediately began arranging for my family's first visit to Las Vegas.

CHAPTER 10

I hadn't spoken much with Vernon Presley yet, but since he was Elvis's father, I hoped he would like me. It was hard for me to find time to talk alone with Vernon because whenever he was in our suite, he mostly talked with Elvis. He only occasionally asked me a question or directed a comment my way. We couldn't converse during Elvis's shows, and backstage, with Sandy at his side, Vernon was usually busy talking with guests.

December 8 proved to be a horrible night when, after Elvis's show, Vernon collapsed in the backstage dressing room. Elvis, myself, Dr. Ghanem, Sandy, and Joe rode with him to Sunrise Hospital, where Vernon was rushed into the emergency room, followed closely by Dr. Ghanem and Sandy.

While we waited, Elvis found an empty wheelchair in a mostly vacant corridor and sat down in it. Someone placed a chair beside him for me and I sat down, too. I noticed Elvis's eyes get misty and he lightly wiped them with the back of his hand. I placed my arm around him, wanting to comfort him any way possible. One night earlier, I'd been afraid I might lose my grandfather. Now here was Elvis, in a similar situation with his own father. I knew how helpless he must feel. Here was a man who thought he could do anything, yet this was beyond his reach. I wished there was something I could do for Elvis, the way he had offered to help me. At this moment, all I had to give him was my love, and that's what I gave.

We said prayers in the hallway as we waited for news. Sandy finally walked out and explained that Vernon had fluid buildup in his lungs, but otherwise he was doing all right. She also mentioned that he would definitely have to stop smoking.

Dr. Ghanem joined us then, relaying similar information. He tried to reassure Elvis and put him at ease. I waited while Elvis went in to see his father. Afterward, the doctors requested that Vernon stay in the hospital overnight.

I had seen Elvis be pensive before, but during our ride back to the Hilton, he was dead quiet. I was determined to comfort him and respect his feelings any way I could. If Elvis wanted to think in silence, I was there to keep him company, or if he wanted to talk, I was there to listen.

As we returned to our suite, Ricky Stanley was waiting for us. He immediately walked up to Elvis and hugged him. Ricky then surprised me with a hug and said, "Thank you for being here, Ginger."

It meant a great deal to me, hearing that. I was grateful if, in some small way, I had actually helped Elvis in a time of need.

A little later, Elvis decided he wanted to meditate—not surprising, I thought, on such an emotional night. He asked Larry and Charlie to join us in our room, where the four of us sat on the bed, held hands, and visualized colors, our hearts and minds focused on healing Vernon Presley.

The following evening, my stomach became unsettled. Whether

this was from the tension I'd felt during the previous night or from something else, I had no idea. Not wanting to worry Elvis, I decided to try a self-healing.

We had been reading in bed together; now I left Elvis and went into the bathroom, where I shut the door and stretched out on the carpeted floor. I took some deep breaths, focused on a color, and concentrated on feeling better.

When my stomach felt less queasy, I returned to our room. Elvis was still in bed, reading, and as I settled in place beside him, he looked up from his book. "Why were you lying on the floor?" he asked.

Completely mystified, I asked, "How did you know I was on the floor?"

Without saying a word, Elvis winked and smiled that satisfied, knowing smile I was becoming familiar with—a smile that intimated some type of sixth sense.

I felt my eyes go wide. Had Elvis somehow performed a healing on me from a distance, through a closed door?

I was beginning to believe in certain powers despite the fact that logic told me otherwise. Now I remembered how Elvis had once said he knew what was about to happen, and where, as if he had the gift of second sight. Had he just demonstrated that gift to me, or was it an innocent parlor trick?

The longer I was with Elvis, the more anything seemed possible.

I had enjoyed watching Elvis tease his band members onstage, and I'd grown accustomed to him changing the lyrics to certain songs in jest. However, during his next show, Elvis seemed to actually forget a few words.

For a moment, I thought maybe he was simply bored by repeating some songs. I quickly dismissed the notion that he would turn in a subpar performance, though, because the Elvis I was getting to know only ever wanted to give his audience the best.

Could his water pills or any pain medication be affecting his memory? It also seemed likely that, with Vernon in the hospital and so much going on around him, Elvis could forget a few words. I was slowly becoming aware of how unforeseen factors could affect a performance.

I waited for Elvis in the dressing room after the show. Before long, he sent for me from the adjacent room. When I entered, I saw two gorgeous women dressed in fur coats seated on either side of a man who Elvis introduced as Prince Adnan Khashoggi. The women seemed completely enthralled by Elvis, hanging on his every word as the men conversed. I sat beside Elvis and listened quietly.

Prince Khashoggi and the ladies had no sooner left when Elvis turned to me and said, "I had to use the bathroom the whole time." As he hastened to the men's room, he glanced over his shoulder at me and grinned. "I bet that's the first time you ever saw a prince and a king in the same room together," he said.

As the door closed behind him, I couldn't help but laugh.

Our prayers were answered on Friday, December 10, when Vernon was released from the hospital. Once Vernon was back at the Hilton, Elvis visited alone with his father in his room. Afterward, Elvis told me he wanted his father to return to Memphis so he could rest from the hustle and bustle of Las Vegas.

At the same time, Elvis was worried about Vernon being on the airplane and having a sudden relapse during the flight. Vernon argued that he was feeling well enough to remain in Las Vegas. In the end, Elvis agreed to let his dad stay through his last show.

Meanwhile, Elvis decided he wanted me to have more clothing and arranged for me to go shopping with Joe's girlfriend, Shirley. She had been a cocktail waitress in Las Vegas, Elvis said, and really knew her way around.

I was excited about the outing. Shirley was energetic and talkative. However, as we rode around Las Vegas in a car together, Shirley immediately brought up Elvis and began asking questions about the two of us. I wasn't one to open up with someone I didn't know. I certainly didn't want to discuss my relationship with Elvis with anyone outside my family. I kept the conversation light and easy, dodging her questions as gracefully as possible.

Fortunately, before long we pulled up to a store called Suzy Creamcheese. It was a high-end boutique filled with clothing like nothing I'd ever seen back in Memphis.

As I browsed through the apparel, Shirley occasionally handed me some pieces she thought were nice and picked out a few for herself. I ended up choosing some clothing that I hoped Elvis would like as well. Shirley paid for our new outfits with money I assumed Joe had given her from Elvis.

We returned to the Hilton and, later that evening, Elvis sent his Lockheed JetStar to Memphis, picking up my parents and siblings; my sister-in-law, Carolyn; and Terry's boyfriend, Tony. Billy Stanley, who had left after Elvis's Anaheim show, was on the flight, too, along with the wife and the son of one of the bodyguards. Everyone arrived in Las Vegas in time for Elvis's second show.

During portions of his first show, Elvis had performed some of his songs while seated on a stool. His leg was still not 100 percent pain-free, and I hoped he wouldn't injure it any further.

Afterward, we returned to the suite so he could relax and, before long, I was told my family had arrived. Excited, I called their room, telling them I'd see them soon.

Close to showtime, a bodyguard was sent to my family's suite and they were escorted downstairs. I slipped into a peach velvet gown, put on my evening shoes, and followed Joe back to the showroom. This time Joe left me to make my own way toward the usual booth.

As I went to sit down, I did a double take as I noticed my brother smiling at me. I had walked right past my family without recognizing them in the booth beside mine! Had I really been away from home that long? Had my new experiences with Elvis over the past weeks completely altered my perception?

Realizing what I'd done, I quickly backed up and joined them.

It was surreal but wonderful to gather my family around me here in Las Vegas. Finally, the people I loved were in one place. Vernon and Sandy soon entered, taking a seat in the booth beside ours.

I had barely begun visiting with my family when the lights dimmed and Joe returned, telling me that Elvis wanted me to sit in the booth with his father.

I was momentarily taken aback. Why didn't Elvis want me sitting with my own family? Knowing how ill Vernon had been, though, I whispered to my family, "I think Elvis wants me to keep Vernon and Sandy company," and moved to the next booth.

As Elvis's intro theme began to play, I was excited for my family. Now they would experience the same incredible feeling I'd had the first time I saw Elvis's show as his guest instead of an audience member. Elvis appeared to put extra effort into his overall performance and, other than a few sound problems, it was a good show. I was extremely happy and proud.

A memorable moment in the show for me was when someone in the audience shouted, "Elvis, I love you!" and he was quick to retort, "Ginger, is that you?" Elvis had mentioned my name in front of the crowd, and my family was right here!

Afterward, my family was escorted to the penthouse suite and I stayed behind with Elvis in his dressing room so he could change. He stepped out, looking incredibly handsome in a blue silk shirt, black pants, and black boots. As usual, he greeted others who'd been waiting and chatted graciously with them.

Once we were in the elevator and heading up to the penthouse, however, I could tell by his nervous mannerisms and little things Elvis said that he was anxious about meeting my family. This was something I again found endearing, if hard to believe. This was *Elvis*! What did he have to feel nervous about?

When we entered the suite, a bodyguard's wife who'd had one drink too many turned to look at Elvis and slipped off her stool at the bar, landing on the floor. Elvis looked slightly embarrassed as he approached my family. They were seated together on the couch.

As I introduced each person in turn and Elvis asked how my sisters had been, I realized I had still never told Elvis that my father met him years ago, when Elvis was first sworn into the army. I related the story now. I also told Elvis that my siblings and I had met him at the fairgrounds when we were little.

Elvis was genuinely surprised. I hadn't expected him to have any recollection of these memories; however, he looked long and hard at my dad and said, "Mr. Alden, I remember you now." He then went on, mentioning the army before going on to discuss other things. Later, when we were alone, Elvis would bring up again that it was pretty neat my family and he had met earlier.

At one point in the evening, Elvis asked someone to bring him the three wise men gifts he had received a few nights back and the conversation turned spiritual.

My mother told Elvis that her father had once been a preacher, years back, which interested him and they chatted a little more. He then politely asked my family if they would mind him continuing his visit with them the next evening, because he was tired but wanted to spend more time with them. He said he would like to treat them to a

French showgirl revue called the Lido de Paris at the Stardust Hotel, then have them return to the Hilton to see his second show.

The following night, my family went to see the Lido, and Elvis's ex-in-laws, the Beaulieus, along with their daughter Michelle and son Don, came to see Elvis perform during his first show. We were introduced backstage and, instead of being seated with Vernon in the showroom, I was surprised when this time Elvis placed me in a booth with the Beaulieus. Mr. Beaulieu was polite, briefly saying a few words to me, but I couldn't help but feel awkward throughout the entire show.

Elvis and I eventually went back to the suite between performances. When I returned to the showroom, I saw that the Beaulieus had stayed to watch another show. My family was sitting, unknowingly, in a booth beside them.

This time I was directed to sit with Vernon and Sandy. This decision baffled me a little, as Elvis had yet to seat me with my family. As always, though, I tried to keep an open mind where Elvis was concerned. By now I knew that Elvis did things in his own inexplicable way. Sometimes I would understand his thinking and sometimes not.

During this second performance, Elvis occasionally sat on a stool, still favoring one leg, but he had a good time and joked heavily with Charlie, which had everyone laughing. At one point, as he leaned over to kiss a member of the audience, Elvis hastily said, "Ginger, it's only part of the show."

He had mentioned my name again! I was on cloud nine!

Afterward, my family joined me in the dressing room and I was finally able to freely chat with them. They were bowled over when I told them about my new car. Elvis visited with a few people in the adjacent room and kept others waiting, as usual, including my parents and the Beaulieus, neither of whom would be introduced to one another. Vernon and Sandy spoke with my parents at one point, and Vernon gave my father a cigar, telling him that his doctors had advised him to quit smoking.

Elvis eventually visited with the Beaulieus. When they had gone, Elvis came out and greeted my family, this time inviting them back to the penthouse, where he gave them a tour of the suite while I waited in the living room.

When they returned, he took me aside. "Put on your white gown and all your jewelry," he whispered in my ear.

I went into my bathroom and did as he requested. Taking one last look in the mirror, I literally glittered from head to toe. Feeling as regal as any princess, I stepped out and was gratified to see Elvis beaming at me from across the room. "There," he said to my family. "I want you to see your daughter in her true attire. It's little Ginger's time to shine."

My family had seen me wear gowns at pageants, but this was the real thing and they were full of compliments. Elvis left the room then, only to return carrying the framed reproduction of a painting of himself by the artist Loxi Sibley.

After we'd admired it for a few moments, Elvis handed the painting to my father. "I want you to have it," he said, once again demonstrating how much he wanted to give to everyone around him. I thought Elvis would be tired after the show, but he continued to visit with my family for a long time, and I was happy to see him enjoying himself.

At some point, the conversation turned to Elvis's love of karate. Gathering my family in a circle, Elvis said he wanted to display some techniques for them.

He asked Ed Parker and Ricky Stanley to come into the room, then carefully placed Ricky in various positions as his "victim" while Ed narrated what Elvis was doing. Ed was fascinating to listen to, and I was mesmerized.

Elvis and Ed also demonstrated a few of their own karate moves on one another, and it was great to see Elvis apparently free from the pain he'd been suffering. It was all extremely entertaining, but it was quite late. My sister's boyfriend, Tony, eventually couldn't help himself and began to yawn.

Elvis shot him a quick glance and said, "Am I boring ya, son?"

Extremely embarrassed, Tony abruptly closed his mouth and replied, "No."

Elvis wrapped up the evening by telling us a story about Barbra Streisand approaching him to work on a remake of the film *A Star Is Born*. There were two reasons he didn't want to do that film, Elvis explained. The first was that he didn't understand why the main character would kill himself. The second reason was that, when Barbra Streisand and the producer, Jon Peters, discussed the movie with him, Jon had yawned.

"Man, I just couldn't see him directing it," Elvis said.

Sunday, December 12, Elvis performed what would be his last show in Las Vegas. Wayne Newton, Lola Falana, Kay Stevens, and Michelle Lee were all in the audience. The presence of so many stars was an added gift for my brother, who, unbeknownst to Elvis, happened to be celebrating his thirty-first birthday that day.

Elvis had a good time cutting up with Charlie onstage that night, and even though Charlie's birthday was a few days away, Elvis sang "Happy Birthday" to him. I only wished I had told him it was my brother's actual birthday, because if Elvis had acknowledged it from the stage, what a gift that would have been!

Wayne Newton visited with Elvis in his dressing room while Wayne's wife, Elaine, chatted briefly with me and my family. After they left, my parents thanked Elvis and returned to their rooms to pack. It was a little tough for me to say good-bye, but I remained with

Elvis an extra day so he could rest, while my parents flew home on the JetStar.

As I looked back on our intense time together in Las Vegas, I wondered what it would be like when Elvis and I were finally apart in Memphis after spending so much intimate time together. We had shared our thoughts and feelings as we discovered new things about each other. He had even spoken of marriage. I had been magically transported into Elvis's world and inhabited it as fully as possible, learning much about his connection to his fans, his life as a performer, his entourage of close employees and friends, and his spiritual quest.

In our exciting weeks together, Elvis had become my mentor, lover, and protector. He had rocked me not only musically, but physically and emotionally. My world, as I'd always known it, was forever changed, no matter what happened next.

CHAPTER 11

I flew back to Memphis with Elvis on the *Lisa Marie*. As the plane touched down on familiar soil, it felt nice to be home. Yet, I also felt slightly displaced after having lived in Elvis's world for almost three weeks nonstop.

David Stanley, another of Elvis's stepbrothers and employees, was waiting to pick us up at the airport. He was close to my age with long, shaggy, dark brown hair and a brawnier build than his two siblings. I had no trouble believing it when Elvis told me David's nickname was Magilla Gorilla.

Driving toward Graceland down Elvis Presley Boulevard, as we neared the front gates, I saw a large nativity scene now sitting in the front yard. I had seen this nativity scene many times in the past. During my childhood, my family would drive around the area every Christmas, marveling at the holiday lights as nearby neighborhoods tried to outdo one another with beautiful decorations. What seemed magical to me then was indescribably wonderful now as I viewed it seated next to Elvis.

As we passed the life-size statues of Mary, Joseph, and Jesus in the manger, Elvis looked my way, shrugged his shoulders, and joked, "Who are those people?"

Inside Graceland, one of the maids greeted us and I noticed a Christmas tree standing in the dining room. From the foyer, I couldn't tell if it was real or not, but it was beautiful. I wondered who had decorated it.

Just then, an older woman with an adorable honey-colored Pomeranian cradled in her arms entered the room and welcomed Elvis home. Elvis introduced her as Aunt Delta. I would later learn that she was Vernon's sister and had been living at Graceland since the 1960s. An aide carried the three wise men Elvis had been given inside and placed them in the foyer near the front door.

Wordlessly, Elvis walked upstairs and I followed him with the unspoken understanding that he expected me to accompany him to his bedroom. I still felt like a visitor on the outside looking in, but it seemed that, for Elvis, me being at Graceland was already the most normal thing in the world.

Although we had taken an extra day in Las Vegas to relax at the Hilton, it had still felt like a whirlwind trip. Now that we were home, I could feel my adrenaline-fueled energy giving way to weariness. I thought Elvis must feel the same way and would want to rest or just be away from the many people who had surrounded him for the past few weeks.

Upstairs, Elvis immediately disappeared into his bathroom. I stood waiting, unsure of what to do. I felt that I needed to go home, regroup, and reflect on all of the new experiences I'd had with Elvis, but I didn't want to leave if that would disappoint him. I also knew that, because Elvis and I had been together nonstop, I would miss him.

Elvis returned from the bathroom, where he had changed into his usual pajamas, and sat down on his bed. Picking up one of his books from the floor, he motioned me over to sit beside him.

If this was what Elvis needed to relax, I was happy to stay until he was ready to go to sleep. However, as I took my place beside him while Elvis read, my eyes wandered to the pictures of Linda Thompson on the shelf. I wondered if he'd simply forgotten they were there. Shaking thoughts of Linda from my mind, I turned my focus back to Elvis.

At one point, Elvis asked about my grandfather having been a minister and said he wanted to speak with my mother again. I called home, said a quick hello, and handed him the phone.

Elvis dove right into a conversation with her about the Bible. "Have you ever noticed how the word *history* broken up means *His story*?" he asked, alluding to history being God's story.

My mother had a strong spiritual faith. She had frequently read parts of the Bible to us, so I knew she'd enjoy this conversation. As they talked, it was interesting to hear some of Elvis's personal observations regarding the Bible. With all of the reading we had previously done, we had not yet touched upon this area.

Their conversation lasted a few minutes, then Elvis abruptly changed the subject. "What kind of car do you drive?" he asked.

As he sat quietly listening, I knew she was telling him about the Dodge Charger they had recently purchased. "That's your family car?" he asked.

When the conversation ended and Elvis hung up, he seemed to be mulling over something. Looking my way, he announced, "I would like your parents to have a new car, a larger one."

I didn't know what to say. He could render me speechless like nobody else.

After thinking about it for a few more minutes, Elvis asked, "Would you mind giving them the Continental? I have another car I wanna give you." This took me totally by surprise.

In the excitement of being with Elvis in Las Vegas and coming home to Memphis, I hadn't given the Continental a thought. In fact, I still hadn't even driven it.

"That's fine," I said, amazed that Elvis would want my parents to have a new car. "But where is the Continental?"

"It should be here," he said. "Someone was supposed to drive it to Memphis."

"Oh. Okay," I answered, smiling as I thought about how, in Elvis's world, magical things like this could just happen.

The Continental was indeed delivered to Graceland. Now Elvis wanted me to drive it home. He called for an aide to escort me.

Eager to surprise my parents, I took a seat behind the wheel of the car for the first time and began following Al Strada toward Graceland's gates. It was a surprisingly harrowing experience. I hadn't realized how big the car was until I was driving it. As I peered over the wheel, the Continental's expansive hood seemed to stretch out forever. It was basically a land yacht! As the car squeezed through the brick pillars and onto Elvis Presley Boulevard, I was worried about hitting any- and everything.

Keeping up with Al wasn't easy, either. He was driving fast, so fast that I had the impression he was just trying to get this chore over with. I wondered if he was tired after the trip, too. Luckily, I made it home with no fender benders.

My parents were at work when I arrived, but my sisters were in the house. It was comforting to see them. At the same time, it actually felt slightly surreal to be at home. I brought my sisters outside, and as they gasped at the sight of the gleaming white Continental, I told them that Elvis wanted me to give it to our parents. They were flabbergasted.

They wanted to hear about Las Vegas when we headed back inside. As much as I wanted to tell them about it, I suddenly realized how exhausted I was. I explained that I needed to rest, because Elvis was sleeping and might call when he woke up. This would be my only chance to get caught up on sleep.

"Can I tell you all about it when Mom and Dad get home?" I asked, then retired to my bedroom. I was practically asleep before my head hit the pillow.

I don't know how many hours I slept before there was a knock on my door. It was my mom. I walked with my parents outside and, as they stared disbelievingly at the Continental, I repeated the words that Elvis had originally said to me: "It's yours."

It was a priceless moment.

I told my family as much as I could about what I'd experienced with Elvis, but I couldn't reveal everything, especially the inexplicable moments when I'd witnessed the self-healing or Elvis's attempts to move objects with his mind. I doubt they would have believed me anyway.

In turn, they shared their own experiences in Las Vegas, and how the trip had taken my mother's mind off her father's health for a bit. It was her first time on an airplane and, although she had a fear of flying, "Once we were inside the JetStar," she said, "I didn't think twice about it."

My parents hadn't been inside their room at the Las Vegas Hilton long before there was a knock at their door. When they opened it, a man stood in the hallway, holding a vase of flowers he said were from Elvis. My mother thanked him and carried the vase into the room.

When she turned back after putting the flowers on a table, she caught the man inching his way into the room. "Is Ginger your daughter?" he had asked.

"Yes," she'd answered, startled.

"Are she and Elvis going to get married?" he asked.

Only then had my mother realized he was probably a reporter, and the flowers weren't really from Elvis at all. "I'm sorry," she told him, "but I can't answer any questions."

The man had tried to step inside the room even more. "I practically had to close the door on him!" my mother reported now.

We laughed about the incident, but I was uncomfortable. Neither my family nor I had any preparation for dealing with the press. I hoped this sort of thing wouldn't happen again.

That was one hope that would go unfulfilled.

"Do you think I still have a job?" I asked her now.

"When I spoke with them, they told me you did," she said.

I breathed a sigh of relief. At least one small thing would still feel normal now that I was back in Memphis.

Later that night, Elvis called my house himself for the very first time. My father asked to speak with him. He thanked Elvis for the car, but told him they honestly felt awkward as it was such a large gift. It was fun seeing the expression on my dad's face, because I could tell from his look of shock and confusion that Elvis was pressing him until he felt all right about accepting the car.

When I got back on the line, Elvis invited me over.

"I'll drive," I said, but Elvis, always the gentleman, insisted on sending someone to pick me up.

Back at Graceland, I wasn't inside long when Elvis took my hand and asked me to walk downstairs with him. I followed him outside onto the porch, wondering what he was up to now. I was rapidly learning to expect the unexpected.

Headlights suddenly appeared from around the side of the house as a gorgeous silver and maroon Cadillac Seville pulled up in front of us. An aide climbed out of the driver's seat, and Elvis turned to me. "Thanks for givin' the Continental to your parents, Ginger," he said. "This is yours."

I hugged Elvis, understanding now why he hadn't wanted me to drive myself to Graceland, then ran over to excitedly look over my new car. It was a customized version of Cadillac's newly introduced Seville with wire wheels, a chrome grille, and a built-in citizen band radio.

Elvis explained that he had originally bought the car for his father. "My dad told me he didn't really have any use for it," he said. I couldn't help but wonder if Elvis had felt a little hurt about this.

Early the next morning, I drove my Cadillac home and slept for a little while. My life had taken a completely new direction. Whether this direction was real and permanent, or just a momentary illusion, I knew that I was willing to take a chance on the relationship I was developing with Elvis.

When I woke, I made the phone call to Larry that I had promised Elvis I would make back when he asked me to stop seeing anyone else. I invited Larry to my home and made it clear that we couldn't see each other anymore. As hard as it was to do, I wanted to be with Elvis now and I had to be truthful about that.

That night, Elvis invited me back to Graceland. I found him seated on his bed. When I entered the room, he made a surprising announcement.

"Linda Thompson called and asked if I was going to spend Christmas with her," he said. "Do you want to spend Christmas with me?"

"Yes!" I answered without hesitation.

He smiled at me. "Good."

I felt suddenly uncertain. Why was Linda still calling him? I'd thought his relationship with her was over. I was happy that Elvis was inviting me to spend Christmas with him, of course, but what would he have done if, for some reason, I'd been unable to? Would he have spent it with Linda? I'd just ended things with Larry and made a commitment to see how things progressed with Elvis. Why had he even told me about Linda's call? Did he want me to be jealous?

Elvis seemed to be tracking my thoughts, which I suppose must have shown on my face, because he pointed to the pictures of Linda. "Why don't you take those down?" he instructed.

Doing this would sure make me feel better. As I began gathering the photos, Elvis went on. "Linda placed those there a while ago, when I was away," he said and asked me to put the photographs in his office bathroom.

I had no idea there was a bathroom off his office at that point; it was one room I'd never seen. I only knew about the bathroom adjoining his bedroom.

Photos in hand, I walked into his office, toward a closed accordion-style door. I had always thought this was a closet. Now, sliding the door open, I stepped onto a floor covered in deep, bubblegum-pink shag carpeting. In the open closet facing me hung a few items of women's clothing. Whose were they?

My stomach was in a knot. Naive as I was back then, I'd had no idea a woman had been staying here with Elvis. Were they Linda's things, or some other woman's?

To my right, makeup and toiletries were scattered across the counter. Liquid makeup had splattered along the bottom of the mirrored wall above it, making me wonder if there had been a small fight of some kind. A vanity chair was tucked beneath the counter, and on the left was a professional salon chair with built-in hair dryer. Beside that was another counter with a sink. That wall was also mirrored. A glass bath/shower stall stood at the end of the bathroom, a misty green toilet across from it. A telephone was attached to the wall. The finishing touch was a tall vase filled with yellow and green feather plumes.

I placed the pictures on the vanity chair, not knowing what else to do with them, and walked out, sliding the door shut.

Back in the bedroom, I sat down beside Elvis, feeling disoriented and upset. Again, he read my emotions easily.

Elvis took my hands in his. "You know, I never could picture myself married to Linda," he said. "She kept asking me, but I always thought that it was the man's place to ask."

He added that Linda had been pursuing a career in California, saying, "Poor Linda. She's gone Hollywood."

I began to relax a little. I had never been there though and said, "I think it would be fun to see Los Angeles one day."

Elvis shot back, "You going to Hollywood would be like throwing pizza to hungry lions!"

I certainly had no plans to go to Hollywood and appreciated that he was being protective of me. Elvis's pronouncement was a little confusing though. Hollywood had been such a big part of his life when he was making movies. Did Elvis disapprove of it? Had something happened in Hollywood to make him feel that way?

Elvis turned on the television and took my hand again. "You don't have to worry," he said. "I told you before. Linda and I are over. I'll see to it that the things in the bathroom are out of there. That bathroom should be for you to use."

I relaxed. Clearly Elvis intended for me to be spending a lot more time at Graceland. I was glad to hear it.

CHAPTER 12

I had a strong feeling that I was going to be more on Elvis's schedule now and knew that I wouldn't be able to continue working and spend time with him. I drove to the dress shop and spoke with the owner about leaving my job. It had been only part-time work, and I decided it was worth putting my career on the back burner to spend as much time as possible with Elvis to see how our relationship developed. Luckily, the owner was understanding and wished me well.

One thing I wanted to do was see my grandfather. I let Elvis know and headed to Arkansas with my mother for a quick overnight trip. It felt good to be driving alone with her. I rarely had her all to myself, even when I was home, and I always treasured our time alone together. Never one to pry, she had always been there to listen.

This trip was no different. As the miles flew by, we talked about what was happening in my life. I knew from an early age that my mother and father had always enjoyed Elvis's music and had a positive opinion of him as a person. I didn't get any sense that my mother had any reservations about our dating or questioned Elvis's character. However, although I didn't really feel the age gap between Elvis and myself mattered, I decided to bring it up with her because I wondered if she had any concerns about it.

"I know there's a big age difference between Elvis and me," I said, stating the obvious, then fell silent to see if she had anything to say about it.

She replied, "I wondered about that, but I didn't say anything to you because it didn't seem to matter to you."

She was being diplomatic, I realized, and doing the same thing I was: trying to assess my feelings before she gave me an opinion. "I don't feel that it's an issue at this point, Mom," I said.

Luckily, she seemed to agree. "Elvis does seem to act like a much younger man. He reminds me of someone more your brother's age," she said, adding that she trusted Elvis and didn't feel any reason not to believe he was sincere about his feelings for me and would treat me right. "As long as you're happy, both your dad and I are happy for you," she said.

It was wonderful to see my grandfather. His illness hadn't progressed, and I hoped our visit to the nursing home lifted his spirits. Because of his age and him having been ill, it was difficult to say goodbye when the time came. I hoped he would be well as we lived far apart and I wasn't sure how soon I would be able to see him again.

"Tell Elvis he'd better take care of you," my grandfather said in parting.

When we returned to Memphis, Elvis called and invited me back to Graceland. Upon entering his office, I noticed the bathroom door was open and, peeking inside, I saw that the toiletries were gone and all of the women's clothing had been removed from the closet. Had Elvis taken them out, or had he asked someone else to do it? Either way, I was happy, feeling that this was a big step. Elvis was letting me know he was serious about us and committed to our relationship as I was. Soon after that, Elvis gave me his private phone numbers and began calling my house daily. Sometimes I phoned him, but this was still Elvis Presley, a busy and important man, so I generally waited for him to call me. As close as we were becoming, I still didn't feel comfortable enough to just pick up the phone on a whim and call him. What if he was working or had other obligations? I wanted to respect his time and privacy.

Now that we were back in Memphis, I wondered if Elvis might switch back to a more normal sleep pattern, but he didn't. Consequently, I alternated between his schedule and my more ordinary hours. I slept at home some nights but mainly found myself at Graceland until early morning hours when Elvis went to sleep, then I'd go home to nap during the day because the odd hours sometimes took a toll on me.

Whenever I arrived at Graceland, Aunt Delta or one of the maids would usually greet me at the front door. The housekeepers were Lottie Tyson, Mary Jenkins, Nancy Rooks, and Pauline Nicholson. They referred to Elvis as Mister Elvis or Mister P, and as time went by, they even began calling me Miss Ginger.

Once in a while, Charlie or Billy Smith opened the door and greeted me. Charlie occupied a room on the first floor of Graceland. Billy lived with his wife and children in a trailer out back. Although they were around Graceland on a regular basis along with aides and a few other family members, my focus was on Elvis, and because he liked keeping me near him, I wasn't spending time alone with any of them at Graceland, the same as in Las Vegas. When I arrived, I was typically told to go upstairs, where Elvis would either be in his bedroom or Lisa's, visiting with other people or watching television alone. I soon met more family members and employees. Minnie Mae Presley, Vernon Presley's mother, lived in the house and slept in a bedroom back by the staircase. She was a tall, thin, sweet, soft-spoken woman whom Elvis called Dodger. She got her nickname when Elvis was young and threw a ball at her, missing her by a few inches. I was very touched when one of the first things Dodger ever said to me was how much she loved Elvis.

Tish Henley, a nurse, worked for Dr. Nichopoulos, and her husband, Tommy, was a caretaker at Graceland, so I saw them every once in a while. Tish and Tommy both lived in a trailer on the property, as did Vernon's younger sister, Nash. Harold Lloyd, a first cousin to Elvis, also worked at the front gate, like Vernon's brother Vester.

In fact, as I gradually sorted out faces and names, I realized that Elvis seemed to have taken on the responsibility of supporting a great many people. Uncles worked as guards, family and friends lived on the grounds, and stepbrothers were on the payroll. Elvis's generosity was legendary, and nowhere was it more evident than at Graceland with his extended family and friends.

Elvis may have had members of his family and some friends living in Graceland and on the surrounding property, but he seemed to prefer staying upstairs in his pajamas and have others visit him. When I came to see him, he never directly asked me not to wander around the house or hang out with the other people, but I strongly sensed he wanted me to be at his side.

This was fine with me. I didn't blame Elvis for wanting to stay in his pajamas and be comfortable. The ornate suits he wore onstage were heavy, tight, and constricting. He once showed me raw spots on his back caused by one of his stage costumes. He also liked to keep the temperature in his bedroom on the cooler side and, when sitting with him in bed, I usually kept a blanket over my legs.

Even in his pajamas, though, Elvis still liked some flash. He often wore a blue-jeweled robe, even over regular clothing. He used a cologne called Zizanie and Neutrogena face soap; even today, those scents make me think of him.

We would often sit on his bed and read for hours. Sometimes we would take turns reading to each other or sit side by side reading to ourselves. Whenever we were reading to ourselves, if the two of us happened to take a breath at the same time, or even sigh at the same moment, Elvis always noticed. Once he said, "It's almost as if we're one."

If I did start reading alone, Elvis would usually put down his own book to see what I was immersed in, and he'd end up asking me about it. I was impressed with his insatiable curiosity and appreciated his continuing efforts to both instruct me and find out what I was thinking.

Elvis and I also spent hours watching television and movies in his bedroom. He had the first Betamax tape machine I'd ever seen, and I loved the novelty of being able to watch any movie on demand. Elvis adored the British actor Peter Sellers, and got the biggest kick out of Sellers's portrayal of Inspector Clouseau in director Blake Edwards's Pink Panther films.

We watched these movies many times, and Elvis would often try to squint his eyes the way Sellers did and mimic Sellers's phony French accent, saying the word *minkey* for "monkey." Elvis also loved to repeat that famous line from *Casablanca*, "Here's looking at you, kid." I was never bored while Elvis and I were watching television because Elvis couldn't watch a TV without talking back to it. I found this quite entertaining. He'd often repeat dialogue, and if a man got rejected by a woman in a film or on a television show, Elvis often shouted out, "Burned!"

He loved comedies like *What's Happening!!* and especially got a kick out of a character named Fish played by Abe Vigoda on the show *Barney Miller*. Elvis found Abe amusing, he said, because "he always looks so disgusted with the world."

He loved the comedy of Redd Foxx, too, and said that I should see him perform live in Vegas someday. Sadly, we would never get the chance.

Whenever we weren't watching something or reading together,

Elvis and I listened to music, or Elvis would sit at the organ and sing. In this way I learned something about his personal musical tastes. Elvis especially admired the American tenor Mario Lanza, and the baritone singer Brook Benton, frequently playing their albums for me. Before that, I'd only heard Benton singing "The Boll Weevil Song" and "Rainy Night in Georgia," and I'd never known about Mario Lanza before. I quickly grew to appreciate his great voice.

When it came to singing, Elvis believed he had been given a divine gift. In his view, he was a messenger meant to bring joy to others.

Even before meeting Elvis, his voice and music had brought happiness to my family for years. One of my favorite albums while I was growing up was Elvis's *His Hand in Mine*. With gospel music rooted so deeply in his soul, I wasn't surprised that Elvis wanted to spend early Sunday mornings watching gospel shows. He loved listening to the singers.

Whenever the TV was off, Elvis left the radio on and tuned to a music station. Music of almost any kind seemed to comfort him. As he often told me, "Music is the universal language."

If Elvis was trying to get me to understand something and a song happened to be playing with lyrics that correlated with a point he was trying to make, he would stop and nod his head toward the radio. "Listen," he'd say, "it's talking to you," as if the song were backing him up.

Not all music was for him, though. Once, a heavy-metal song with a shrieking guitar began to play on the radio. Elvis got up to use the restroom, and as he passed by the radio, he paused for a second, looked at it, and said, "Boy, I'll break your Goddamn fingers!"

I cherished those early mornings when it was just Elvis and me alone upstairs at Graceland. If he got an idea for a song, he'd go over to the organ in his office and ask me to sit beside him. I sometimes sat on the floor to give him more room on the bench.

Elvis loved playing around with the various instrument sounds built into the organ. Once, he turned on the drums and joked, "Someone better let that guy outta there."

As the drumbeat pounded away, he laughed and started singing, "You poor worthless, foolish . . . foolish . . . fool."

Other times, he was serious, putting a great deal of emotion into different songs as he experimented with them. Elvis sometimes tried reaching various notes he thought he never could hit, too. Thrilled one time when he hit an unexpected bass note, he said, "My God, I've never sung that low before."

The indirect lighting along the edge of the ceilings in his bedroom and office was always on. Many times as I watched him at the organ, where he was bathed in soft light and lost in song, dressed in his jeweled robe, I'd feel like one part of me were there and another part of me were viewing this scene from a distance. I still couldn't quite believe that I was with Elvis, and hearing him sing never ceased to be special.

While Elvis and I were upstairs, his aides mainly hung around downstairs on call. This seemed to be a relatively undemanding job when Elvis wasn't on tour. Dean Nichopoulos, Al Strada, Steve Smith, and either David or Ricky Stanley alternated work shifts. I no longer saw Elvis's stepbrother Billy around.

David Stanley, Elvis's youngest stepbrother, called Elvis Boss. David was married to a young girl named Angie, whom I had yet to meet, and sometimes when he was on duty, he would come upstairs to talk to Elvis about his marital problems. Elvis told me it bothered him that David was going through this; he had faith in the sanctity of marriage. I would give them privacy as Elvis tried offering David the best advice he could. As David began to do this more frequently, however, Elvis told me that he was getting frustrated because none of the advice he gave David seemed to be changing things or helping David resolve things in his marriage.

Although I didn't see much of Aunt Delta, her Pomeranian, Edmund, had free rein of Graceland and periodically wandered around upstairs. Charlie occasionally popped in and out of Elvis's bedroom, usually telling dirty jokes, and often I could tell he had been drinking. Billy Smith, Elvis's cousin, was a frequent visitor upstairs as well; he and Elvis shared a similar sense of humor, and Elvis often called him Marble Eyes.

Dr. Nichopoulos had stopped by a few times, nervously jingling his car keys against his pant leg while chatting with Elvis. Elvis referred to him as Dr. Nick, and I thought how nice it was to have your doctor check in on you.

Before leaving Graceland to go home after spending an evening with Elvis, I sometimes noticed sleep medication packets left for him. This surprised me because Elvis wasn't on tour. Why would he have difficulty sleeping if he was at home? I didn't think much about this at first, though; I trusted Dr. Nichopoulos to keep an eye on Elvis's health and felt reassured knowing there was always a nurse on the property.

Elvis had two telephones on his bedside table. A gold one served as a private line, the one I called when I phoned Elvis and that I assumed he used when he called me. The other phone had buttons marked for various rooms in the house. By pressing a button marked "kitchen," Elvis could relay to the maids what we wanted to eat. Sometimes he asked me to be the one to call downstairs. I wasn't accustomed to giving people orders and knew it would take me a little while to get used to it. When I did relay what Elvis requested, I always made sure I said please and thank you.

Elvis had simple tastes in food and especially liked Lottie's cooking. She prepared wonderful steaks with special seasoning and hamburgers with their buns steamed in butter, which Elvis called Lottieburgers. One night at dinner, I had my first taste of Canadian bacon with crowder peas, another of his favorite meals.

I got so used to our meals being brought to the bedroom that I found it difficult to imagine Elvis sitting at a table to eat. In fact, during the many months we spent together, that was something I would never witness.

One evening, well past midnight, I was home with my family and fast asleep when a rumble in the distance woke me. Our dogs began barking, and the rumbling sound slowly became more of a roar, growing louder and louder until it finally stopped nearby.

From my bedroom, I heard doors inside our home opening. Terry, who shared a room with me, sat up in bed. "What's that?" she asked.

We both put on robes and went into the den. Shortly, our mom, Rosemary, and father appeared. My dad went to the front door and opened it. Meanwhile, I peeked out of our music room window to see what was going on. There were no streetlights in our neighborhood and it was pitch-black outside.

My father turned on our front porch light and stepped outside while we anxiously watched him from inside the doorway. The sound of rustling in the grass drew our attention.

A shadowy figure emerged out of the darkness and into the light. It was a motorcyclist clad in black leather. It wasn't until he stepped onto the porch and removed his shiny black helmet that I saw it was Elvis!

Al Strada stood behind him. I had never seen Elvis travel anywhere without an entourage, so I figured there must be bodyguards waiting around the corner, unseen. But only Elvis and Al came inside, and Elvis took a seat on the sofa in our den. Just when I had been thinking this incredible man couldn't surprise me more than he already had, he succeeded. Here was Elvis at my house! Not at Graceland, not in an arena, not in a hotel penthouse, but sitting in our den like he was a neighbor from down the street!

This was the first time Elvis had seen anyone in my family since Las Vegas. We were all so stunned to have him show up at our house like this, at such a late hour, that we didn't even think about getting out of our pajamas. Elvis didn't say a word about how late it was. Luckily, it was a weekend, and neither of my parents had to get up for work the next day, but I doubted Elvis had thought about that. This was my boyfriend and my parents couldn't help that he kept odd hours. The fact this was Elvis, also gave him a little more latitude. After we'd chatted for a few minutes, Elvis eventually began talking with my mother about the Bible. She brought out the large, worn, family Bible she often used to read to us. Elvis went over a few passages, directing most of his comments to my mother, and asked if he could write inside the Bible.

"No, I don't mind," my mother said. I could tell he had piqued her interest.

Elvis wrote the word *ask* above the title "Genesis, The First Book of Moses," and then began reading about God creating heaven and earth. He underlined certain lines and wrote down a few words, dissecting them as he had done once before with her on the phone, shortly after our return from Las Vegas. He then moved on and began underlining verses in the Book of Revelation.

The visit lasted quite a while, and I loved seeing Elvis enjoying himself with my family. It was a much more relaxed and intimate setting for us all to be together than it had been in Las Vegas. I was happy that my parents were finally getting the chance to witness a little of Elvis's spiritual quest and to see him as I had over the past weeks, as a man who was bright, interesting, and charming.

Near dawn, Elvis decided it was time to go and went to use our restroom. Al had been sitting quietly in the room with us. Now my parents asked him a little about himself. Al said that he wasn't that happy with his job, but said he was working to help support his mother in Los Angeles. I understood how Al's job could sometimes be difficult.

Elvis wanted others around him to pick up and go whenever and wherever. He wanted to have his employees at his beck and call. Hearing Al talk reminded me that, even now, Al was at work for Elvis. Being at my home was a paid job! I could see where nights like this wouldn't necessarily be fun or exciting for an aide.

When Elvis returned, I followed him outside. "Thank you for coming over," I said as we walked together toward his motorcycle. "Your bike is beautiful."

"I'll take you for a ride sometime," he said.

Then, strapping his helmet back on, Elvis climbed onto his motorcycle. Al got into a waiting car. I stood on the lawn to watch them leave, smiling as I watched Elvis ride off into the night.

A few days before Christmas, Elvis asked if I would help him shop for his relatives. He had arranged for Goldsmith's Department Store in Memphis to reopen after public hours. Goldsmith's was located in the Southland Mall, not far down the street from Graceland. Elvis's cousin Patsy Gambill and a bodyguard accompanied us.

As we turned into the mall's parking lot, we were greeted by a police officer waiting in his car. One of the mall security guards opened the door to Goldsmith's while the police officer waited outside.

It felt eerie to walk through the department store, empty now except for us and a few sales clerks patiently waiting for this one shopper. I had been in Goldsmith's many times, but this was shopping Elvis-style and completely different.

We had been in the store for only a few moments when Elvis said he'd like to buy me some nightgowns and robes. I was surprised that he wanted to buy something for me and by the intimate nature of the gifts. I followed Elvis and the guard to the lingerie department, where I browsed through the sleepwear while the men made small talk close by.

Above: A picture taken of me around age two and a half. Who would've known Elvis Presley would one day enter my life and give me the nickname Little Two?

Photo courtesy of Ginger Alden

Left: My first-grade picture that Elvis requested and kept in a frame on his bedside table at Graceland alongside another photo of me. My permed hairdo I could have lived without!

Photo courtesy of Ginger Alden

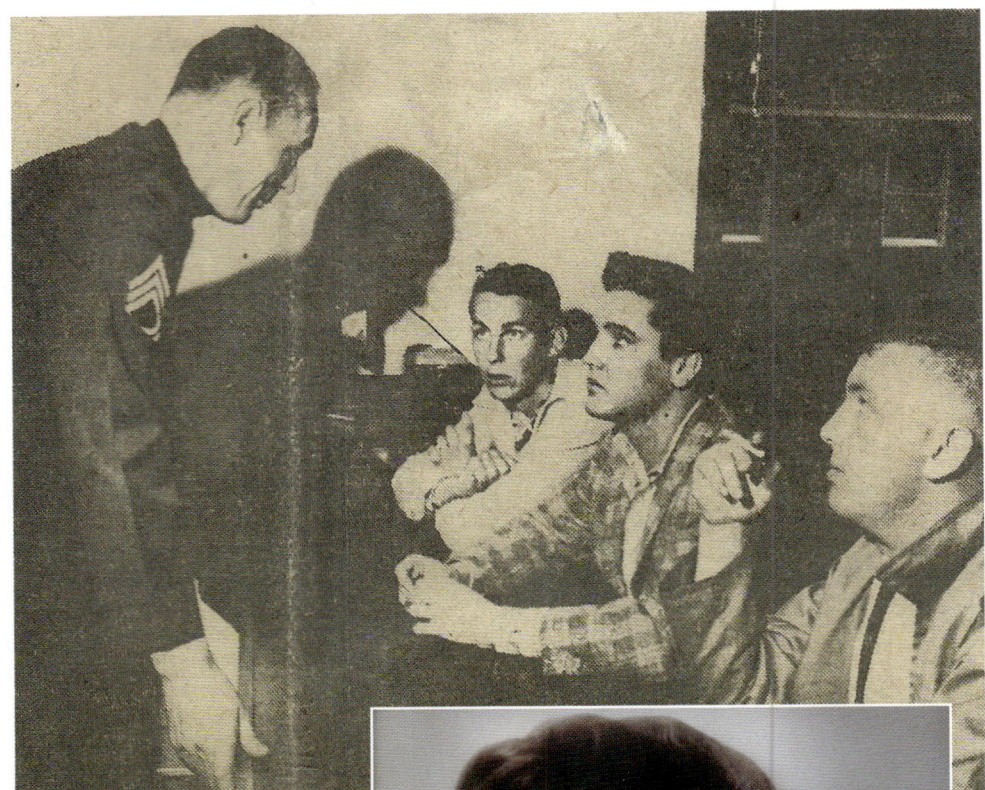

Above: Elvis listening intently to my father speaking, shortly after they first met at Kennedy Veterans Hospital in Memphis, Tennessee, on March 24, 1958. Little did the two of them know that they would be in each other's lives again eighteen years later.

Photo courtesy of Ginger Alden

Right: My mother proudly serving her country. The photo was taken when she first entered the army in 1943.

Photo courtesy of Ginger Alden

My sister Rosemary, Dad, Mom, my sister Terry, and me during the Miss America pageant in Atlantic City, New Jersey, in September of 1976. We couldn't have been any more proud of Terry!

Photo courtesy of Ginger Alden

My brother, Mike, inside Elvis's JetStar, heading to Las Vegas on what was my family's first trip to see one of Elvis's shows.

Photo courtesy of Jo Alden

Elvis's personal identification bracelet that he wore for many years and surprisingly gifted me with on our first flight together to Las Vegas.

Photo courtesy of Ginger Alden

Elvis's wonderful sense of humor shows in a couple of personal checks made out to me. My father had given Elvis a dime so he could make a phone call when he entered the army. I couldn't help but smile remembering my dad's story when Elvis gave me the Christmas check for ten cents.

Photo courtesy of Ginger Alden

Elvis and me holding hands, with Ed Parker in the foreground, after arriving in Pittsburgh, Pennsylvania, on December 31, 1976, before his New Year's Eve show. Usually shy about being photographed, I was also sad here because my grandfather had just passed away the day before. *Photo courtesy of BobKleinMedia.com*

Elvis onstage during his New Year's Eve show in Pittsburgh, Pennsylvania, on December 31, 1976. It was a fantastic show! I was so proud of his performance and happy that he was wearing the cross necklace I had given him for Christmas.

Taken by Donna Gaffin, from the Russ Howe Collection

Elvis and me walking toward my parents' Lincoln Continental, leaving the Ramada Inn in Harrison, Arkansas, on January 3, 1977. We had earlier returned to the Ramada after my grandfather's funeral.

Photo by Bill Doshier Jr., courtesy of Harrison Daily Times, *Harrison, Arkansas*

Elvis entering my parents' Lincoln Continental after my grandfather's funeral. He had changed into the jeweled robe that he so often loved to wear.

Photo by Bill Doshier Jr., courtesy of Harrison Daily Times, *Harrison, Arkansas*

Right after asking me to marry him, Elvis surprised me with this beautiful engagement ring at Graceland on January 26, 1977.

Photo courtesy of Ginger Alden

During their chat, Elvis accidentally referred to me once as "Sheila." He quickly caught himself and said, "Ginger."

When I hastily turned around, wondering who Sheila was, Elvis glanced at me with a "sorry about that" look.

This threw me for a moment, but I went back to shopping. It was only much later that I learned Elvis had dated a woman named Sheila Ryan for a few years, not long before meeting me.

I selected some nightgowns and robes, then followed Elvis over to the fur coat section, where he began looking through the coats. He seemed to know what he liked and I started to feel like he didn't really need me along as he picked out a coat and had Patsy try it on.

Looking through a few more, Elvis singled out a black-and-white mink and one more made of white rabbit fur. He asked me to try them on so he could see if they would fit some of his relatives. I slipped into each coat and turned around, briefly modeling them while Elvis watched and mulled them over. He then purchased all of the coats while I browsed close by.

Back at Graceland, Elvis gave Patsy the coat she had tried on and I knew Elvis's other relatives would be pleasantly surprised by the gifts he had waiting for them. I wondered if he was this generous with his family every Christmas, and decided he probably was. Elvis was his family's real Santa Claus. In fact, I'd begun to see that every day with Elvis could feel like Christmas.

I left Graceland shortly after sunrise. On the way home, I wondered what I could give Elvis for the holidays that he didn't already have. I couldn't possibly repay him in kind for the generous gifts he'd given my family and me.

At first, because of everything we'd been reading, I considered having a special turban made with a large stone in its center, but I didn't think I'd have enough time. I went to sleep for a while, still pondering ideas, and later went shopping with Rosemary.

In a nearby mall, I finally purchased a gold chain necklace with a large cross made out of a gemstone called tiger's eye. It was a simple gift compared to most of Elvis's jewelry, but I liked it and hoped he would, too.

That night, Elvis called to once again invite me to help him choose coats for some relatives. I went to Graceland, and from there, for the first time, I got to ride in his Ferrari. The bodyguard, Sam, squeezed into the backseat with Elvis's cousin Billy and Billy's wife, Jo. I sat in the passenger seat with Elvis at the wheel.

Soon we were zooming along on the expressway toward downtown Memphis. Elvis drove at a speed I had never dared to drive. It was scary, yet exhilarating. I never doubted his ability to handle the car.

We flew past a parked police car. Luckily, for some reason the officer didn't pursue us. I wondered if he recognized Elvis's Ferrari. As fast as we were going, I doubt the police could have caught us anyway.

Arriving downtown, Elvis wheeled into the parking lot of a store called King Furs and came to a quick stop. Relieved, I opened the door and got out, releasing the others from their confinement in the backseat. As Sam started to get out, he made a comical suction noise, pretending to remove his fingers from the tight grip he'd had on the back of my seat. I laughed, but I was sure he'd experienced that kind of ride with Elvis before.

Inside the store, Elvis's attention went straight to a full-length white mink coat hanging on a rack in the back. He asked the salesperson to pull it out and wanted me to try it on.

While his cousins and bodyguard stood around, I stepped in front of a three-way mirror and slipped into this incredible coat. In the reflection I could see Elvis, now seated in a chair behind me, watching and looking quite pleased, with a great big smile. The salesperson handed me a white mink hat, and when I lifted my hair to tuck up under it, Elvis jumped up and walked toward me. Putting his hand on the back of my neck, in a childlike voice he said, "Now let me see that neck . . . now that's a chicken neck!"

He was clearly getting a kick out of teasing me and I had to laugh. Later he would tell me, "I'm self-conscious about my own neck. It's too thin. That's why my jumpsuits and shirts are designed with high collars."

Elvis purchased the white mink coat and hat without bothering to look at anything else. On the way out the door, he told me they were mine. Astonished, I thanked him. It was clear he hadn't gone out tonight to shop for anyone else but me.

He waved a hand. "I wish they'd had a full-length black one for me," he said. Had the salesperson heard him, I'm sure the clerk would have bent over backward to find one.

The five of us returned to the car, where Elvis peeled out of the parking lot with me holding on for dear life, smiling at my new nickname, Chicken Neck. It wasn't glamorous, but it was mine.

Back at Graceland, Elvis went into the dressing area of his bathroom and returned with the two coats he had purchased the previous night. He asked me to take off the coat I was wearing and, when I did, he put one of the coats around my shoulders, giving me a soft kiss on my neck.

"These are yours, too," he said.

I was dazed by the extravagance. What about his relatives? Was this his plan all along? I had never given any thought to owning a fur coat, and now I had several. No question about it: Elvis liked to do things big. He couldn't just give me one coat; he had to give me three!

"Thank you, Elvis, they're really beautiful," I said, simply, for what more could I say? This had been another one of his plans and he was beaming.

Caught up in the moment and obviously proud of what he had done, Elvis suddenly wanted me to call my family and invite them over to see what he'd given me.

It was after midnight when I called home but I knew that my family would be okay with late-night calls coming from Graceland. It was all part of this new adventure we were having with Elvis as our guide. I spoke with my mother and told her that Elvis had something he'd like to show the family. I knew they'd be curious but only my mother and Rosemary were able to come over. Elvis asked me to lay all three coats out on his bed and so I carefully arranged them on his bedspread. When Rosemary and my mom arrived, he invited them upstairs. Of course they exclaimed over how beautiful the furs were. My mother was wowed because this was her very first look inside Graceland. Elvis graciously took her on a brief tour while Rosemary and I waited in his bedroom.

When they returned, we followed Elvis into his office, where he sang and played the organ for all of us. Not long afterward, a man walked into the room. I'd never seen him before. Elvis said hello and the two of them disappeared into the dressing area of his bathroom. I wondered if he was talking business. For Elvis, the world was awake when everyone else was asleep, so I knew that was possible.

Given the late hour, my mother and Rosemary told me they didn't want to overstay their welcome. They prepared to leave. Elvis reappeared before long, however, and my mother thanked him for inviting them over and said they should be going.

We had all started walking downstairs when Elvis stopped midway on the staircase and said, "Oh, I almost forgot something." He opened his hand.

In his palm glittered two diamond rings. "You won't find these in a Cracker Jack box," he teased, handing my mother and Rosemary each a ring.

They stared at Elvis, speechless for a moment. Then my mother shook her head. "Elvis, I'm sorry, but we can't—" she began, but Elvis cut her off.

"Mrs. Alden, I really want you and Rosemary to have these," he insisted.

I had already learned that there was no force that could match Elvis when he was intent on being generous. My mother and sister finally realized that and graciously thanked him.

I was touched by his gesture and wondered if the stranger who had arrived had brought the rings. I saw my mother and sister to the front door, then took Elvis's hand as we headed upstairs, thinking I'd never met another man so joyful and enthusiastic about sharing the bounty of his life with everyone around him.

I eventually went home to get some sleep, but when I woke that afternoon, Elvis called and told me he wanted to get his dad a new car. Apparently his generous mood had lasted through the night. "Would you come with me to look for one?"

"Of course," I said.

I drove back to Graceland, and together we went to a local dealership. It didn't take long for Elvis to decide on a four-door truck for his father.

His kindness didn't stop there. Elvis also bought a new car for one of the dealership's employees before we left. As always, the combination of being able to surprise people and give them magnificent gifts never failed to put a smile on Elvis's face. He wanted to make people happy and wow them while doing it.

Lisa flew to Memphis to spend the holidays at Graceland, where she divided her time between Elvis and playing with the children of Sandy Miller, Tish Henley, and Billy Smith. I was still a new person in her father's life and she was a little quiet around me at first, but I felt confident we'd get to know each other better over time. Due to Elvis's nearly reversed sleep patterns, he allowed Lisa to stay up quite late, but he was a great dad. He especially loved tucking her into bed, often saying to me, "Let's go say good night to Lisa."

On Christmas Eve, I was watching television with Elvis in his bedroom and left to use the restroom. The TV was off when I came back and Elvis seemed absorbed in reading a book.

As I was walking around the foot of his bed, I noticed sparkling lights dancing all along the walls and ceiling. I looked toward the headboard and saw a beautiful diamond necklace with matching watch and bracelet propped upon my pillow. The bedside light had been turned its way and was aimed down to shine on the jewelry.

I caught my breath. I had received so many incredible gifts already and wasn't expecting anything for Christmas. Elvis pretended to read for a few more seconds. Then he glanced up from his book and joked, "I wish it had been designed for a man, because I would have bought it for myself."

Taking the jewelry from my pillow, I leaned over to hug him. Once again, I wanted to tell him this was too much. However, now that we were closer, I understood Elvis would be hurt, or even a little angry, if someone turned down a gift from him—especially if the gift was something he'd put a lot of thought and effort into choosing and how he would present it.

Still, I tried. "This really isn't necessary, Elvis," I protested. "You've already given me the coats, and I feel bad because I don't have your gift with me." I'd been prepared to give it to him on Christmas Day.

Before he could respond, Lisa came in. She sat on the bed in front of us and Elvis turned the TV back on. Lisa began watching it with us. Elvis lovingly observed her for a moment and then tapped me on the shoulder, motioning for me to watch Lisa as she periodically glanced about the room and back at the television, oblivious to the two of us.

"We have the same look in our eyes," Elvis said softly.

I settled against the pillows, thinking it was touching that he saw himself in his daughter.

The house was quiet early on Christmas morning. Lisa was still asleep, and because Elvis was going to bed, I told him I would go see my family, exchange gifts with them, and bring his present back with me later in the day. I also had a small silver bracelet to give Lisa.

I visited with my family at home, then returned to Graceland. I expected to see Elvis as I usually did, relaxed and dressed in pajamas, with his hair a bit mussed. When I returned this time, however, he was sitting in his bedroom dressed in nice clothes and with his hair styled.

I sat beside him on the bed. "Merry Christmas," I said, and handed him his gift. As he unwrapped the necklace, I held my breath.

Elvis took the cross out of the box, looked at me, and smiled. "I love it," he said and all my fears disappeared. He then asked me to fasten it around his neck.

Vernon and Sandy came over later that evening, and we met with them in the dressing area of Elvis's bathroom. I sat on the bed, surrounded by Elvis's clothing, while Elvis took a couple of nearby chairs and placed them across from me for his dad and Sandy. As the four of us were visiting, Lisa joined us and I was able to give her my small gift, too.

If any kind of traditional gift-giving ritual happened around the tree at Graceland, it must have happened before I got there, because Elvis seemed totally content to stay up in his bedroom and spend this part of Christmas day with me. We watched television, talked, and visited with Lisa.

After tucking Lisa into bed that night, Elvis and I went back into the bedroom and I thanked him again for my beautiful gifts.

"I like women in furs," Elvis said, and told me he'd once bought a child-size mink coat for Lisa, but his ex-wife, Priscilla, didn't want her to wear it and returned it, thinking it was too extravagant for their daughter.

Elvis's family didn't have much money when he was growing up, and I felt that was part of the reason he wanted to spoil Lisa and many of the other people he loved with such extravagance. However, I could definitely understand his ex-wife's point. What child needed a mink coat? On the other hand, how many children had Elvis as a father?

Since Elvis seemed sensitive about the returned gift, I chose not to say anything. His impulse had been a generous one, and I didn't want to add to any hurt feelings.

CHAPTER 13

Elvis's next tour was scheduled to start December 27 in Wichita, Kansas, and would end on New Year's Eve in Pittsburgh, Pennsylvania. I was looking forward to it. Although I'd flown from San Francisco to Anaheim and into Las Vegas with Elvis, this would be my first time to really get the feel of being on the road with him.

While I was home packing, Larry Geller had flown in and given Elvis more religious books. Elvis gave some copies to me when I returned to Graceland, and I was happy to be included. I had begun to enjoy our ritual of reading together and talking about the various ideas that we found intriguing in these books. I was also glad to find Elvis rested and ready to go. Vernon, Sandy, and Lisa were coming, too, so I thought Elvis would be even more inspired to perform.

While others rushed around preparing for our departure, I remained upstairs with Elvis and Larry, looking over some of the new books. It was obvious from listening to the men talk that Elvis and Larry had been studying spiritual material for quite a while. Because of their extensive shared knowledge about religion and philosophy, I wasn't able to contribute much to the conversation; however, I definitely found the dialogue thought-provoking even though I knew it would take me time—maybe years—to make sense of the different philosophies that fascinated Elvis.

Later, I would see that Elvis wasn't simply on a spiritual quest, but striving to broaden his general knowledge as well. Many times on tour, he would ask someone to hold a dictionary and challenge him with words to spell or define.

During Elvis's concert in Wichita, he sat behind the piano and played a beautiful song titled "Unchained Melody." I'd never heard it before and loved it, feeling the song's lyrics about love and longing spoke to the deep, soulful connection between Elvis and me. Larry Geller told me later that it had been quite a while since he'd seen Elvis sit at the piano and perform the way he did that night.

Despite the pace and demands of having to travel from one city to the next, on this tour Elvis seemed free of the health problems that had plagued him in Las Vegas and he was in a great mood. His voice was in fine shape as well, and his overall improved state was reflected in the quality of his performances.

Other people noticed this as well. I happened to be standing beside Larry before one show and he leaned over and said, "I don't know what you're doing, but whatever it is, keep doing it."

Hearing this certainly was an ego boost, but whether Elvis felt better because of our relationship or not, it was wonderful to see him doing well. I was also extremely happy to see that, during his shows, Elvis continued to wear the necklace I'd given him.

Elvis seemed attuned to my presence even when he was busy performing. While he was onstage in Birmingham, Alabama, I was deeply touched when Elvis lowered his head toward the microphone and said, "I'm gonna do this song for you, sweetheart," then sang, "The First Time Ever I Saw Your Face."

Speaking to me directly in the middle of the song, he interjected, "Listen to me," and then, "You gotta listen to me." Elvis sang the song beautifully, and I was falling ever more deeply in love with him.

Not everything went smoothly on that tour, though. Elvis was still worried about his father's health, especially on the road, and periodically made comments to me about it. Unfortunately, my attention was fractured by personal concerns of my own, after checking in with my family and learning that my grandfather was now experiencing complications due to pneumonia.

We were in Atlanta, Georgia, on December 30. I tried to rest before Elvis's show that night, but I was having trouble sleeping and woke shortly after 2 P.M. I started thinking about my grandfather and tossed and turned while Elvis slept. Finally I decided to place a call to my parents, who were at his nursing home, to see how my grandfather was doing.

When my mother came on the line, I could tell she'd been crying. "Grandpa passed away about ten minutes ago," she said.

"I'm sorry, Mom," I managed around the lump in my throat as I heard the pain in her voice.

Had my urge to call her been a premonition or merely a coincidence? My mother told me she'd just been discussing when to have the funeral with our relatives. "We were thinking of having it on January third," she said.

A wave of sorrow washed over me when I hung up. It was really impossible for me to sleep now, but I didn't want to disturb Elvis, so I lay quietly beside him. When he woke up, I told him the sad news.

Very concerned, Elvis wanted to help in some way. He called my mother, gave her his condolences, and said, "I want your father to have the nicest casket possible." He even offered to pay his funeral expenses.

My mother thanked him, but said my grandfather had set aside money to pay for his own funeral. Everything had been prearranged. Their conversation ended with Elvis assuring her I would be at the funeral.

During Elvis's show that night, I couldn't shake my lingering sadness. I felt so sorry for my mom. I also felt terrible about not having been able to see my grandfather one more time to say good-bye.

Elvis was in tune with my emotions. While we were flying into Pittsburgh for his next concert, he encouraged me to talk about my grandfather by asking me questions. I shared a few family memories and, to my surprise, found myself laughing with Elvis. I was glad. I knew that Elvis had a show coming up and I didn't want my grief to affect his mood. I put on a brave front and was determined to keep a smile on my face.

We stayed at the Hilton in Pittsburgh. The next evening, I was getting ready for Elvis's show when he called me into his room. Two of his stage costumes were on his bed, one with multicolored blue stripes and the other with the image of a black eagle on its front and back.

"Which one do you think I should wear?" he asked.

I was flattered. He'd never wanted my opinion about his stage outfits before. Since it was New Year's Eve and not an ordinary night, I pointed to the jumpsuit with the eagle, the symbol of America.

Before we left, Elvis asked me to wear my full-length white mink coat and matching hat. I put them on, comforted not by the coat, but by the fact that Elvis had earlier lifted my spirits and was doing everything he could to show how much he cared about me.

The atmosphere in the Pittsburgh Civic Arena was supercharged when we arrived. People were ready to celebrate New Year's Eve with Elvis, and their excitement buoyed my spirits. Chairs had been placed on one side of the stage for Lisa, Vernon, Sandy, and me, but Lisa chose to sit in my lap during the concert. I wrapped my arms around her, happy to have her close.

Elvis's performance that night was energetic and nothing seemed to be hurting him. Soon after the concert started, he introduced his father, then Lisa. I helped Lisa stand so others could see her.

As he eventually took a seat at the piano, Elvis said, "I want to dedicate this song to my daddy, Lisa, and Ginger." He proceeded to play "Unchained Melody." As always, Elvis's voice and those haunting song lyrics touched my soul.

It was a fantastic show. The evening was made even better when we returned to the Hilton and Elvis received a phone call from President Jimmy Carter, who wanted Elvis to serve as a special adviser to the youth of America. By the proud look on his face and the excitement in his voice, I could see how honored and touched Elvis felt by President Carter's request, and I was thrilled for him.

Being on the road with Elvis was amazing, the experience made even more surreal because we were traveling from city to city and from hotel to hotel. Every morning, I'd have to remind myself where I was when I woke up.

On the way back to Memphis, Elvis told me he'd have a six-week break from performing. He was coming down from the excitement of the tour, his mood even lower because Lisa was going back to her mother in Los Angeles. Still, once we'd returned to Graceland, I couldn't stay long, either, since I had to attend my grandfather's funeral.

"Would you like me to go with you?" Elvis offered as I was leaving.

I was astonished. Elvis had just finished a tour and I knew he must be exhausted. "Aren't you tired?" I asked.

He shook his head. "I'd like to be there."

I felt very moved that Elvis would make time to support me. My plans had been to drive from Memphis to Arkansas with my siblings, but now I was stymied. If Elvis came, there wouldn't be enough room in the car. Maybe my brother should take his car, too. But then there were his bodyguards: I had yet to see Elvis go somewhere without one.

Once I was back at home, I phoned my parents, relaying the news that Elvis would be coming to the funeral with me. My parents informed us that the weather in Arkansas wasn't good, and on January 2, the city of Memphis was walloped with a terrible snow and ice storm.

I called Elvis. "I don't think we're going to make it to the funeral," I said, worried. "The weather's so bad." Elvis wouldn't let that faze him. "If I have to call the president," he said, "I'll see that you make it to your grandfather's funeral."

"Elvis, how is this going to work?" I asked.

He was silent for a minute, then said, "We're all going to fly in on the JetStar. I'm sending someone to escort you to Graceland."

It was close to midnight. I phoned my brother, telling him to bring his family over to my house. Before long, there was a knock at our door.

I opened it, expecting to see one of Elvis's employees, but instead recognized the man standing on our front porch as our local sheriff, Gene Barksdale. The bright flashing lights of five police cars illuminated the night sky behind him.

The sheriff introduced himself. "I'm here to take you and your family to Graceland," he said.

This was our escort? Sheriff Barksdale stepped inside, along with several deputies, each man removing his hat as he crossed our threshold. I couldn't help smiling, thinking that Elvis was probably chuckling to himself right about now, as he imagined the shocked expression on the faces of me and my siblings.

My family and I gathered a few belongings, entered the police cars, and slowly made our way to Graceland in a caravan. Elvis was waiting in the foyer with Charlie, Lamar, his stepbrothers, aides, bodyguards, and Joe. They were all prepared to go with us on the JetStar. Having just come from a tour, I knew these men couldn't be too happy about this new travel plan, especially given the weather.

Elvis told me that the runways at Memphis Aero were being deiced so we had to wait a little while. He invited the sheriff and his deputies inside for coffee. Right before the police left, Elvis presented Sheriff Barksdale with a gun from his personal collection.

I introduced Elvis to my brother's daughters, Amber and Allison. As he looked over the huge group of people he'd assembled, Elvis realized there wouldn't be enough room for everyone on the JetStar. He ended up chartering a Learjet out of Nashville to fly into Memphis for my brother, his family, and a few others.

Before long, I was in the air with Elvis on his plane, along with my sisters and a few more from the entourage. Our flight was turbulent enough that some of the guys periodically voiced a concern. As we were flying into Harrison, Arkansas, the JetStar approached the runway, but we didn't land because the conditions were too rough. Milo made a second attempt.

Most of us were uptight, save Elvis, who calmly told everyone not to worry. Deep down, I didn't really think anything bad would happen, either, because we were with him. During my time with Elvis, I had begun to believe he truly was special, and that God wasn't going to let anything happen to him.

Due to ice and snow, the JetStar skidded a bit when finally touching down, but we arrived safely. Milo came back from the cockpit and informed Elvis that he had told the pilot of my brother's plane to go ninety miles north into Springfield, Missouri, because of the weather. Milo felt their plane wouldn't have the braking power the JetStar did to land on this shorter runway.

My parents were waiting for us as we exited the plane. "Mrs. Alden, I'm very sorry about your father," Elvis said warmly when he greeted my mother. She thanked him and he then sent the JetStar to Springfield to pick up my brother, his family, and the others.

Rental cars were waiting for everyone. We followed my parents to a Ramada Inn, where they were staying with some other relatives. Elvis had reserved a few rooms for the rest of us. My siblings and I gathered with my parents in their room. I visited with them for a while and then joined Elvis in his room. Elvis had brought books and his jeweled robe with him; now he put on the robe and sat on the bed, where we read together, talked, and rested for a few hours.

The service, scheduled for 10 A.M., would take place in a small community called Mount Sherman twenty-five miles away. I knew this relatively early morning start time would throw Elvis off his usual schedule and hoped it wouldn't prove too difficult for him.

When Elvis ordered breakfast, I became increasingly concerned about our timing. It was almost time for us to get ready to leave for the service, and Elvis didn't seem to be in any hurry. Al Strada eventually brought our food. Elvis turned on the TV and the two of us began eating. Suddenly there was a knock on the door. Al opened it and my mother was standing outside.

"The state police have made an extra effort to make the road to the funeral more passable," she said. Then, noticing Elvis in his robe and our breakfast in front of us, she gently reminded us of the time, and said it was quite a drive to the service.

This was enough to nudge Elvis into fast gear. We finished eating and, as various members of his entourage began checking in with him, I left so he could get ready.

It was cold outside. I put on my long white mink coat, then joined my family, waiting for Elvis. Before long, he stepped out of his room with a few books in hand, wearing a dark, high-collared coat and blue scarf around his neck.

My parents had driven their Lincoln Continental to Harrison. Now they offered it to Elvis, telling him they would take one of the rental cars. "That's fine," Elvis said.

Charlie, David, and Ricky took the backseat of the Lincoln while Elvis and I sat up front. With Joe behind the wheel, we pulled out of the parking lot and headed toward the Mt. Sherman Assembly of God Church.

The weather conditions were still treacherous. The ride was slow along the two-lane, ice- and snow-covered road and grew worse as we entered Newton County, where the area became hilly and the road more winding.

We finally reached the small town of Jasper, turned onto another narrow road, and began our ascent up the snow-covered mountain toward the church. The road looked so slippery that I couldn't help voicing my concerns about being able to make it up to the church.

"If I can land my jet on that icy runway, I can also land on top of that mountain," Elvis assured me.

Five slick, nail-biting miles later, we finally pulled into the small graveled parking lot of the country church. My grandfather had donated the land for this church, helped build it, and preached in it, too. Organ music was softly playing when we walked inside. Although we were fifteen minutes late, the minister had waited for us before starting the service.

It was a small church with only six pews on each side. We quietly took seats in the back. The Reverend Maddox stepped forward and began singing "How Great Thou Art." There was a hint of nervousness in his voice until suddenly, Elvis began singing along, and then Charlie joined in. I was initially surprised that Elvis would sing, but he did it softly, not trying to take over the service, and the reverend's voice grew in power as Elvis subtly nodded his head at him.

The Reverend Martin Villines and the Reverend Guy Jones, both friends of my grandfather, handled the rest of the service, with the

Reverend Villines giving the eulogy. Near the end, Elvis leaned my way and, with his eyes fixed on my grandfather's casket, said under his breath, "Son, you're on your own."

It was a line I remembered from the film *Blazing Saddles*. I wondered if he was trying to make me laugh. At times, Elvis dealt with tension by injecting humor, and in a strange way, hearing him say this did lighten my mood for a moment.

When the service ended, we stepped outside the church. Everyone was very courteous and polite. One of my cousins began speaking with Elvis as cars began to line up behind the hearse. Elvis continued talking with her, which prompted my mother to mention that it was time for us to go.

Before returning to our car, Elvis quickly mentioned to my mother, "Mrs. Alden, you know this church reminds me of the church I went to when I was a little boy."

We then drove the two miles to the cemetery for a short graveside service.

After it was over, Elvis once again was kind and gracious with everyone, taking time to speak with a few relatives and telling one of my cousins that the weather reminded him of his days in the service in Germany.

We returned to the Ramada Inn, where we gathered our belongings and Elvis changed back into his jeweled robe. My parents were going to drive the Continental back to Memphis, but Elvis asked my mother if she'd like to fly back with me and my sisters. My mother accepted the invitation when my father said he didn't mind driving because it was only a six-hour trip home and someone had to bring the car back. My brother decided to accompany him. Once we were back in Memphis, the JetStar would return for my sister-in-law, nieces, and the others.

Elvis had my mother ride with us on the way to the airport and took a seat across from her when we boarded the plane. During the flight, the two of them began conversing about various things. I heard him tell her at one point that his favorite cousin, Bobbie Jane, had died around the same time as my grandfather.

I was startled by this revelation. Had Elvis chosen to go to my grandfather's funeral instead of his own cousin's? He'd never said a thing about it to me! My mother, siblings, and I told him how sorry we were. Elvis also mentioned that he'd like to take a vacation to his home in Palm Springs, California, and invited my mother, sisters, and me. I was thrilled. It would be wonderful to see him in a relaxed atmosphere after his hectic schedule.

Unfortunately, my mother had to work and Terry couldn't come. But Rosemary was between jobs. "I'd love to go," she said, and I was glad she and Elvis would have a chance to get to know each other better.

I thanked Elvis once we were alone again at Graceland. His tremendous act of kindness in attending my grandfather's funeral, especially given all of the effort it had entailed, would forever hold a special place in my heart.

CHAPTER 14

True to his word, Elvis immediately planned our getaway to Palm Springs for January 4. This left little time for Rosemary and me to pack.

Somehow we managed to get together our clothes and return to Graceland for the trip. I had imagined we'd be flying to Palm Springs on the JetStar, perhaps with an aide or two and a bodyguard along for the ride. However, when we arrived at the airport with Elvis, I saw the *Lisa Marie* ready to go.

Charlie; Lamar; Joe; David, and his wife, Angie; Ricky; Al; and a few others were waiting for us on the plane. I couldn't believe Elvis traveled with this many people on vacation! Then again, I reminded myself, Elvis always did things his own unique way, and grand gestures seemed to be the norm with him. He also seemed determined to surround himself with people, bringing a little bit of home with him on the road.

It was Rosemary's first time on the *Lisa Marie* and Elvis gave her the grand tour. This would also be her first trip to California. Rosemary was more audacious and outspoken than Terry or I. She didn't seem the least bit intimidated by either new experience. I also quickly learned that, if anyone could match wits with Elvis and Charlie, it was Rosemary.

When Charlie appeared with drink and cigarette in hand, firing off jokes, Rosemary kept up with him joke for joke. I loved having her with us and watching her cut up with them. Rosemary really knew how to make Elvis laugh, and it made me happy to see him so relaxed and comfortable with my big sister.

We landed at the Palm Springs airport near dawn. The glitz of Las Vegas was nowhere in sight, only the serene desert with spectacular mountains in the distance. We exited the plane and the group divided, most going on to a hotel while Elvis, one of his aides, Charlie, Rosemary, and I rode to Elvis's home on Chino Canyon Drive.

I loved the house. It was a low, sprawling, Spanish-style white stucco home with a roof tiled in a warm terra-cotta color. The property was surrounded by a black iron fence.

"Not much yard," Rosemary said as she noted the lack of grass.

Elvis laughed. "That's why I had some of the rocks painted green."

Excited to show us the house, Elvis led us down a hallway to the right. We passed a front bedroom and stopped outside a smaller room with a couch and bar inside. Elvis turned to Rosemary. "Which room do you want?"

Rosemary glanced at Charlie. Then, looking pointedly at the room with the bar and sofa, she said, "Charlie, this one's yours."

We entered the master bedroom at the end of the hall. Like the one on the *Lisa Marie*, this one was decorated in blue, apparently one of Elvis's favorite colors. Elvis then led us back toward the entryway and into a living room with a fireplace and large windows.

Continuing through the room, Elvis took us outside to a free-form pool surrounded by a patio. Viewing the calm landscape with its backdrop of mountains, Elvis put his arm around me. As we stood there together for a few moments, quietly absorbing the serenity around us, I was deeply content.

Back inside, Elvis led us to a den with couches, pinball machines, and a television. When Rosemary and I both complimented the bright, multicolored carpeting, Elvis laughed and said, "The carpet was a gift from the Mafia."

Was he joking? Like everyone, I'd heard stories that the Mafia controlled a lot of what went on in Las Vegas, but I didn't really know anything about that. Still, it made sense to me that Elvis might have at least met some members of the Mafia because everyone from fans to fellow entertainers sought out Elvis's company, if only to be seen with him. It certainly wasn't out of the realm of possibilities that someone in the Mafia had given Elvis the carpet as a gift to impress him. On the other hand, I'd never overheard any conversations or seen Elvis involved in any activity that would lead me to believe he was actively involved in the Mafia in any way, and I never would.

Elvis had brought his books to Palm Springs. I'd brought mine, too, and I'd adopted his habit of making notes in the margins and underlining text that I found interesting or wanted to understand better. I still never felt my beliefs as a Christian were being tested, only that Elvis was trying to introduce me to different ways of thinking and exploring different ways of looking at the universe.

Eager to have Rosemary share what we were reading and discovering, Elvis invited her to join us in the bedroom and gave her a few books as well. The three of us read for a little while, but Rosemary wasn't used to Elvis's sleep patterns and returned to her room before too long to rest.

Even on vacation, Elvis needed some help going to sleep. A little while after Rosemary left us, an aide brought in what I assumed was a sleep packet. I decided it had to have been prefilled back in Memphis, since no doctor or nurse was staying with us here in the Palm Springs house.

That afternoon, Elvis and I were awake but still sitting in bed when there was a knock on our door. It was Rosemary. She came in, saying, "Elvis, your lock just got taken!"

Rosemary told us that she'd been awakened by female voices outside, shouting, "Elvis!" She'd looked out her window and had seen women gathered by the driveway gate, removing what looked like a large, unlocked padlock from it.

I couldn't believe Elvis's fans already knew he was here—or that they'd be that daring. It wasn't clear to me if any bodyguards had arrived at the house yet, but Elvis didn't seem worried.

He thanked Rosemary and shrugged off the incident as if he'd encountered similar acts many times before. I actually thought it was kind of funny at the time and didn't feel Elvis's safety was really at any risk.

From watching Elvis perform onstage, I had seen firsthand how much his fans wanted a piece of him—a scarf, a ring, and so on. With Elvis's singular celebrity, which he had been experiencing for over twenty years, I knew that he was used to this kind of behavior from people. He understood it was just a way for his fans to try getting closer to him because they loved him that much. Most of the time, he seemed to accept their attention as a compliment rather than any real threat to his safety.

Just as they had at Graceland, the members of Elvis's entourage congregated in Palm Springs. Elvis's stepbrothers and Al alternated between staying at the Palm Springs house with us and in a hotel, catering to Elvis's needs. I rarely saw the bodyguards and was unsure where they were staying, but when they were at the house I suspected they gathered in the den.

I knew what Charlie and Joe did for Elvis, but I couldn't figure out Lamar's role. The few times I'd been around him, he was plainspoken and direct, and Elvis usually bounced jokes off of him. Finally I asked Elvis, "What does Lamar do for you?"

"I don't know," he said. "Remind me to ask him later."

Sure enough, when Lamar came to say hello the next time, Elvis looked at me with a grin, then back at Lamar. "Lamar, remind me to ask you something."

Looking perplexed, Lamar said, "Okay."

I smiled at Elvis, feeling I had the answer to my question. It seemed Elvis liked Lamar for entertainment purposes and was just generous in including Lamar whenever he went places.

I wouldn't get to know these men much better during our time here as they continued to mainly speak with Elvis when stopping by our room to greet him. However, during that time I did get to know some of the comical nicknames Elvis gave a few of his employees and friends. He sometimes called Charlie Hodge Slew Foot. Lamar Fike was Lard Ass because of his weight. In private, Elvis told me he called his aide, Al The Atheist and that his bodyguard Dick "had the personality of a rhinoceros." Despite his generosity and habit of joking around with these men, the black humor of these nicknames made me wonder if he was completely happy with some of them.

For instance, one evening, Rosemary rushed into the bedroom to announce that she'd been sitting in the living room when David's wife, Angie, came running in, looking terrified, with David in close pursuit. David had been carrying what Rosemary recognized as a dog training stick.

"Lamar was in the room, too," Rosemary said, "and Angie was trying to hide behind him." Apparently David and Lamar had exchanged strong words.

Rosemary was also worried because there were some guns lying out in the open close by on a table. She was afraid someone might really get hurt.

"I want David in here now," Elvis said, and yelled for David to come into the room. Clearly angry, Elvis asked us to step outside while he talked to David. I went to Rosemary's room with her. A little while later, Elvis called us back in, looking embarrassed and shaking his head. He said he couldn't understand Ricky, Billy, or David sometimes because "they're on different wavelengths."

Occasionally, I would see that the guys weren't all that pleased with Elvis either. Even though Elvis, Rosemary, and I were relaxing, it was still work as usual for them and a little resentment would show itself from time to time. When Elvis was hungry, for instance, he would usually ask me to tell one of the aides what he wanted. One time when Al was on duty, I saw him seated in another room and gave him Elvis's order. Al rolled his eyes, stood up, and walked into the kitchen without saying a word to me.

Al's reaction surprised me. Was it because it was me asking him to do something or because he was mad at Elvis for some reason? Or was he just tired of his job? I remembered the time Al had come to my house and told my family that he wasn't overly happy with his job at Graceland and worked mostly to support his mother.

Rosemary had a similar experience once, when she walked into the kitchen and heard Al and Ricky lightly bickering over which one had to reheat Elvis's food. Neither one wanted to do it. Elvis often wanted his meals reheated, typically after getting caught up in conversations and letting his food get cold. It didn't seem to be a difficult job, but I guess for some of them, it was trying their patience.

Just as he did at Graceland, Elvis chose to relax by staying inside and reading or watching television rather than going anywhere, hanging out by the pool, or socializing. It would have been nice to leave the house, even just to take a ride around and tour the area, but I understood that Elvis had to be tired after his tour and then going straight on to my grandfather's funeral. Besides, for Elvis, going out in public was never an easy task; as the padlock incident had proved to me yet again, everyone wanted to get close to Elvis.

The only exception to this was our trip to see Colonel Tom Parker, Elvis's manager, who had a home nearby in Palm Springs. One afternoon, Elvis told me that the colonel's wife, Marie, was very ill and he wanted to visit her. We arrived at the colonel's home and as I followed Elvis to the front door, I noticed a number of statues of elephants in all different sizes.

"Why do you have so many elephants?" I asked when the colonel stepped outside to greet us.

"An elephant never forgets," he said. Then, smiling, he added, "I want Elvis to buy me a ring with an elephant on it."

I couldn't tell whether he was joking or not, but decided he must be. The colonel and Elvis began to chat. As we walked around the side of his home, he showed me his backyard. Carousel horses sitting atop poles rose from the shrubbery surrounding a pool. We followed the colonel inside, where Elvis told me he would be right back. He and the colonel left me while they visited with Marie in another room. I wondered how long Marie had been ill, and thought how nice it was of Elvis to see her. They returned a short time later, and Elvis said goodbye without lingering to socialize. I didn't know the details of their long history at that time; from our visit, I couldn't tell if he and Colonel Parker were close. So far, their relationship seemed to be mostly centered around business.

I accepted his choice not to socialize much with Colonel Parker and some of the others along with us, and didn't push Elvis to do otherwise, figuring when he felt ready, he would do so. It was just nice being with him in a different environment and it was great having Rosemary with us as well.

As I became closer to Elvis, getting to know him way beyond the image of the superstar, there still were constant little reminders of who he was. On January 6, Rosemary and I were in Elvis's room with him when he got a phone call from Colonel Parker. After listening for a few minutes, Elvis hung up, looking stricken.

"Frank Sinatra's mother just careened off a mountaintop," he said.

Dolly Sinatra, eighty-two years old, was one of four people killed when their Learjet took off from Palm Springs and crashed into the San Gorgonio Mountains. She was heading to Las Vegas to see her son's opening show at Caesar's Palace.

Elvis was using dark humor in the face of tragedy, but I could tell the accident upset him. When he mentioned wanting to offer one of his planes to Frank Sinatra, it struck me that, among entertainers at this level, there must be a certain camaraderie. Elvis felt comfortable offering help to Frank Sinatra in the same way I would offer to help if something happened to one of my friends or neighbors.

Elvis spent a lot of time flying in his own planes, both large and small, and his father had flown in on one to see his Las Vegas shows. Private planes carrying celebrities had gone down several times over the past twenty years; although I never thought anything would happen to Elvis, I found myself wondering if this was something that ever worried him. I thought back to my grandfather's funeral, and felt thankful once again that we'd made it safely.

While his plane travel didn't cause me great worry, I was concerned about his health.

When it came to mealtimes, Elvis and I enjoyed eating similar things such as hamburgers, steak, and omelets but I continued to notice certain foods were being brought to Elvis in larger than normal portions. Sometimes Elvis was seduced by the temptations of these larger portions and sometimes he wasn't. I hoped to move us toward a healthier diet, but I just didn't know how because he was used to getting what he wanted.

Elvis *did* like yogurt though and sometimes asked for some, which I encouraged. I wasn't a nutrition expert, but thought yogurt would be good for him. I hoped to find other foods like this that I thought would be more beneficial for him to eat as well.

One afternoon, I entered Elvis's bedroom and found him talking on the phone. As I crossed the room, he looked up at me and said into the receiver, "Tell her how to take care of me," then held the phone out to me. "It's Priscilla."

I took the receiver, confused, as Elvis sat by watching. "Hello," I said.

A female voice instructed, "See that he eats right and gets plenty of rest."

"Okay," I said, quickly handing the phone back to Elvis and wondering if that was as awkward for Priscilla as it had been for me. But I did think it would be nice to have allies when it came to helping Elvis with his diet, even if one just might be his ex-wife.

Elvis continued his conversation and I went into the bathroom to give him some privacy. I wondered how often he spoke to Priscilla. I'd been unaware of what their relationship was like, but now I reminded myself that Elvis and Priscilla were raising Lisa together; it was only natural that they'd talk once in a while.

Having left the door slightly ajar, I heard Elvis say, "Really, Priscilla. Ginger is one of the prettiest girls I've seen in a long time."

I suddenly felt ten feet tall, hearing him compliment me, but then I had to ask myself why he was telling Priscilla this. Did he want the women in his life, past and present, to be jealous of one another?

Shortly, I heard Elvis hang up the phone. I returned to sit on the bed with him. To my surprise, he opened up a little about his relationship with Priscilla without me even prompting him.

"I'll always love Priscilla because she's the mother of my child," he said, "but I let her go. What hurt me was that her boyfriend, Mike Stone, said that I couldn't see Lisa."

I saw the wounded look on his face and could only imagine how that had felt, knowing how much he loved his daughter. I took his hand. It meant a lot that Elvis would share this intimate detail of his life with me and I was glad that he was talking about his emotions so openly. I hoped he'd always feel this comfortable sharing himself with me.

Throughout our entire stay in Palm Springs, the flow of people in and out of the house continued nonstop. Typically the visitors would include Lamar, Joe, Elvis's stepbrothers, various girlfriends and wives, bodyguards, and a few unfamiliar women.

But, no matter who was at the house, Elvis seemed more interested in the new books his hairdresser had given him than he was in socializing with any of his employees or guests. He wanted to spend his time reading with me in the bedroom and asked only Rosemary to join us.

Elvis had the charisma and persuasive ability to draw you into his activities, and Rosemary was soon getting excited about the books, too, saying she liked the mystery of the spiritual philosophies we were studying. I wondered how often, or even if, any of the others among Elvis's family and friends ever read with him. I had yet to hear anyone other than Larry mention the books or get drawn into discussions about the philosophical and religious ideas that interested Elvis.

One of his favorite books was *Autobiography of a Yogi* by Paramahansa Yogananda, the story of Yogananda's lifelong exploration of the mysteries of the saints and yogis. Elvis seemed fascinated by Yogananda; he was also reading *Only Love*, by Sri Daya Mata, which dealt with Yogananda's teachings, and *The Road Ahead*, by Swami Kriyananda, a book that illuminated Yogananda's world prophecies.

Elvis also admired David Anrias's book *Through the Eyes of the Masters*, which expounded on the belief that a person could incarnate in another person's body. Over time, Elvis would tell me he thought Koot Hoomi, one of the masters from the book, was incarnate in himself, and pointed out a photo with the master dressed in a high-collared jacket similar to his own favorite style at the time.

Elvis felt there was some force inside him, guiding him to teach and bring joy to others in various ways, especially through music. He was reading these books not only to understand his own life but to help others as well. Having witnessed some mystical things with Elvis already—and there would be more of those events ahead—I was beginning to wonder if the kinds of miracles we were reading about were possible. I wasn't ruling anything out.

Elvis's endless fascination with Eastern philosophers led him to believe that we in the West could only benefit from studying their teachings. "India has the spiritual, and we have the natural resources," he explained. "They have to meet at some point."

When I looked over Elvis's books with him, he often asked if I understood what we were reading. Sensing his deep need for me to be in synch with him, I usually told him I did. I wanted to and always tried my best, hoping in time that I would achieve as deep an understanding of these subjects as Elvis did.

Elvis took special care to explain his intellectual and spiritual interests to me. He had studied chakras and at one point he showed us a book on them. I learned that the word *chakra* came from the Sanskrit language and meant "wheel center." A chakra channeled life force, feelings, memories, and thoughts.

The *kundalini*, or "life force," was like a spiritual energy residing in a resting body, Elvis said, a sleeping serpent in the root chakra located at the base of the spine. To demonstrate this, Elvis placed his hand at the bottom of my spine, forcefully applying pressure while explaining that, if this spiritual energy was aroused and released, its power was enormous and could bring one to an enlightened state.

Shaking his head from side to side as if saying, "Man, oh man, if I could only do this," he told me it took a lot of time and training to learn how to release that energy.

Elvis also eagerly taught me about acupressure, which he explained could help relieve tension. Taking hold of my foot, he pressed his fingers on different pressure points, showing me how each had an effect on the rest of the body. Elvis had strong hands and it hurt a few times, but overall, I found it really relaxing. More and more, I was finding his beliefs persuasive. Elvis was awakening my own curiosity as he introduced me to these different concepts.

During one of our reading sessions, Rosemary began to feel nauseous, which led Elvis to try a healing on her. He asked Charlie to join us and the four of us went into her room.

Rosemary lay down on her bed. Charlie held her hand and Elvis hovered his own palm close above her abdomen. Staring intensely at his hand, Elvis said to Rosemary, "Think of the color green for healing."

He waited for a couple of moments, then quickly lifted his hand high in the air, shaking it, seemingly trying to cast away her ailment.

Watching him brought me back to my own experience in Las Vegas. I realized I was almost holding my breath, willing Elvis's healing to work on my sister. I wanted her to feel better and truly wanted to believe in this alternative healing technique. I also wanted things to go well because it was so important to Elvis.

In any case, it worked! After a few moments, Rosemary said, "I feel better now," and got up.

Elvis began talking about the power of concentration then and asked Rosemary and me to follow him out to the backyard. The sun was coming up as we walked past the pool and over to a nearby shrub.

Placing one of his hands near the leaves, Elvis watched them and waited for some subtle movement. I didn't see anything happen.

After a short time, Elvis turned his attention toward the sky. Raising his arms and turning his palms upward, he began focusing on some clouds overhead. A few moments passed, then the clouds parted a little. Elvis looked back at Rosemary and me with a subtle smile.

"That's wild!" Rosemary said.

Welcome to Elvis's world, I thought. I was starting to feel that maybe Elvis was right. Maybe we all really did possess abilities we're not cognizant of; maybe if we trained and learned to focus, we could more fully tap into the power of our minds. Who was I to say no to that?

The way Elvis viewed life and his place in it led me to believe that he thought he had developed a keener awareness of his own spirituality and of the unseen layers of living than most people. I don't think Elvis thought of himself as God-like. However, from his insatiable curiosity and intense studies of different religious practices and philosophies, it was clear he felt he had achieved a higher consciousness, one that gave him unique insights and an enlightened view of the powers we all might possess if we were willing to follow his path. Even today, many years later, I still think the opportunity is open to all of us, but it would take much time and study, which is not usually available to the average individual who faces a normal workday and raising a family.

Elvis's mind was always churning. He was either orchestrating events or trying to understand them. I remember one afternoon, Elvis was dressed, as he usually was, in his pajamas, and began pacing back and forth in front of me, circling his bedroom. "What do you notice about my walk?" he asked.

I watched him carefully for a few seconds, trying to find something out of the ordinary. I didn't see a thing. "One leg is shorter than the other?" I joked.

Again, Elvis was being surprisingly serious. He pointed out that his walk was very catlike, and let me know his animal title in karate was Mr. Tiger.

"I fight the way a tiger does, light on my feet," he explained.

I had seen for myself how Elvis had interwoven karate into his shows. Now it occurred to me that Elvis literally prowled from one side of the stage to the other so his audiences could see him. I wondered if his iconic pacing might have somehow been developed while learning karate.

The deliberate way Elvis was demonstrating his stride at that moment made me think that even this simple act of walking was something he was acutely aware of. With Elvis, every detail mattered.

He also loved to talk about the people he knew or events in the news, especially when something mysterious had happened.

While we were in Palm Springs, at one point Elvis became animated when talking to Rosemary about Claudine Longet, the ex-wife of singer Andy Williams. Claudine had gone to jail briefly earlier that same year for the shooting death of her boyfriend, a skier known as Spider Sabich. Claudine claimed it was an accident, but Elvis thought there was more to it. He didn't stop at pure speculation, either: Elvis actually phoned a friend, a private investigator named John O'Grady, and had Rosemary listen on a separate phone line while they discussed different theories concerning the case.

Elvis also loved to postulate about possible foul play in the death of Bruce Lee, the martial arts expert. Given Elvis's passion for karate, I wasn't surprised that he was fascinated by Lee's death—and by some supposedly special techniques one could employ while fighting. For instance, Elvis told me about the possibility of generating an invisible wall of resistance out of projected energy, a protective shield with a special characteristic: It could soak up the energy of an attacking foe and repel it back on itself.

Only a few people knew how to execute this, Elvis said excitedly, and called Charlie into the bedroom for a demonstration. Elvis stood up and put his hands out in front of him, focusing intensely as if controlling some kind of energy. Then, after taking a few deep breaths, he asked Charlie to run at him.

Charlie backed up and came charging full force at Elvis, only to fall smack back down onto the floor, as if he had run into an invisible wall. I started to laugh, thinking they must have done this to entertain me, but both men seemed deadly serious. I quickly stifled my laughter and was left feeling bewildered. Had Elvis really learned some special mind trick in karate that allowed him to create an invisible force field?

I had my doubts about this particular demonstration that day, but seeing how serious Elvis was about it, I began to think that certain inexplicable things might actually be possible. *Welcome to Elvis's world*, I thought again. One simply had to be there to understand.

CHAPTER 15

Elvis kept the curtains closed in his Palm Springs bedroom, helping to blur any difference between night and day. My days were no longer dictated by the rise and fall of the sun, but by when Elvis went to sleep and woke up. Elvis, Rosemary, and I had been so completely immersed in various books and our discussions that each day had melded into the next. The calendar was completely forgotten.

It wasn't until we woke one afternoon and an aide wished Elvis a happy birthday that I realized it was January 8. Elvis was forty-two that day, and I felt terrible that Rosemary and I hadn't been able to buy him anything.

We eventually got dressed and went into the living room, where members of his entourage and a couple of unfamiliar women were waiting to greet him with birthday wishes. Elvis chose to spend the evening visiting with everyone, occasionally reading to them passages from some of his spiritual books.

Later that night, Elvis announced that he was going to have Robinson

Department Store reopen for all the ladies. He wanted to send us on a little shopping spree. It felt odd to be leaving Elvis on his birthday, but I thought maybe Elvis just wanted to be alone with the men.

Elvis provided spending money for each of us, giving Rosemary and me a little extra. We headed out accompanied by a bodyguard.

Once inside Robinson's, I found a purse I liked, then set off to find a gift for Elvis. I browsed the aisles, but Elvis wasn't the kind of man you buy a tie or a pair of cuff links for off an ordinary store shelf or rack. Nothing caught my eye, so I decided I would use the rest of the money to get Elvis a gift back in Memphis. I didn't know what that would be yet, but I hoped to find something different. We eventually returned to the house, where the rest of his birthday was low-key and spent doing one of the things Elvis loved most: reading to me, Rosemary, and a few others.

The next afternoon, Elvis, Rosemary, and I started watching *The Gong Show* on television. It was an amateur talent contest and the three of us were having fun, laughing at some of the show's contestants and their often-absurd talent, when Joe Esposito came into Elvis's bedroom, walked over to Elvis, and whispered something in his ear.

"That's okay. You can say it in front of Ginger and Rosemary," Elvis said. Looking slightly uncomfortable, Joe repeated, "Linda called and was wondering if you're going to pay the rent on her apartment in Los Angeles."

I was completely taken aback. Elvis had been paying Linda's rent? Why? And for how long? Elvis was watching me closely, as he did sometimes, studying my face for a reaction, but I tried not to let my surprise and concern show.

Elvis looked at Joe and shook his head no.

Looking back at me he said, "It's not fair to you." Joe walked away.

"Well, Elvis, it wouldn't be right," I said, remembering that Elvis had asked me to commit myself 100 percent to him, and feeling like he should do the same for me.

Elvis kept his eyes on my face. "I bought Linda a house not long ago to put some distance between us," he said.

Had Linda lived at Graceland full-time until then? I wondered, but I didn't ask. I was too busy trying to absorb this new twist.

Elvis then looked at Rosemary. "How can I get her to stop calling?" he asked.

Rosemary shrugged. "Change your number, maybe?"

He grinned, but I was unable to smile. I continued to ponder all of this and what it meant for Elvis and me.

When Elvis had told me in Las Vegas that he and Linda were just friends, I had believed him. After all, he'd been publicly dating other women, and that seemed to say his relationship with Linda must be over. However, I was sure the articles of clothing and toiletries inside Graceland had been Linda's. Plus, she had called before, asking to spend Christmas with him. It seemed that Linda was trying to hang on, no matter what Elvis did.

Now I took comfort in the fact that, even though Elvis had been helping Linda out by paying her rent, he'd just said in front of Rosemary and Joe that he wouldn't do it anymore, and he certainly wasn't trying to hide the fact that Linda had called. I chose to trust that Elvis was being honest with me about the relationship being completely over for him.

Unfortunately, I would still feel uncomfortable every time I saw Sam, Elvis's bodyguard and Linda's brother. Sam and I were friendly with one another, but I couldn't help wondering how he truly felt toward Elvis—and toward me.

Elvis spent a great deal of time trying to understand numbers, customs, signs, theories, and how the universe's patterns were interrelated. He even liked to dissect names. Sometimes he'd put his glasses on upside down and say our names backward, calling himself "Sivle" and me "Regnig." And, when I told Elvis my middle name was "Lita," he seemed pleased to note that *Ginger Lita Alden* and *Gladys Love Smith*—his mother's name—contained the exact same number of letters in them.

It was illuminating to talk about philosophy and numerology with Elvis, but it could be tiring. One morning, after having been up all night with Elvis, Rosemary and I simply couldn't focus anymore. We began to miss words, skip sentences, yawn, and joke around.

I thought Elvis had to be tired, too, but instead of appearing to need sleep as much as we did, he told us that we had just given up and didn't want to continue reading with him.

"Elvis, I can't keep my eyes open," I said, feeling bad but wanting to be completely honest. "We're just tired."

It wasn't easy to reason with Elvis when he had his mind set on something. Now, determined to continue his studies, Elvis said, "I'll get someone else who *will* read with me, then."

He called for Charlie to come to his bedroom while Rosemary went off to her own room. Charlie entered, looking as exhausted as I felt, and sat on the foot of our bed. Elvis began reading to him.

Unable to keep my eyes open even a second longer, I lay back against the pillows and dozed off.

I woke as Charlie got up to leave. When Elvis finally went to sleep, I hoped he understood I was trying my best to be there for him.

Elvis could be just as compulsive about eating certain foods as he was about studying his books. Early the next morning, I noticed that, between visits from some of the guys, Elvis must have eaten at least eight containers of yogurt over a short period of time. We finally went to sleep, but Elvis woke up shortly and decided he wanted more yogurt. He asked me to get it or have someone bring it to him.

His request concerned me. I had yet to see Elvis do any exercise at all during the weeks we'd spent together, except when he was onstage. Now, after spending so many hours with him nonstop in Palm Springs, I was concerned about him overeating. I was just trying to look out for his health.

"I don't think you need any more yogurt," I said.

Elvis went back to sleep without pressing the issue. So did I, thinking all was well.

A short time later, a deafening bang echoed throughout the room. I bolted upright and saw Elvis standing at the foot of the bed, holding a 57 Magnum pistol in his hand. I risked a glance behind me and saw a bullet hole in the wall above the headboard. My heart was going a mile a minute. I looked back at Elvis, trying to wrap my mind around the idea that he really had just shot a hole in the wall.

By way of explanation, Elvis said he had asked for yogurt again and I hadn't responded. "It was an attention getter," he said.

Bewildered, I told him I was asleep and didn't hear him.

Meanwhile, around us the house was silent. Nobody else appeared to have heard the gun go off. Or, if they did, they weren't coming to see who'd been shooting what.

Extremely hurt, I began to cry and ran into Rosemary's room, almost bumping into her as I shut the door. She'd been coming out to see if I was all right, her eyes wide with fear. She looked as scared as I felt. "What happened?" Rosemary asked. "I was just on my way to your room."

I was having trouble catching my breath. My pulse was still roaring in my ears as I told her about the gun and the inexplicable reason Elvis had given me for firing it.

Rosemary's reaction was immediate. "My God! We're leaving right now," she said.

I couldn't move and I was still having trouble breathing. My mind flooded with questions. Why had Elvis shot a gun in our bedroom?

Had his sleep medication momentarily caused him to lose touch with reality?

I couldn't come up with any rational explanation for Elvis's behavior. Rosemary decided to go see where Elvis was and stepped into the hallway.

After a few seconds, she returned and closed the door. "I looked out the window and saw Elvis standing alone by the pool," she reported.

I didn't know quite what to do or how to feel as Rosemary and I sat in her room, unsure of what might happen next. Now that I felt a little calmer, deep down, I didn't really think we were in any danger.

Before long, there was a knock at the door. When Rosemary opened it, Elvis was standing in the doorway, dressed in his robe and wearing his glasses, a deep look of remorse on his face.

I was seated in a chair beside the dresser. Elvis stepped inside and sat down in the chair on the opposite side of the dresser. The three of us were silent for a few moments.

Then Elvis stood up, took one of my hands and one of Rosemary's, and led us to the bed. The three of us sat down.

Continuing to hold our hands, Elvis bowed his head and closed his eyes. "God, don't let us lose it," he prayed aloud. "God bless my family and Ginger's family, and please don't let us break up."

Obviously, he was concerned about the lasting effect this incident could have on us. I could offer him little comfort, though. I was still in shock and extremely hurt by what he had done. I had completely shut down emotionally. I was numb.

Fortunately, Rosemary seemed to understand what I was feeling and took over. "Elvis, you can't do this kind of thing," she said.

Grasping for common ground, trying to play peacemaker between us, she started talking to Elvis about some of my likes, such as motorcycles and horses. "You should do some of those things together," she ventured.

Elvis listened silently, still holding our hands. Was he absorbing this?

Finally, I dared to speak. "I was only trying to help you," I said quietly, almost under my breath.

Elvis looked down at the floor, took off his glasses, and held them between his fingers. Silence hung over the three of us for a few moments. Taking my hand again, he said, "I'm sorry, Ginger."

I sensed, on a deep level, that Elvis honestly was sorry. It felt like our relationship had been put to some bizarre kind of test, and all for the sake of more yogurt! I was acutely aware that my feelings for Elvis were like none I'd ever felt before. I'd been completely consumed by him, and now I had reached a point in my life where I couldn't picture my future without him. I loved Elvis.

Did I think he would intentionally harm me? No. Did I think Elvis was used to getting what he wanted? Yes.

Some ironic little voice inside my head observed that one good outcome of this whole scenario was that Elvis didn't get to have any more yogurt. I forgave Elvis that day, but I suspected more challenges lay ahead.

I went to sleep, still grappling to understand this very complex man and hoping that he might now understand me a little better, too.

Late the following night, Elvis decided with his usual combination of impulsive action and determination that we both needed to have our teeth checked. He flew in Max Shapiro, a dentist from Los Angeles, to make a house call.

Dr. Shapiro was in his sixties and brought his fiancée, Susan, a woman in her twenties, to Palm Springs with him. When they arrived, I thought, "Wow, this woman is a lot younger than the dentist," then caught myself.

Probably a lot of people seeing me with Elvis thought the same thing about us, I realized, but it just seemed different with us. Maybe this had to do with how Elvis looked and acted. He could be like a big kid sometimes. The only times I was actually aware of our age difference was when we were reading together and he was teaching me something.

Elvis sat in a chair in his bedroom and Dr. Shapiro examined his teeth. When Dr. Shapiro finished looking at Elvis, I took a seat. The dentist said he could lightly file a few of my lower teeth if I wanted, just to even them out a little. I was fine with that and tilted my head back in the chair.

As Dr. Shapiro worked on my teeth, he mentioned that he'd been thinking about getting married, but he and Susan didn't know where the right place would be.

"Do you have a marriage certificate?" Elvis asked.

"Yes, we always carry it with us," Dr. Shapiro said.

"Why don't you get married here?" Elvis suggested.

Dr. Shapiro stopped working on my teeth and I sat up. The dentist was obviously caught off guard, but he loved the idea and so did Susan.

Elvis was euphoric. He immediately began making plans, telling us that Larry Geller could legally perform marriage ceremonies. He called Larry and asked him to come to Palm Springs, then quickly had an aide summon a jeweler to the house so Dr. Shapiro and Susan could choose their wedding rings.

When the jeweler arrived, he displayed various pieces of jewelry in front of Elvis on the bed. Dr. Shapiro and Susan chose some rings. Like a kid in a candy store, Elvis began pulling the price tags from a few rings, picking out rings for me, Rosemary, himself, and a couple of other people, with seemingly no regard for the cost.

This whole time, Elvis and I were still in our sleepwear. When Larry arrived, Elvis didn't bother to change, so I didn't either. Dressed in our pajamas and robes, Elvis and I went into Charlie's room for the ceremony.

Rosemary, Charlie, and David joined us there. With Elvis acting as best man and me as maid of honor, the wedding got under way with Larry officiating. Elvis was beaming as Dr. Shapiro and Susan began reciting vows they had previously written for one another.

During the ceremony, I noticed some movement from David. As he stood beside Rosemary, he turned and looked at her suddenly with a big grin on his face, trying to hold in laughter. I could see that the marriage ceremony was affecting David slightly differently from the rest of us.

Unable to contain himself any longer, David got down on all fours and began slowly crawling out of the room. Lucky for David, Elvis was so happy and excited about being able to make this wedding happen that he didn't notice. I would have hated to have anything spoil the moment for Elvis.

Dr. Shapiro and Susan thanked everyone when the ceremony was over. This was such a kindhearted thing for Elvis to do and it was wonderful to be a witness. I was also impressed and amazed he'd been able to pull everything together so quickly and easily.

Surprisingly, the groom wanted to finish working on my teeth a little more afterward, so I returned to the bedroom with Dr. Shapiro and resumed my position in the chair.

After he and Susan left, Elvis asked Larry and Rosemary to come into the bedroom.

Clearly still energized by the wedding, Elvis discussed the ceremony. He loved the idea of saying verses to one another. He picked up *The Prophet*, and read again from its passages on marriage.

At one point, he stopped reading to look over at me. "Ginger, if you and I were to get married, would you consider having Larry marry us?" he asked.

I was blown away. Wow, I thought, he's bringing up marriage again! This was the first time he'd mentioned it since Las Vegas. I knew he and Larry were friends and Larry looked happy about the idea. "Sure," I said. I was excited.

Elated, Elvis continued going over his spiritual books. The four of us talked well into the early morning hours. That night, all of the excitement about the wedding and our feelings about marriage continued to swirl around us. Elvis had once again reconfirmed wanting to marry me. Hearing him talk like this made me feel the two of us drawing ever closer to creating a future together.

CHAPTER 16

After spending a little over a week in Palm Springs, Elvis decided it was time to return to Memphis. We all packed up and headed for the airport.

As we entered the *Lisa Marie*, the pilot was having a problem with the engine and the interior lights weren't working. Rosemary and I followed Elvis toward the back of the darkened plane, where the three of us sat down at the conference table.

The lights suddenly came on and Elvis looked at Rosemary, shocked. He had mistakenly taken hold of her hand in the dark. Quickly letting go of it, he said, "Good God, Ginger, where are you?" He grabbed my hand and the three of us laughed.

Elvis, Rosemary, and I moved into the bedroom, and after a little while, the plane took off safely. Once in the air, Elvis said to me, "You need your own room and a private phone line."

Surprised, I realized I must have mentioned to him at some point that I shared a room with Terry. I was amazed that he remembered this.

Elvis wasn't done pondering my living situation, apparently, because then he said, "I don't like it that you have to drive so far to see me. I'd like you to have a home closer to Graceland."

I stared at him in disbelief, touched that he wanted me to live closer to him, but stunned by what I thought he might be proposing. Was Elvis really thinking what I *thought* he was thinking? Elvis knew that I lived with my family, so I didn't think he was suggesting that I leave them to buy a home closer to Graceland for me to live in alone. This must mean that he was talking about a new home for my entire family!

This idea was so over the top that I found it difficult to digest. My parents had just purchased our home. It was modest, certainly compared to Graceland, but we didn't really need a new house, and I didn't think of the one we had as being too far away from Graceland. However, I was extremely flattered that he was thinking about how to make my life more comfortable.

Luckily, Elvis quickly moved on to another topic, so I didn't have time to protest or give him any sort of answer immediately. He did that sometimes, I noticed, enthusiastically flitting from one idea to the next as he bared his thoughts to me. Sometimes it almost seemed like he just wanted me to share what was going through his mind, minute by minute, as a way of letting me know him.

I saw signs that Elvis had a growing concern about my safety. This was part of his protective nature with me. He knew I usually drove around alone so upon our return to Memphis he gave me a Smith & Wesson .22/.32 Kit Gun. He told me to keep it in my car when traveling back and forth to Graceland. This "gift" didn't surprise me as I had learned that Elvis loved to collect guns, and he owned a great many of them. He enjoyed showing them to me on occasion. Among the guns he brought out were a Derringer with a mother-of-pearl handle, various Magnums, an ivory-handled revolver, and even a machine gun. I thought the guns were really amazing, and especially liked the small pearl-handled Derringer.

I readily agreed to keep the gun in my car. My father kept a revolver and a rifle in our home for protection, but I had never been taught how to use a gun. I wasn't afraid to have one, though, and it did make me feel more secure. What Elvis was appreciating, and I was not yet aware of, was that my world had changed. I was now in his world where you needed bodyguards, as people could come at you in unexpected ways.

A perfect example of Elvis's protective instinct would happen months later when I noticed a strange car parked in front of our house with a man inside. He sat there for a long time and I wondered if it was a reporter or photographer. Elvis happened to call at the time and I innocently mentioned that a reporter might be outside my home. "I'm coming over and I will smash his Goddamn lens out," Elvis fumed. Before I could say another word, the phone went silent and I became worried about a possible confrontation. Luckily the car left, but not long before Elvis's Ferrari came flying around the corner of our street. All was okay that day, and Elvis simply ended up visiting and taking my sister Terry for an exhilarating ride in his Ferrari.

Now that I was home, I was able to go shopping for Elvis's birthday present. Elvis had once told me he used to own a monkey named Scatter, so I bought something fun to remind him of that favorite pet: a statue of a monkey holding a candle. I also purchased a large mirror with the outline of Elvis's face etched on the front. In honor of his love for the way Peter Sellers, as Inspector Clouseau in the Pink Panther films, said the famous line from *Casablanca*, I wrote, "Here's looking at you, kid," on a card and taped it to the front of the mirror.

Elvis was tickled by the gifts. He placed the monkey on a shelf in his bedroom and propped the mirror against the wall. They would remain in those places throughout the rest of his life.

Elvis continued to keep to his custom of mainly living upstairs at Graceland, but I was glad to see that he seemed mostly free of stress. We continued enjoying our evenings reading and watching television together. We happened to see an episode of *Saturday Night Live* in which the comic Andy Kaufman appeared as a guest and did his impression of Elvis.

Peering over the top of his reading glasses, Elvis addressed Andy on the television screen. "You better get it right, son," he said.

We laughed and had fun rooting for him. In the end, Elvis thought Andy did an "all right job," and told me, "You know impression is the highest form of flattery."

If I wasn't at Graceland, Elvis and I usually spoke on the phone twice a day, usually right before falling asleep and again upon waking. I had grown more comfortable with calling him, but most of the time I still waited for his call, not wanting to wake him.

Shyly, I also began to say "I love you" to Elvis on the phone. My family and I loved one another, of course, but we rarely expressed that verbally, so this was a big step for me. However, if I didn't tell Elvis I loved him first, he usually asked me if I did.

During my visits to Graceland, I was finally becoming a little better acquainted with Elvis's extended family and friends. Some of their roles still confused me though. I didn't sense that his cousin Billy Smith was on the payroll or had a particular line of work. He just seemed to be on hand to do things for and with Elvis whenever Elvis wanted him to. Billy was the son of Travis, the guard at Graceland who my father once had been friendly with many years back. Travis had since passed away.

On one of Billy's visits upstairs, he told me that before Elvis had met me, he and Elvis had been out riding motorcycles once, and after returning home, Elvis laid across his bed and said, "There must be someone out there for me."

This made me feel good, thinking that maybe I was this person Elvis had been waiting for. I had certainly come to feel we were meant to be together.

On occasion, Billy's wife, Jo, came to Graceland with him. She had dark eyes, pale skin, and pitch-black hair. She was usually dressed in black and Elvis teased her by calling Jo his "assassin." Sometimes the two of them would kid around and cut sharp glances at one another, as if each knew what the other one was thinking. As Billy's wife, Jo had been a part of Elvis's life for a long time. She and I were always friendly with one another but we didn't have any time alone together to become good friends.

George Klein visited every once in a while, and he was always nice. On occasion, Vernon made appearances. He maintained an office in a building behind Graceland, along with Patsy Gambill. If he and Elvis needed to go over business or some private matter, sometimes they'd ask me to leave the room, then summon me back afterward. I respected their privacy and never minded this.

During one of these visits, Elvis asked his dad, "Doesn't Ginger look a little like Mama when she was young?"

Mr. Presley thought a moment. "Yes," he replied. I smiled back shyly, regarding this again as a compliment. Elvis smiled right back at me, as if satisfied that what he had told me on the plane was confirmed by his father.

We continued to meditate together alone in the bedroom, and sometimes while Elvis read, I would rest my head against his chest, feeling safe, and gently stroke the side of his face with my hand. I loved those peaceful moments. Every once in a while before stepping into his bathroom, Elvis would announce, "I'm going to meditate and clear my mind." He had also said this in Las Vegas a few times before disappearing into the bathroom and closing the door.

It seemed that Elvis occasionally needed a retreat, to just be on his own. For him, this sanctuary seemed to be his bathroom suite.

One day, we were casually sitting together in Elvis's room and chatting when, out of the blue, Elvis asked, "Would you like to move in?"

This was completely unexpected and I was more than flattered. I knew this was an offer that many women around the world would jump at, but as much as I had come to love Elvis and think of him as part of my life—and my future—to just move into Graceland without being married first was something I didn't believe in or feel was appropriate to do at the time. Although this was 1977 and cohabitation was becoming more acceptable, I came from a pretty conservative background. My sisters and I had been brought up to believe that you lived with someone only after you were married. I may have been behind the times in that way, but even being on the road with Elvis was a daring thing to do for me, and I didn't take these actions casually.

Hoping he would understand, I looked him in the eye and nervously said, "Elvis, it just isn't my way."

Fortunately, Elvis seemed okay with that. He smiled and said, "Fine, I respect you for that."

Late on the afternoon of January 18, just a week or so after returning from Palm Springs, Rosemary and I decided to see a movie near Graceland. I briefly considered asking Elvis to join us, then dismissed the idea as impractical. From my parents' description of their movie-watching experience with Elvis back in the 1960s, I knew Elvis usually rented a whole theater if he wanted to see a film undisturbed, without drawing the attention of fans. Besides, I hadn't heard from him yet that day, so I figured he was still asleep.

As Rosemary and I were leaving for the movie, I asked my mother to tell Elvis where I was if he should call. We were getting out of our car at the theater when Steve Smith, one of Elvis's aides, intercepted us and said Elvis wanted us to skip the movie and go shopping for my family. This was something I didn't quite understand. For a moment, I wondered if Elvis had done this because he didn't want me to see a movie on my own. But why would Elvis feel that way?

I looked at Rosemary. I didn't want to abandon my plan with her. This really put me on the spot and I didn't know what to do. Elvis had made another of his grand gestures and I appreciated that he was thinking of my family. However, he really didn't need to buy them anything else. Now Steve was standing in front of me, expecting me to go with him. Do I tell him, "No, thanks, we're going to the movies?" I had a strong feeling that Elvis would be offended by that.

I turned to my sister. "Do you mind if we see the movie another time?" I asked.

Rosemary shrugged. "It's okay," she replied. The two of us then followed Steve to Goldsmith's Department Store.

Once inside, Steve told us that Elvis wanted us to buy mink coats for our family—and for ourselves. Me, too? Elvis had already given me beautiful coats! However, knowing Elvis as I did by now, I felt certain that if I didn't select something as he'd requested, he would only bring me back to the store.

I picked out coats for my mother, Terry, and my sister-in-law, then chose a simple black mink for myself. Rosemary found a less expensive fox fur coat she liked, but since it wasn't a mink, she asked Steve if it would be okay.

Steve called Elvis from a phone inside the store, then relayed to

Rosemary that Elvis had said "only minks." She put the fox coat back and selected a mink.

We followed Steve to Graceland and carried the coats upstairs, where Elvis was in his pajamas and seated on his bed. We laid the coats in front of him.

He looked over our purchases approvingly. As if Elvis hadn't already been generous enough, though, he said, "There isn't one for your father or brother."

I thought he was going to take us back to a store, but Elvis walked over to a closet by his bathroom and began browsing through it. Pulling out a sheepskin coat and a long, brown mink, he laid them among the others. Then he stepped into his loose blue jumpsuit, pulling it up over his pajamas, and secured his black studded belt around his waist. Finally he put on a pair of shiny black boots and tucked his Magnum 57 inside the belt.

"Let's go to your house," Elvis said.

I quickly phoned home to tell my parents we were on our way to see them. An aide gathered the coats and piled them into the Stutz. Elvis slid behind the wheel and Rosemary and I climbed inside the car. We left Graceland with bodyguards following in a separate car.

Driving down a two-lane country road near our home, Elvis told us he had noticed another car following ours for quite a while. With no streetlights, it was pitch-black out; I supposed he'd seen the headlights behind the bodyguards' car.

Elvis suddenly pulled over to the side of the road. I looked back nervously and saw the headlights from the bodyguards' car. Sure enough, another car was behind that one. Both cars pulled over behind ours.

Before the bodyguards could exit their car, Elvis jumped out of ours and began walking briskly toward the car in question. Worried for his safety, Rosemary and I turned around and tried to see what was happening through the back window of the Stutz.

In the headlights, I saw the figure of a man walking toward Elvis. The bodyguards stepped between them. When the stranger innocently showed them a pen and paper, Elvis politely gave the man his autograph and returned to our car.

As he eased into the driver's seat, Rosemary asked him, "Aren't you afraid to do that?"

Elvis pointed to the gun inside his belt. "Why do you think I carry this?"

At my home, Elvis surprised my family with their new coats. They stood in our den, quite stunned, and almost in unison, said, "Elvis, you shouldn't have done this!"

A look of complete contentment suddenly graced his face. "I wanted to," he said.

Pleased by their reactions, Elvis was in an upbeat mood, and later asked Terry to play something on the baby grand piano in our music room. She chose a classical piece, "Toccata," by Aram Khachaturian, which she had performed in the Miss America pageant.

We gathered around the piano and Elvis stood beside Terry, carefully watching her hands on the keyboard. I was glad Elvis was now getting to see the musical side of my family.

"Toccata" wasn't the easiest piano solo to play and Elvis applauded when Terry finished, telling her that he thought she was extremely talented. He then sat beside her on the piano bench and began playing and singing "Unchained Melody." To see Elvis having a good time at our home warmed my heart. His love of music and his enjoyment of family were all the more evident during moments like these. I longed to share many more days like this with him.

The next evening, Elvis called to see if Terry, Rosemary, and I would like to spend the night at Graceland. Terry was out with her boyfriend, but Rosemary said she'd love to come. Although I had driven to Graceland many times before, this time Elvis said he was worried about me driving after dark, so he sent someone to pick us up.

Since our time together in Palm Springs, Elvis and Rosemary had enjoyed kidding around with one another. I tended to be more reserved, but both of them had a wicked sense of humor.

That night, the three of us were sitting in Elvis's bedroom watching television when Elvis jokingly made an off-color remark.

Rosemary brightened. "Could you imagine if you acted like that in some of your movies?" she quipped.

Elvis laughed. Rosemary then suggested the opening sequence for a new film, one that would be nothing like most of his All-American, apple-pie musicals. "It opens on the gates of Graceland," she began, "with peaceful music playing in the background and birds chirping. Faintly, in the distance, you hear the roar of a car engine getting closer and closer, and suddenly your Ferrari comes smashing through the closed front gates. You get out with a cigar in your mouth and walk inside. The maids are all cowering. Going upstairs, you find Ginger chained to a wall saying, 'Elvis, don't hit me anymore!' "

Elvis thought the idea of him playing a bad guy on film was hysterical. The three of us joked around, putting different twists on the story, changing the ending of the movie each time to make it and Elvis's character more outlandish.

We just sat around talking and laughing, and when Elvis heard Rosemary wasn't dating anyone steadily he asked, "If you could go out with anyone, who would you like to go out with?"

"Well, I like Burt Reynolds," Rosemary said.

Elvis winked at her and said, "That can be arranged, you know."

My sister, a woman of many words, was suddenly speechless.

We continued clowning around for a while. Then Elvis put on a tape of *Monty Python and the Holy Grail*, and after we'd finished watching it, Elvis told Rosemary she could sleep on the bed in his dressing area.

When we woke that afternoon, Elvis decided to drive Rosemary and me home. We left Graceland with his aide Steve. As we pulled into our driveway, Elvis noticed some dust on my Cadillac.

"You shouldn't let it get dirty," he said. It was only a little dust but I didn't want Elvis to think that I wasn't appreciative of my gift or a person who wouldn't take care of it so after that, a couple of times when I thought the car looked slightly dusty, I washed it in our driveway before going to Graceland. At home, we visited with my parents in the den, where at Elvis's request my mother brought out her large family Bible again. Elvis pointed out a few new things he had discovered. He dissected the word *Genesis*, saying "Genes-is," and jotted down some notes. He also underlined verses and shared his thoughts with us on the meaning behind them.

When we started getting hungry, Elvis sent Steve to get some food for everyone from McDonald's while he continued talking with my family. After a little while, he wanted to play the piano, so we all moved into our music room.

Our kitchen table wasn't large enough to accommodate everyone, so when Steve returned, my mother brought some plates into the den. Elvis and I sat beside my parents on the sofa.

While we were eating, Elvis said he'd like us all to live closer to Graceland. This was the first time I'd heard him mention the idea since our flight from Palm Springs.

"I'm worried about Ginger driving back and forth to see me," Elvis said, "and I'd like her to have her own room and phone."

Still addressing my parents, Elvis added, "As you get older, you don't need the burden of a house note hanging over your heads. You should be able to retire, play golf, or do whatever you want. I'd like you to look for a house close to Graceland."

My parents clearly didn't know what to say to this offer, but they politely thanked him. Despite Elvis's enthusiasm for buying them a house, I think the idea didn't seem real to them. They had worked their whole lives to own a modest home. They hadn't been living in Elvis's world, where you could buy mink coats, new cars, or three rings on a whim.

In addition, the friction in my parents' marriage hadn't improved. This affected my siblings and me, naturally, since they'd been going through difficult times for quite a while. However, I kept this to myself, not wanting to violate my parents' privacy, and hoping that things between them might somehow improve.

It was getting late and Elvis said he would like to stay over at our home. The fact that he felt comfortable enough to want to do this meant a great deal to me, but I knew my family had to be panicking, thinking as I was, Where would he sleep?

There was a king-size bed in the room Terry and I shared, but my mother had been busy decorating the rest of the house and had yet to buy curtains for the bedroom window. She had pinned a large sheet to the wall in order to cover the window.

Luckily, Rosemary jumped in, offering Elvis her room. She asked if he'd like to see it. He stood up and Rosemary and I walked him down our hallway.

Rosemary's room was decorated in tune with the 1970s. She had affixed crackled mirror squares to one wall, and her bed's headboard and a dresser, both dark wood, had detailed sections covered in red velveteen. She'd chosen red for her curtains and bedspread, too, and a swag lamp in the corner glowed a soft red.

Looking at Rosemary, Elvis said, "Your room looks like a brothel," then said he was kidding. He didn't mind that, but Rosemary's bed looked too short—his feet would probably hang off, he said. Next, noticing her television in the corner, Elvis asked what kind it was.

Rosemary walked into the room and turned it on. "It's a good one."

It was a black-and-white television set. When Elvis saw that, he said, "You need a color one."

Despite our embarrassment about the sheet covering our bedroom window, Terry said she would stay with Rosemary and Elvis could sleep in our room. It was the only choice. My father soon went off to bed, but Rosemary, Terry, my mother, and I stayed up talking and reading with Elvis in the den.

Later, the doorbell rang. I looked out our front window and saw Al standing on our porch. To my surprise, he was holding a brand-new color television set. Now I put the pieces together: Steve had earlier made a call from our house, and Elvis must have arranged for this then.

Al carried the TV into Rosemary's room, took the old one and left. Rosemary thanked Elvis, expressing her utter disbelief. I smiled, knowing exactly what my sister was feeling.

As everyone grew tired, my mother brought out a blanket for Steve, who said he'd sleep in the recliner. My mother said good night to us, and when she left the room, I knew she felt as I did, that she could trust Elvis as a gentleman, and that I would never engage in anything inappropriate under my parents' roof.

Rosemary and Terry headed to Rosemary's room, and Elvis and I went into mine. I had been alone with Elvis many times before; still, it felt awkward sleeping with Elvis in my bedroom at home.

When we got up that afternoon, Elvis said he had a recording session in Nashville and wanted me to go. I dressed and gathered some clothes. Before leaving home, Elvis told my family it was the first time he had spent the night in someone else's home in a while.

"I feel like I have a family, because you're as nutty as I am, and I feel no jealousy here," he said.

I wondered if Elvis felt there was some jealousy at Graceland, either directed at him or between members of his family and staff. I would never fully know what he meant, nor would I ever ask. I was just glad that my house was a place where he felt comfortable.

We flew into Nashville and settled into our hotel. I stayed in my bedroom while Elvis went into the living room area of our suite and began lightly rehearsing with a few others. I heard someone strumming a guitar. Elvis began to sing, and then everything fell quiet suddenly.

Shortly after that, Elvis came walking into my bedroom, rubbing his throat. He told me it was beginning to feel sore.

I felt sorry for him, knowing how concerned he always was about losing his voice. I wasn't aware of anything that was going on behind the scenes. I didn't know what he was supposed to be recording, how important it was, or who was waiting on him, and Elvis hadn't told me. But that was okay: I knew the quality of his singing mattered to Elvis in every song. That's just who he was.

He talked with his staff. A doctor came to see him, and we spent the next couple of days reading and watching television together in his room, hoping his throat would feel better.

At various times, Elvis told me that he didn't want to record if his voice wasn't perfect. Finally, he said he was afraid to continue and ended up canceling the session. We flew back to Memphis. With three weeks off before touring again, I hoped he'd have time to recuperate fully before his next round of performances.

CHAPTER 17

Back at Graceland, Elvis stayed upstairs, as usual, and tried to be extra protective of his voice. Instead of reading to me as he often did, he let me take over and read to him over the next few days so he could rest. Others still came and went, visiting with Elvis upstairs as they usually did, but now Elvis made a point of speaking softly, taking extra measures to care for his throat. Before long, luckily, Elvis was feeling and sounding much like his usual self.

The rings Elvis had given me in Las Vegas were a tad large on my fingers, and Elvis had noticed that I'd been wearing tape wrapped around the bands to hold them on. One evening, he told me that he wanted to know my correct ring size and mentioned that he'd asked a local jeweler to come over and measure me. Before long, the jeweler walked into Elvis's bedroom and introduced himself as Lowell Hayes. Lowell measured my finger, he and Elvis shared a friendly visit, and before long, Lowell left.

A short time later, I went into the bathroom. When I returned to Elvis's bedroom, I discovered that he'd propped a magnificent necklace with the letters *TLC*, all in diamonds, on my pillow. Once again, he'd aimed the overhead reading light on it to make sure it sparkled. I was blown away. I had noticed these tender loving care necklaces worn by women in his family, female band members, and a girlfriend or two of certain entourage members. This one was unique though; it looked larger than the others and the only one I'd seen made with all diamonds.

I was deeply moved by this beautiful, singular expression of Elvis's affection. He fastened the necklace around my neck, telling me, "I had this made especially for you, Ginger."

Having this necklace meant that I'd been truly accepted as a part of Elvis's inner circle. Although I had felt this sentiment from him for a long time, I was happy now to have something that would signal this message to the people around us. Turning back to him, I told him how much I loved it and thanked him.

Elvis smiled and winked. "I don't give these out to just anyone," he said.

I continued to spend a lot of time at Graceland, but one afternoon, my niece Amber asked me to take her to a local hamburger restaurant, and I suddenly realized that I had been so focused on Elvis that I had neglected seeing my friends or hanging out with my family.

Wanting to spend some time with Amber, I happily picked her up and we went to the restaurant.

As we were finishing eating at a back table, I noticed a woman at a nearby table stand up and fold a newspaper she had been reading. I glanced at the front page of her paper when she walked by and was startled to see a picture of someone who looked remarkably like me!

I hurriedly paid our bill and raced out of the restaurant with Amber.

We headed straight to a nearby store. There, lined up on magazine racks beside every cashier stand, was the *National Enquirer* with a large black-and-white photo of Elvis and me, captured on tour, gracing its cover.

I was shocked. Me, on the cover of a national paper? Tabloid or not, I was awestruck and thought it was a nice picture of the two of us, too. I purchased a copy and rushed home to show it to my family, figuring they'd get a kick out of seeing me on the cover with Elvis.

Because I had devoted most of my free time to seeing Elvis, I'd barely gone out much on my own. Naively, I had thought that any pictures snapped of Elvis and me on tour or in a car, coming from and going to Graceland, were just being taken by Elvis's fans. Being in the media spotlight was something new to me, especially because we honestly hadn't been out that much in public yet.

I soon realized I was now of interest to the press. One day, I was at home and planning to take a drive with my family when I noticed a strange car parked on the street in front of our home with the engine running. A man was sitting inside it. Who was this? Was this a photographer or a reporter?

Just in case, my sisters and I donned sunglasses before walking to the car to make it more difficult for someone to tell who was who. Sure enough, the car followed us.

My dad randomly drove around for a while, but eventually had to stop and get gas. The car that had been following us pulled up at the gas station, too, and the driver got out. He approached our car and peered into the backseat.

"Which one is Ginger?" he asked.

Determined to protect my privacy, my sisters and I pointed at one another. The man walked away, not looking too happy. I was glad he couldn't hear my heart thudding against my rib cage. I knew we wouldn't be able to keep this up for long though as the word was definitely out: I was with Elvis.

On the night of January 26, I was watching television with Elvis in Lisa's bedroom. He left the room at one point and was gone for long enough that I looked to see where he was.

I found Elvis talking on the phone in his bedroom. I returned to Lisa's room and watched some more television, then heard a commotion as others came and went upstairs, speaking in private with Elvis.

It wasn't like him to avoid me. As more time passed, I started to feel odd and began worrying that something might be wrong. When Elvis finally returned to Lisa's room, he took my hand without saying a word and led me into his dressing area.

I was all the more puzzled as he guided me toward a black chair in front of his bathroom window, where Elvis asked me to sit down. As soon as I was seated, he knelt before me with one hand behind his back.

"Ginger, I've been searching for love so long," Elvis said, "and never in my wildest dreams did I ever think I would find it in my own backyard. I've been sixty percent happy and forty percent happy, but never a hundred percent. I've loved before but I've never been in love. Ginger, I'm asking you: Will you marry me?"

Elvis brought his hand out from around his back. In it was a small, green velvet box.

Nearly overcome by emotion, my voice quavered. I was glad I was sitting down because I wasn't sure my shaking legs could have supported me. "Yes," I managed, holding on to the beautiful words he'd just spoken.

Elvis placed the box in my hand, which was now trembling. Inside it was the most magnificent ring I had ever seen, with a huge center diamond surrounded by six smaller ones.

I kissed Elvis, feeling my eyes brim with tears. He delicately took the ring from the box and slipped it onto the ring finger of my left hand. It was a perfect fit.

Now I remembered the jeweler, Lowell, Elvis had called to the house to measure my finger. I realized he must have planned this then.

With a hint of nervousness in his voice, Elvis asked me to hold up my hand so he could see what the ring looked like. Commenting on how beautiful it was, he said, "God will come through me and tell me when the time is right for our wedding. Are you ready? Can you cope with my lifestyle?"

"Yes," I answered, still naive but ready to do whatever that entailed.

"There will be a lot of people jealous of you," Elvis went on, "but you should always be a lady, and if negative things are ever said, just bow out gracefully."

"I will," I said, clueless at that bright moment in our lives as to just how deep and biting those jealousies would become. I was also unaware of how close some of the people around Elvis were to the other women in his past, and how loyal they would remain to those women. I only knew that I loved Elvis and hoped his feelings for me were as deep as what I felt for him. I was willing to wait to marry until the time felt right to Elvis, and intended to leave it all up to him. But, for now, having a ring on my finger made me realize that he was as deeply committed to our relationship as I was. We were going to build a future together and I was never happier.

When we walked out of his bathroom, I was surprised to see Charlie and Billy Smith standing in Elvis's bedroom. I blushed, knowing they must have been in on the secret and were waiting for us to come out and tell them our news.

Beaming, Elvis said to me, "Show them the ring."

I was proud to, and in such a daze, my hand almost rose on its own.

Elvis took hold of it and shook his head. "Boy, oh boy," he said.

Charlie and Billy hugged and congratulated us. Then Charlie presented us with a small backgammon set and said, "This is a little engagement gift." This was so sweet of him, and I hugged him again.

Shortly afterward, Elvis's stepbrothers, Ricky and David, entered the room to give us their hugs and congratulations as well. *Everyone knew!* The overwhelmingly cheerful response was comforting, but I wondered if these men would ever really accept me as Mrs. Presley, or if they felt that Elvis getting married might bring some change in the dynamics of their relationships with Elvis.

Every few minutes, Elvis would tell me to hold up my hand so everyone could see the ring. I think I was still in a state of shock because each time he did this, I had trouble keeping my hand from trembling.

After everyone had finally left us alone, Elvis and I sat on the bed. He asked me to raise my hand several more times, so he could look at the ring again.

"It looks like a car headlight," Elvis said proudly at one point.

"I think it's beautiful," I countered, leaning over to kiss him. I was so overwhelmed, I couldn't take my eyes off the ring. At first I was dying to call my family and let them know, but then decided it would be fun to do it in person.

Elvis wanted others in the house to see the ring and know we were engaged. He called for Aunt Delta and the maids to come up. With each new arrival, he proudly again asked me to hold out my hand, even aiming the overhead reading light so the ring gleamed and sparkled, giving them a better look. Each one enthusiastically congratulated us.

It wasn't until after Elvis's death that I would learn the center diamond in my engagement ring was the diamond from his custom-made TCB ring, which Elvis always wore onstage. The jeweler, Lowell Hayes, had made it for him and years later he described on his website how this engagement ring came to be. Elvis had called him at one o'clock one morning telling him that he wanted Lowell to make an engagement ring for me with a diamond that looked like the one in the middle of Elvis's TCB ring. Lowell protested, saying he didn't have a diamond like that, but Elvis called him back half an hour later and said he had to have the ring that very night and pleaded with him to make it.

Lowell reported that he'd called diamond dealers in New York then, but they all reported that nobody could get a diamond of that size on such short notice, since the diamonds were kept in vaults overnight. Once Lowell had delivered the bad news to Elvis, though, he had pondered the problem some more, and realized they could use the diamond from Elvis's TCB ring and find another to replace it later. Elvis was thrilled with that idea.

Lowell had driven to Graceland to collect the ring and went back to the jewelry shop to remove the diamond and make a mounting for it. He centered the TCB diamond and added three diamonds on either side of it, then drove back to Graceland to present the ring to Elvis—all on the same night. When I heard this story, I was once again reminded that the rules in Elvis's world were a lot different from the rules governing everyone else.

It had been an extraordinarily unforgettable night. By the end of it, I had come to believe with certainty that all of the things Elvis had been saying to me about us being soul mates and us having a future together were absolutely true. I was committed to Elvis heart and soul.

The following afternoon, I woke eager to share my news with my family, but there were a few more people to announce it to at Graceland first. Elvis and I went downstairs to show the ring to his grandmother. Dodger was sitting in bed when we entered her room. When Elvis told her we were engaged, she took my hand in hers, smiled sweetly at Elvis, and said she was happy for us.

Elvis was still as excited as he'd been the night before; now he wanted to show his father the ring. I followed him out the back door. I hadn't seen that much of Vernon at Graceland. He usually spoke to Elvis by phone and I felt nervous about his reaction to our news. He was a nice man, but from the little I'd been around him, I knew Vernon could be blunt. I was slightly intimidated by him. What if he didn't like the idea of me being Elvis's second wife?

For whatever reasons—mostly due to the chilly weather, the fact that we'd been touring, and Elvis's preference for his bedroom—I had never actually been in the backyard of Graceland before, though I hadn't really thought about that until now. We walked through a pasture behind a racquetball court, and I saw some horses in the distance before entering Vernon's property through a gate in the fence surrounding his backyard. Elvis had built a two-story white house with black trim for his father on Dolan Drive, which ran along one side of the land surrounding Graceland.

After Elvis showed Vernon the ring, his father embraced us both and congratulated us. I immediately felt relieved. I didn't sense that Vernon was really surprised, though, which made me wonder if Elvis had spoken to him at some point about giving me a ring.

As he had earlier with me, Elvis told his father that God would tell him when the time was right to set the date. We visited for a bit. Before long, however, Elvis said to me, "Let's go see your parents." I was happy and couldn't wait to tell them the news!

I didn't even give my family any advance warning of our arrival. They were plainly surprised when they opened the door and saw Elvis and me standing together on the front porch.

I kept my hand behind my back until we were in the den, where Elvis turned to me and said, "Show them your hand."

I was still finding it difficult to hold my hand steady as I brought it from around my back. My parents looked at the ring, then back at us, speechless.

"We're engaged," Elvis said, effectively making what he had told my mother on the phone in Las Vegas an exciting reality. I was touched to see that he seemed a little anxious as he waited for their reaction and approval.

I wish I'd brought a camera to capture the completely stunned look on my parents' faces. My mother broke the silence finally, smiling and saying, "I'm so happy! And what a beautiful ring! I've never seen a diamond that large!"

My parents hugged the two of us. Serious, Elvis then said to them, "I'm going to take good care of Ginger, don't you worry."

Making direct eye contact with Elvis, my father smiled and said, "I'm sure you will." He shook his hand.

Then Rosemary and Terry came in, and when we'd announced our news to them, the elation and congratulations started up again!

Elvis and I stayed another hour or so, relaxing at my house and basking in my family's excitement. When we returned to Graceland later, I couldn't help but wonder what Vernon really thought, so I asked Elvis, "What was your father's reaction to our engagement?"

He replied, "My daddy only asked, 'Son, does she do little things for you?' And I told him yes."

It felt good hearing his answer, since I had tried to pamper Elvis in small ways, such as ordering food for him, rubbing his back, reading with him, and even placing cotton balls in his ears so he could sleep better.

According to Elvis, his father had then responded, "Good. What could a forty-year-old woman do for you, like what can a sixty-year-old do for me? Nothing."

I didn't agree with what Vernon said, but didn't comment. Of course I was glad that Vernon was comfortable with the age difference between Elvis and me, but hearing his words made me think that maybe Vernon brought Elvis up believing that's what a man needed, a younger woman to take care of him since Elvis was with me and

Vernon was with Sandy. I was glad to take care of Elvis—but equally glad that Elvis seemed keen on taking care of me, too.

A few nights after our engagement, Elvis returned to my family's home to visit and, while he was there, invited his jeweler to come over.

When Lowell arrived, he brought TCB and TLC necklaces with him. As he had done with me, Elvis slipped the symbolic necklaces over the heads of each of my family members. He wanted my family to know they were now part of his inner circle and family. And this was his way of making sure that others knew it as well.

Impulsive, extravagant gestures remained the norm for Elvis. On the spur of the moment, he invited my whole family to Las Vegas again. He called the sheriff, and the sheriff called the mayor of Memphis to see if the district chief would give my brother permission to take the following day off from the fire department.

The power of Elvis worked and the chief said yes.

We flew to Las Vegas, where we all stayed at the Hilton and Elvis gave each member of my family a hundred dollars for gambling in the casino. Elvis preferred to remain in his room with me again and I now felt that Elvis got bored sometimes and just a change in location relaxed him. It would have been nice to see one of the Las Vegas shows, but I understood that, if Elvis went out, it would be a big deal. I was confident that one day, if I asked him, we would see some shows together. I didn't mind staying inside with him that night, and I felt especially happy knowing my family was being treated to a wonderful time.

The two of us kept to our usual patterns and spent our time watching television and reading together in our hotel room. This time Elvis had brought *The Impersonal Life*, a book by Joseph Benner. It was a small book about self-discovery and looking within for true spiritual guidance. Elvis was seriously interested in the concepts and eager to share them with me.

One never knew what Elvis might say or do, and at one point during the night, Elvis asked me to sit with him, close my eyes, and practice saying, "Be still and know that I am God."

As we sat, chanting this phrase in an attempt to bring inner peace, Elvis suddenly got a cramp in his toe that didn't let up. So much for inner peace! He finally jumped up from the bed and, still holding on to his foot, began hopping around. He was laughing and cursing through the pain, which made me get tickled, too.

It took a little while for the cramp to go away, and it was pretty funny to watch how Elvis kept his sense of humor while in agony. As others were being entertained in showrooms across Las Vegas, I was getting a uniquely private performance as Elvis danced for me!

Later, we connected with my family and visited with them for a while. We were in Las Vegas for only one night and before I knew it, we were on our way back to Memphis.

Not long after we returned to Graceland, Elvis again brought up his wish to buy my family a new home. He also mentioned again that I should have my own room and phone line, so he could "easily get in touch with me." I was still uncomfortable about Elvis buying a house for my family.

I hadn't pursued the idea, nor had my family, but Elvis remained determined to follow through with this. He decided to take matters into his own hands one day and contacted his cousin GeeGee, asking him to set up an appointment with a Realtor to look at a home. Elvis also invited my parents to come to Graceland so they could go with us.

My mother showed up, accompanied by Rosemary and my niece Amber. My father was working a late shift. We rode along with Gee-Gee and Patsy to a two-story home in the Whitehaven area, a neighborhood closer to Graceland.

Two Realtors gave us a tour of the home. It was an older house and still occupied. As we walked around the first floor, Elvis said, "Well, don't look at it as it is, because there will be a lot of repairs that will need to be made on it. Picture it in a different light, with new carpeting and bathroom fixtures."

We went upstairs. When I saw that the house had five bedrooms, I realized the house must be much more expensive than the one we lived in now. Elvis peered at the backyard through one of the upstairs windows. "You need a pool," he said. "The backyard looks small, and there's no room for a pool."

Elvis had been holding my hand the whole time. When he let go, Amber quickly took my hand. Elvis shot her a look. "Amber, watch it," he said with a grin. "You're getting too close."

Before we left, Elvis told my mother, "Keep looking to see if you can find one in the neighborhood with four or five bedrooms. I'd like you to have one closer to Graceland, but you have to live in the house. It should be something that pleases you and has a room for each of you."

With the difficulty that my parents were having in their marriage, I knew the last thing they would be focused on was looking for a new house, but we could all tell Elvis was extremely serious about doing this. His benevolent spirit continued to astonish me.

CHAPTER 18

Learning how to be part of Elvis's life was like running next to a fast-moving train, grabbing a door handle, and jumping on board. That express train showed no signs of slowing down.

His new tour began in Florida on February 12. Elvis wanted me to see how he prepared for his shows, so at one point he asked me to join him in his bathroom on the *Lisa Marie*. There he mixed up a saline solution, tilted his head back, and poured the salt water down each nostril. This made him cough and helped clear his throat.

Another time aboard the *Lisa Marie*, Elvis asked me to come into his bathroom before that night's show. He leaned against the sink and handed me a black eye pencil. He wanted me to touch up a few gray whiskers on his sideburns and a couple of gray hairs in his eyebrows. I never thought of his gray hair as detracting from his sex appeal in any way, but Elvis obviously didn't like it.

I started to pencil in a small area. Our faces were close together; Elvis began staring at me and making subtle, comical facial expressions.

He wouldn't stop even when I begged him to, and I started laughing so hard, my hand shook in the middle of giving him his touch-up.

When I was finished, Elvis turned around to look in the mirror. "My God," he said in mock horror. "I look like Groucho Marx!"

Needless to say, he had to tone it down a bit. We laughed as he wiped some of the color off and then Elvis shared a tip he'd learned working in films, showing me how to apply mascara a certain way to make your lashes look longer. I never could have imagined that I could learn makeup tips from a man, but here I was, still learning something new from Elvis every day.

Because we were touring from one city to the next, Elvis and I usually didn't know what day it was. However, on Valentine's Day I got a pleasant surprise: Elvis gave me not one, but *four* different Valentine's cards!

I knew someone else must have picked out the cards, but it still touched me that he'd thought to do this. Inside the cards, Elvis had underlined certain verses and written some beautiful personal words.

A few nights later, I again looked over the cards Elvis had given me. Maybe because of the romantic things Elvis had said and done, I started thinking about my parents' marriage crumbling, reflecting on how their love had gone wrong and wondering why it hadn't lasted. Here I was with Elvis, both of us looking forward to marriage, while theirs was possibly coming to an end. The thought made me sad.

Elvis could tell something was bothering me. "What's wrong?" he asked.

I hadn't wanted to burden him with any discussion about my parents' marital problems before, but I felt that part of being in a loving relationship meant being honest with someone. I hoped he would open up to me if something was bothering him, so I decided not to hide it anymore. I broke down, telling Elvis that my parents just weren't compatible with one another.

Elvis was surprised. After I'd described what was going on at our house, he said, "Those are unpleasant conditions to be living under, and I don't want you living in that."

I appreciated his sympathetic ear and concern, but I wasn't asking Elvis to do anything about it. He had asked me what was on my mind, and I had honestly opened up to him, I explained, adding, "Elvis, this is a situation that I believe only my parents can solve."

I learned it was impossible for him to be a passive listener, as he seemed determined to want to help. "I'd like to speak with your mother about what's going on," he said. "I want to invite her and your sisters to see my last few shows."

On February 19, Elvis flew them first-class on American Airlines into Johnson City, Tennessee. During his show there, Elvis introduced me to his audience, along with my mother, Rosemary, and Terry.

The next show was in Charlotte. On the flight between Tennessee and North Carolina, Elvis took time to talk with my mom about her marriage. He listened patiently to everything she was willing to share.

I knew Elvis couldn't change how my parents felt about each other, but I deeply appreciated how much effort he was putting into trying to comfort her. He told my mother that he hoped things would work out, and asked her to keep looking for a house.

"It will be one less thing to worry about," Elvis promised her.

During the Charlotte show, he introduced me again. This time, going down the line with my family, he said, "and all the little Aldens," acknowledging Terry as Miss Tennessee. With a mischievous look, he then started walking toward Terry.

Terry began shaking her head and, under her breath, I heard her say, "No . . . No."

Elvis ignored this. Looking straight at her, he asked Terry to join him onstage. He had stopped his whole show to single her out.

Terry finally stepped up onto the stage beside him, blushing furiously.

"Play that weird piece you play," Elvis teased.

"No," Terry said.

But Elvis motioned for her to do it, and finally she took a seat behind the piano, where she quickly played part of "Toccata."

As Terry stood to leave, she turned to Elvis and jokingly said, "I'll get you for this," forgetting his microphone was in his hand. We later had a good laugh wondering if any others had heard her.

The performance in Charlotte was Elvis's last show of the tour. We flew back to Memphis afterward, where he could enjoy nearly a month off.

Once we were back in Memphis, Elvis continued to visit my parents' home, sometimes by motorcycle and not always under the cover of darkness. I never knew when Elvis might appear. If I was at home sleeping and heard the roar of a motorcycle, I always woke up wondering if it could be him.

I could tell he was getting real comfortable with my family, which made me feel great. Occasionally, Elvis would enter our house and, right off the bat, would ask, "Where's Rosemary?" Looking for her, he'd march down the hall and flip on her bedroom light.

One time my brother happened to be at the house when Elvis came to visit, and Elvis brought up the possibility of training Mike as a guard to work for him. My brother thanked him and said he would certainly consider it.

On another occasion, Elvis decided to approach my father about my parents' marriage. He sat with my dad in Rosemary's room and talked with him for a little while. Later, Elvis told me he didn't know if their conversation had helped fix anything, but it was a start. I was amazed by how caring and good-hearted he was with both of my parents.

Elvis really seemed to be taking them on as his own family now that we were engaged. I thought that boded well for our future as a couple, because family was so important to both of us.

I had never lost my love of motorcycles. I was thrilled, therefore, when we were at Graceland one night and Elvis finally asked me to ride with him. He called for Billy Smith and, when Billy entered the room, Elvis looked at him and said, "Saddle up the Harley hogs."

Billy left, and figuring that Elvis must own a few Harley-Davidson motorcycles, I asked him why he called them that. "Because they hog the road," he said.

As usual, he left his pajamas on, stepped into his blue jumpsuit, buckled his black stage belt around his waist, and tucked one of his guns inside it. Going into his dressing room, he returned with his black leather jacket and handed me another one, saying, "Here, I want you to have this."

It was a beautiful jacket in silver leather, with multicolored flames and a black eagle painted on its back. Elvis handed me a helmet and we walked downstairs.

Stopping by his grandmother's bedroom, we said a quick hello and continued out back. I thought it was sweet that Elvis usually checked on Dodger whenever he was going out.

The minute I put the helmet on, Elvis looked at me and began to laugh. "You look like a lollipop head," he said.

I was amused as well, knowing my head was on the small side and the helmet was huge on me.

Billy and a couple of the guys got on motorcycles and, straddling his own, Elvis said, "Come on, Chicken Neck. Get on."

I did, and we slowly took off down the driveway. My neck couldn't support the weight of the helmet and I kept banging my head into Elvis's. He started laughing, and pretty soon we were nearly hysterical because every time he slowed down, my helmet would go *clank* against his.

We rode up and down Elvis Presley Boulevard, where Elvis playfully yelled to a couple of passing cars, "Get off my street!" He was enjoying himself, and I was having a blast.

At one point, Elvis had to use a restroom, so we stopped at a gas station. Some fans had followed us; stepping off the motorcycle, Elvis signed a few autographs. He always took time with his fans.

Before long, we were back on the motorcycle and we rode around some more, circling through parking lots, then returned to Graceland. It had been a fun night, and I hoped there would be many more like it.

I was now actively envisioning a future with Elvis, and I delighted in imagining the life we would share, a life that I hoped would be enriched by pets and children. Soon I took one step closer to that future. I'd always loved Great Danes, and I'd been entertaining the idea of getting one. I was surprised when I mentioned this to Elvis one day and he told me he'd owned Great Danes in the past. I thought it was neat that we both liked the same breed.

Excited by the prospect of sharing and caring for a pet together, I told Elvis that, when the dog was a puppy, I could keep it at my parents' house, and after he and I were married, it would have room to run at Graceland. This got us talking about dogs, and I could tell Elvis had a soft spot for animals by the way he reminisced about some of the pets he'd owned over the years. My parents had allowed us to have a variety of pets and, as we traded stories, he suggested that we get one.

I later found a listing in our local paper for some puppies. One day, unbeknownst to Elvis, I drove to a home in Sayreville, Tennessee, and purchased a black male Great Dane with a small white star on his chest. In honor of Elvis's opening theme to his concerts, I decided to name him Odyssey.

I couldn't wait to show him to Elvis! I brought the puppy to Graceland. Gawky, with large paws and long legs, Odyssey was big at just a couple of months old. The puppy didn't have any experience with stairs, so, hoping no one would see me, I stood over him, took one paw at a time, and slowly helped Odyssey walk up the front stairs.

Elvis and Billy were chatting in Lisa's room when I arrived. I entered the doorway, lugging my new puppy with me, and said, "This is Odyssey."

Surprised, they started laughing. Billy began joking around, calling the dog Oddball.

I was a little sensitive about it, which Elvis noticed. He gave Billy an annoyed look and said he thought Odyssey was cute. Billy left the room then and Elvis apologized. He said he'd looked in the paper, too, where he'd seen the same ad and was going to call.

Over the next few days, I divided my time between trying to train Odyssey at home and going to see Elvis. He was clearly thinking about what our future would look like together, too, because one day, Elvis said, "You have to learn that you are the lady of the house."

"Okay," I agreed. It warmed me to hear this. Although I didn't live at Graceland yet, it was wonderful to know that Elvis was already thinking of me in this way.

At the same time, I was a little worried, wondering how I could easily slip into this role without disturbing or offending those who were running Graceland behind the scenes. I didn't want to step on anyone's toes. I hadn't had any opportunities to hang out downstairs and visit with the other people who were regulars in the house, so I hadn't formed a close relationship with any of them.

In addition, I also came from a middle-class upbringing, one where you cleaned your own house and cooked your own meals. Having maids and aides at your beck and call any time of day or night was still a novelty for me, one I'd been trying to get used to while being with Elvis. I was confident, though, that the more time I spent at Graceland, the more comfortable I would start to feel that I would know the right things to say and do as his wife.

Meanwhile, Elvis continued to demonstrate his growing trust and commitment to me by giving me the remote control for an electric gate that opened onto the back of his property. A side road led to the gatehouse at this rear entrance, where a guard was always on duty. Elvis often used this road when he wanted to come and go from Graceland privately. Now he wanted me to be able to arrive or leave without notice whenever I wanted. It was a small step, but a big gesture; one more way of him saying, "I want you to have full access into my life."

Another evening, Elvis glanced about his bedroom with a thoughtful look and suddenly announced that he wanted to redecorate his home. He grew excited as we started talking about the possibilities.

"Graceland should come alive again," Elvis said cheerfully. "After we're married, I want to redo my bedroom first." He paused with a sigh. "Then comes the monstrous task of downstairs," he said, turning to me then and taking my hand. "I want it to be a lot of what you like, too," he said.

"That'll be fun," I agreed, excited about the prospect of redecorating Graceland. Although the idea of this undertaking was a little intimidating, I felt sure Elvis would guide me through it successfully. This was something we could do together that would make me feel more a part of his home. Interior design also appealed to my artistic side.

"What colors for downstairs?" he asked.

I thought about this for a minute, then replied, "Green would be pretty, with some plants and maybe a large aquarium."

Elvis nodded. "Okay." He said another one of the things he'd like to do was redecorate the ladies' bathroom in his office. He asked me to choose colors for that also.

"Turquoise and white would be nice," I said at once. I'd always loved that combination for a bathroom.

He then brought up redecorating his Palm Springs home and putting in a screening room, making it like a small movie theater with king and queen chairs for the two of us.

Talking about how he wanted to change some things caused me to truly begin visualizing the details of what our life together could be like for the first time. I was thrilled and swept up in his vision, adding my own ideas here and there.

One afternoon, I woke at Graceland before Elvis did and decided to go downstairs to look around a bit. If we were going to redecorate the house, I wanted to be able to consider our choices, and I didn't feel like I knew the downstairs rooms that well because most of my time had been spent upstairs.

I walked into the dining room and began looking at some objects arranged on a shelf in a built-in corner cabinet. At one point, I turned around and was startled to see the maid, Lottie, seated at the dining room table, watching me. I hadn't heard her come in.

"Hi," I said.

Lottie smiled and greeted me in return, but I felt some trepidation, as if I'd sneaked into a room I wasn't supposed to be in at all. For me, trying to feel at home at Graceland was like trying to feel at home in the White House. I turned back and continued to examine the objects on the shelves, a little self-conscious now.

"You can change anything you want," Lottie said, surprising me.

Elvis must have said something to her about me being the lady of the house, I thought happily as I turned around to smile at Lottie again.

"It's all fine," I replied. I hadn't come downstairs to start changing things. I just wanted to look around a bit. I also wanted Lottie to feel comfortable with me. Although I appreciated how deferential she was acting, I knew myself too well. I would never feel comfortable ordering her or any of the other staff around, lady of the house or not.

CHAPTER 19

Toward the end of February, Elvis asked, "Have you ever been to Hawaii?"

I was aware that Elvis had made a few movies in Hawaii and had performed a concert there years ago, but I didn't know if he'd been back recently. Elvis still didn't know how little I'd traveled before meeting him, I realized.

"No," I answered.

A smile crept across his face. "I'd really like to take you there," he said.

Wow, I thought. That would be a dream come true! I'd always wanted to go to Hawaii. "I'd love to see it," I said.

And so it was settled: Elvis decided he wanted to leave on March 3 and graciously invited my whole family. Only my sisters would be able to make this trip, and my parents offered to take care of Odyssey.

The evening of our departure, I was sitting with Terry and Rosemary in the living room at Graceland, packed and waiting for Elvis to finish getting ready upstairs, when the doorbell rang. One of the maids opened it.

A man, dressed in a suit and carrying a briefcase, stepped into the foyer, accompanied by a woman. Walking past my sisters and me, they went upstairs, leaving us wondering who they were.

Not long afterward, someone asked me to come upstairs. I entered Elvis's office and saw him seated at his desk, talking with Charlie and the two strangers. Elvis introduced the man to me as his attorney, Beecher Smith, and the woman as Beecher's wife. Elvis's will was lying on the desk in front of them.

"I need witnesses, and you and Charlie are close by," Elvis said.

This was the first business document I'd ever seen placed before him. It was obvious that Elvis didn't want to be bothered with it, since he started making comments about Hawaii and seemed anxious to leave.

I noticed that, on the last page of his will, the year 1976 had been crossed through and 1977 was written in its place. Elvis didn't read anything in my presence. He just quickly signed the will and then Charlie, Mrs. Smith, and I signed as witnesses. I never wondered about the will or the timing of Elvis signing the document at that time. I just looked at it as a little bit of business that Elvis had to do before leaving.

A little while later, we were on the way to the airport, all of us excited about the trip. I mentioned that it was an extra-special treat for Terry because it was her birthday. What a great birthday gift! Elvis smiled broadly and wished her a happy one.

I had become aware at Graceland that Charlie and Billy and Jo Smith were also going to Hawaii, but it wasn't until we arrived at the airport and boarded the *Lisa Marie* that I realized how many people were actually gathered for the trip: aides, stepbrothers, wives, girlfriends, bodyguards, Lamar, Larry, and even Dr. Nichopoulos and his entire family were all on board the plane. Discovering this reminded me once again that Elvis's generous impulses weren't reserved only for me and my family, but bestowed on all those around him.

Elvis greeted everyone and then asked me to join him at the back of the plane. I suspected he felt most comfortable being in the bedroom during takeoff. After the *Lisa Marie* was in the air, we moved up front to visit with various members of the group. Elvis had never met some of the girls who were coming along. One of them was Lamar's date. She had a funny sense of humor, and she hit it off with Rosemary and Terry.

A little while into the flight, my sisters told me they had been chatting with her when Lamar took hold of her hand and she looked at them with a tolerant smile. She had then rolled her eyes at my sisters behind Lamar's back, as if to say, "This is something I have to do."

It was obvious, I thought, that this woman had come along on the trip only to meet Elvis. She later confirmed this by telling my sisters that she didn't really want to be with Lamar.

We landed in Oakland, California, where Ed Parker and his wife, Leilani, boarded the plane. With their addition to our group of travelers, I thought there had to be at least thirty people now on board! Before long, we were in the air again and soaring over the Pacific Ocean.

During this portion of the trip, Elvis mainly stayed in the back of the plane with my sisters and me with the door closed. He was in a silly mood. At one point, he started talking about rats and said he thought his aide Dean looked like one.

Cutting up and laughing, Elvis joked about rats, cheese, and other people on board he thought looked like rats. My sisters and I had him pretend he was in a movie with cameras rolling. As if envisioning rats all around him, Elvis hunched his shoulders and, with a panic-stricken look, suddenly shouted, "Rats! Millions of them! They're all around me, crawling all over my body!"

Elvis had us all in stitches. It was great to see him having so much fun. The three of us egged him on and he continued to act out various silly scenarios with rats.

After a while, Rosemary, Terry, and I went up front to get a snack and a drink. Following us out, Elvis took a seat in the room just outside the bedroom, and Dr. Nichopoulos walked back and began chatting with him.

My sisters and I got our refreshments and headed back toward the bedroom. Elvis was still in a conversation with Dr. Nichopoulos and, as we passed them, Rosemary looked at Elvis.

"Would you like some cheese?" she asked.

He laughed, shushed her, and said, "Get out of here, Rosemary."

Elvis soon joined us in the bedroom and asked Rosemary, "So what's going on up front?"

"Oh, not much," she said, then casually told him what a few people were doing, including Charlie, saying that he was talking to Ed about some of the books Elvis had been reading.

When she mentioned this, Elvis asked, "Charlie's doing *what?*"

Elvis then told us that Ed was a devout Mormon, and said he was worried about Charlie drinking and saying the wrong things about his books. I sensed that Elvis didn't want to upset Ed or disrespect him in any way.

Elvis called for Charlie to come to the back. When Charlie walked in, Elvis said, "Charlie, man . . . be careful how you talk about my books with Ed."

Charlie looked puzzled. "I wasn't doing anything wrong," he said, but Elvis didn't want to hear it. Looking a little hurt, Charlie slunk out the door.

As we approached Hawaii, Elvis began rhapsodizing about the islands. Later, Elvis whispered to me, "Can you imagine if we got married here? It would blow everybody away."

I froze for a moment. *Is he seriously considering this?*

Then, as if reminding himself, Elvis said, "God will tell me when the time is right, though."

When the *Lisa Marie* touched down on the island of Oahu, Elvis made the moment all the more magical as he began softly singing "Blue Hawaii," to my sisters and me. I couldn't believe we were actually here!

As I followed Elvis outside onto a mobile stairway, the first thing that hit me was the overwhelming fragrance of flowers. Hawaiians greeted us and placed beautiful leis around our necks after we descended the steps.

My sisters and I rode with Elvis in a limousine from the airport while the rest of the group followed in a small bus. About twenty minutes later, we pulled onto the grounds of the Rainbow Tower at Hilton Hawaiian Village. It looked like a tropical paradise with its gardens, ponds, and waterfalls.

Elvis had reserved a suite of rooms on the thirty-first floor and arranged for Terry and Rosemary to be in a bedroom across the living room from ours. A few of the guys came in to help us settle in our room. They brought in the bags, laid out Elvis's books, and left a contact sheet so we'd know who was on duty and when.

Elvis eagerly took me by the hand and led me onto the suite's balcony, where I took in the unbelievably gorgeous, postcard-perfect view of Waikiki Beach below and, in the distance, a volcanic crater that Elvis said was Diamond Head. I couldn't wait to see it all up close.

Rosemary and Terry were going downstairs to look around, but before they did, Elvis remembered Terry's birthday and thoughtfully called a jeweler to come to our suite with a selection of pieces. Generous as always, Elvis picked out a beautiful ring and gave it to Terry.

My sisters eventually left and a few other people stopped by our suite to greet us. Before long, however, Elvis went into the bedroom and sat on the bed, where he picked out some books and appeared to be ready to read and relax.

Could he really want to read now, I wondered, when there was so much to see? Then it hit me: We'd been up almost twenty-four hours.

I was too excited to feel the effects of jet lag or our sleepless night. Now I realized that Elvis was probably getting tired, so I joined him on the bed. We read for a little while and then slept.

When we woke up, I thought Elvis might have something planned for us to do or something he might want to show me, since he'd been here before. He surprised me, though, by saying I should go with Terry and Rosemary to the beach in front of the hotel.

I wanted Elvis to come with us so badly, but how far could he walk outside without being recognized and most probably mobbed? Not far, I realized. Still, I hated the thought of just leaving him sitting here alone inside while the rest of us went out and enjoyed ourselves. There had to be a way to get him out of the hotel.

My sisters were back in the suite by now. The three of us tried talking Elvis into sneaking downstairs incognito. Rosemary suggested a wig and different glasses, but he shook his head.

"Nah," he said. "I don't wanna wear that."

It was a beautiful hotel, but now I wondered who had arranged for us to stay in this particular place—a hotel where Elvis clearly couldn't go outside and relax because there were too many people around.

When a few members of his entourage showed up in the suite to visit with Elvis, knowing he wouldn't be alone, I decided to accompany my sisters to the beach. It truly was paradise, complete with palm trees and clear turquoise ocean. Rosemary stayed in the shade, but Terry and I picked out a spot on the sand where we could lie down on our towels and soak up the sun.

Rosemary was the smart one, it turned out. Terry and I were both oblivious to the strength of the sun's rays in Hawaii. We weren't on the beach long, but when we returned to the suite, Terry—who was fairer than I—discovered that her body and face were seriously sunburned. Her lips had blown up like little sausages! This was years before collagen would become fashionable, and Terry was mortified.

My face was also badly burned and my eyelids were swollen. The two of us were extremely embarrassed.

The minute Elvis saw us, he asked Larry to come to the suite to try some healing techniques on Terry. Larry arrived and Terry lay down on her bed. As Rosemary and I stood by watching, Larry and Elvis placed their hands a few inches above Terry's back and legs, telling her to think of healing colors.

Elvis mentioned something about aloe vera gel and requested an aide to find us some; he told Terry she should spread it over her sunburn. Neither my sisters nor I were familiar with the gel, but Terry was in pain and I hoped that one of the things Elvis and Larry were kindly trying to do would comfort her. Before long, someone brought up some gel and Terry and I liberally applied it. It did help us feel a little better.

Hawaiian music continuously played outside by the beach. Later that evening, my sisters and I dared Elvis to go on the balcony and sing along. He walked out; I stepped up beside him, and he began to sing. It was another perfect moment, as the flames from tiki torches softly lit the beach below us and I gazed out over the ocean while listening to Elvis serenade us.

At one point, I decided to call our parents to let them know we had arrived safely. I went with Rosemary and Terry into their room and dialed an operator to place a collect call. Elvis walked in and asked what I was doing.

"I'm trying to reach our parents."

He took the phone from my hand and said into the receiver, "This is Elvis Presley and I'm trying to get connected."

Of course the operator didn't believe him. My sisters and I started laughing as he began singing in an effort to convince the woman.

It worked. Within seconds, I was speaking with my parents and letting them know that we were all fine.

Elvis relaxed for the rest of that evening, visiting with a few people in our suite, and then we went to bed. When we woke the next day, he decided to send me shopping with Rosemary and Terry.

Still wondering when, or even if, Elvis would ever go outside, I put on a crocheted halter-top and some jeans. As I started to leave, Elvis stopped me.

"Ginger, I don't want you to go out like that," he said.

Confused, I looked at him for a minute, wondering what was wrong with my outfit.

"I'd like you to wear a shirt over it," he added.

Why was he saying that? Was he being protective? Did he not want other men looking at me?

This was the first time I'd ever seen Elvis react this way to something I had chosen to wear. I was flattered by his concern, no matter what had provoked it.

"Okay," I said. I put a shirt on over my top and left with my sisters, who said they'd gone downstairs earlier and run into Lamar's date, who was "as red as a lobster."

The other woman had told them she purposely got sunburned the first day so Lamar wouldn't touch her. She also had a pack of gum with her, and said she was constantly telling Lamar that she was going out for gum so she didn't have to be in the same room with him. Terry and I got tickled as we realized that, for us, being sunburned was painful, but for Lamar's date, it was apparently a relief.

While others dined out, my sisters and I ate in the suite with Elvis. After dinner, some members of the group came in to visit and later Elvis mentioned something about mai tais. This surprised me. Except for Charlie enjoying a cocktail, and a bottle of vodka I'd noticed once partially sticking out of a backpack Ricky carried on tour, I had yet to see Elvis or others around him drink.

When my sisters and I told Elvis we'd never had mai tais, he asked one of the guys to order some sent up to the suite. My sisters and I each had one, but Elvis drank three. Not long afterward he began marching in place. We all started laughing, especially when Elvis stood up on the couch and started walking back and forth across the cushions.

His face soon flushed red, though, and Elvis quickly sat down, telling us he shouldn't really drink because he had high blood pressure and was taking pills for it. I was glad he told us. I'd had no idea.

Later on, Elvis called for a jeweler to come up again. This time he picked out puka shell necklaces for everyone, including himself. Kindly thinking of my mother, Elvis purchased one for her, too.

He also made the decision that night to rent a beach house so he could have some privacy. I was glad, feeling that now he'd be able to go outside and have fun with the rest of us.

Well into the early morning hours, my sisters and I were alone with Elvis. He was still in a jovial mood and brought up rats again. He was having fun, talking loudly and every so often shouting out something to do with rats. I loved cutting up with him, seeing him act like a big kid and having such a good time with my sisters. I was happy that Elvis seemed to have left his cares behind on the mainland.

Before going to sleep that morning, Elvis told me that, if I wanted to look around in the hotel shops downstairs later, I should, because we would be leaving that afternoon to view some houses.

When Elvis and I woke, I asked my sisters if they wanted to accompany me. Terry was still in pain from her sunburn so she opted to stay in her room, but Rosemary said she would go.

The two of us browsed through the stores downstairs for a while. When we returned, Terry met us in the living room and told us that Elvis had knocked on her door and come into her room. He had wanted yogurt and handed her his list with the entourage's room numbers, asking her to call someone to get him some.

She had gone into the living room and started calling. No one was answering in any room, and Elvis began getting irritated as she went through the complete list.

"None of them checked to see if I needed anything," Elvis had told her angrily. "These aren't friends here."

Wanting to help him, Terry had gone out into the hall and spoken with a guard stationed by the elevators, requesting yogurt for Elvis. It was soon brought up to the room.

Luckily, Elvis was in a better mood by the time I saw him, but I was sure he would have some hard words to say to a select few—if he hadn't already.

To look at beach houses, Elvis got dressed in a light blue jogging suit, a navy nylon jacket, a pair of sneakers, and a terry-cloth hat. It was different to see him dressed like this. Jeans were popular, but I had yet to see Elvis wear any. Now I asked him why.

"Because I had to when I was little," he replied. I suspected wearing jeans reminded Elvis of a time in his youth when his family had little money and that was all they could afford.

I gathered a few of my things and left the hotel with Elvis, my sisters, and a few of the others. It was a half hour ride to the other side of the island. From the windows of the limousine, I drank in the lush green countryside. The beauty of the island was beyond amazing.

We arrived at a private home and walked through it with a local liaison. In one room was a large window with a bizarre feature: When you pushed a button nearby, it looked like it was raining outside.

Elvis sat on a couch, relaxing for a moment and contemplating the house. Joe Esposito had come along with us. He had a camera with him and began taking pictures of Elvis.

Rosemary had taken a seat on the floor nearby and was paying attention to some others who were chatting. Suddenly, I noticed Elvis cut his eyes over at her. Rosemary looked back at him, smiled, then turned her attention elsewhere.

A big grin spread across his face as he continued to watch her. Shortly, he stood up and, as he walked past her, he suddenly turned and pounced. Rosemary fell backward with Elvis on top of her.

Someone snapped a picture of their spontaneous tussle while we all laughed. Then Elvis stood up and helped Rosemary to her feet.

Elvis decided he didn't care for this first house, so we went to see another.

The second home was close to the beach and had access to a neighbor's nearby pool. Elvis liked it and immediately decided this was where we would stay. He put my sisters in a bedroom close to ours, and placed Billy and Jo Smith in a room at the end of the hall. Dr. Nichopoulos would be in a room on the other side of the home and, as usual, Elvis wanted an aide or two staying at the house also. The remainder of the group would stay at the hotel.

Before long, the rest of the group arrived at the house and Elvis decided he wanted to go to the beach. It was so warm out, we found some scissors and cut off the long sleeves to the jacket of his jogging suit. I assumed someone would be going back to the hotel to bring our suitcases. Meanwhile, a group of us walked with Elvis down to the water, where he and I sat on some small foam boards on the sand.

A few people took a dip in the ocean, but Elvis and I remained on the beach, peacefully enjoying the serene view and watching the others swim. It felt wonderful to relax with him out in the sunshine.

Before long, Joe pulled out his camera again and began taking more pictures. Beach mats were soon brought down to us and we rolled them open to have more room to sit or lie down. I had a Polaroid camera with me; out of respect for Elvis's privacy, I had yet to take any photos of him. However, now that I saw Joe snap away, I decided to snap a couple of shots, too.

A few others began shooting photographs as well. Elvis sat with various people, joking and cutting up for photo ops. A short time later, Rosemary told me that when she'd been sitting beside Elvis, he had confessed to wishing only Polaroids were being taken. The problem with film being developed, he explained, was that the person doing it could then decide to sell the photographs. This was another reminder that his celebrity had sometimes taken away some of his enjoyment from ordinary activities that the rest of us take for granted.

Elvis and I finally fell asleep near dawn. When I woke that afternoon, Terry told me that when she and Rosemary first opened their bedroom door, they had seen a huge hunk of cheese sitting on the floor in their doorway. I laughed, pleased that all of our joking about rats seemed to have left quite an impression on Elvis! Someone had gone out earlier and bought some tops for Elvis to wear, but they were short-sleeved cotton sweatshirts. It was so warm out that I took some scissors and cut the neck out of one, making it larger so he could get it over his head more easily, and hoping the more open neckline would let more air in for him and keep him cooler.

I didn't know if Elvis had any shorts or a swimsuit with him, since he chose to wear a pair of lightweight pants, but I decided to look for some shirts that were made of a lighter material for him. He arranged for someone to take my sisters and me shopping and we browsed around at some nearby stores. I purchased a few shirts I hoped he would like.

When we returned, I found out that Elvis and some of the guys in the group had played touch football while we were gone. I hated missing the chance to see them play, but I could tell it had gotten rough at times, because Elvis's cousin, Billy, had a swollen knee.

I was standing in the kitchen a bit later when Joe's girlfriend, Shirley, came in. I hadn't spoken much with her since our shopping venture in Las Vegas, but we were always cordial whenever we saw each other. As we talked, Shirley said she'd had lunch with Priscilla Presley not long ago, and that Priscilla had asked her if Elvis and I were engaged. This surprised me; I hadn't known she was close friends with Priscilla.

"What did you tell her?" I asked.

"I told her, 'Well, she has an engagement ring,'" Shirley said.

I knew the news of our engagement must have circulated throughout the entire group by now, but I suddenly realized that I had no memory of ever being congratulated by Shirley, Joe, Dr. Nichopoulos, Lamar, or a few others who regularly surrounded Elvis. This certainly was strange and inexplicable.

"Have you set a wedding date?" Shirley asked.

"No."

"You should mention marriage to Elvis, to push him a little," she said. "You should bring it up more."

I didn't like this idea. I remembered Elvis once telling me that he thought when it came to marriage, it was the man's place to ask, and Elvis had already told me a few times that God would come through and tell him when the time was right. I wanted him to be sure. A red flag went up. Was Shirley trying to help me or hurt me?

"Shirley, I don't want to do that," I said, feeling awkward. We dropped the subject and I left the kitchen a few minutes later. Unfortunately, now when it came to Shirley, I felt my guard had to be up.

Elvis had started rising a little earlier during the day and was spending more time in the fresh air. However, he still often wanted me to read with him inside, and when he did go out, he didn't hang around by the pool for very long and he never seemed to want to go swimming.

With so many other people around and the strong possibility of some taking photos, I sensed that Elvis remained fully clothed because he didn't feel comfortable about taking his shirt off. I guessed maybe he was self-conscious about the scars on his back left by some of his stage suits. But I had seen him without his shirt on and he looked good.

From time to time I tried to coax him into the water, but because I couldn't get him into the ocean, I tried to enjoy myself anyway and usually swam with Terry.

Elvis and I had yet to try any of the local Hawaiian delicacies. He was mainly sticking with certain foods he liked—familiar comfort foods like pizza and cheeseburgers—though he did drink a fair amount of papaya juice, which was so readily available.

The first time Elvis ventured out among the general public in Hawaii was for a shopping trip to a local mall. Amazingly, we actually made it into one of the stores without anyone noticing who he was.

We browsed the aisles together and came across some large candles shaped like pyramids. Intrigued, Elvis decided to purchase a few. He also found a mother-of-pearl crucifix on a stand that he liked.

I was looking around the store with my sisters when Joe came over and told us not to show Elvis anything expensive because he would probably buy it. According to Joe, Linda Thompson had once pointed out a costly bubble gum machine to Elvis even after Joe had asked her not to show it to him.

"Sure enough, Elvis bought it, and he didn't need things like that," Joe said.

I wondered if Joe always managed Elvis's spending money. On the one hand, it was nice that Joe seemed to be watching over it, but on the other hand, should Joe be saying what Elvis should or shouldn't have? Joe didn't know us well, but my sisters and I weren't the sort of people who would take advantage of Elvis's generosity or tell him to buy things. It put a little damper on the enjoyment I'd been feeling while looking at things with Elvis, because the prices on most items in the store weren't visible and I was now afraid to comment or point out anything at all.

In a second shop, Elvis admired some amazing jeweled robes. He began choosing some for my sisters, Jo Smith, himself, and me. Suddenly I noticed people gathering outside the store and knew word must be spreading that Elvis was here. Elvis spotted them at the same time and decided it was time to leave. I certainly understood others wanting to see him, but I did wish he could have stayed out for a little while longer.

I never knew Elvis to personally carry a wallet; after he'd chosen the robes, a member of his staff got in line to pay for his items. As we stood near the counter, a man was buying something. Elvis asked who it was for and the man, understandably stunned to see Elvis standing beside him, said it was a gift for his wife. Elvis then paid for the man's item as well.

On the way home, Elvis wanted to show us a tourist attraction, so he asked our driver to stop at an area called the Halona Blowhole. This was a natural occurrence created by lava tubes from volcanic eruptions. As we watched from a lookout area, waves crashed against the formations below us, and every once in a while some ocean water sprayed high into the air.

Before long, some of the other tourists gathered at the sight recognized Elvis and approached us. He kindly posed for pictures and signed some autographs before leaving.

Hawaii was an amazingly beautiful place, but in addition to the stunning scenery, it was also a wonderful opportunity for Elvis to relax and have fun. There was a Ping-Pong table in the house, and once I challenged Elvis to a game. I thought it would be fun and it would do Elvis good to get some exercise. I went to where he'd taken his customary pose on the bed with some books and asked him to play.

"No, I don't want to," he said.

Taunting him, I said, "You can't. That's why."

Elvis grinned as I kept at him. Finally, he walked with me into the room with the Ping-Pong table and we started to play.

We hit the ball around a few times, but then Elvis started slamming the ball so hard at me that it became impossible to return his shots. Some of the aides were in the room with us; later, one of them told me he couldn't believe it, as he'd never seen Elvis play Ping-Pong before.

I wasn't sure you could actually call the game we'd been playing Ping-Pong, but it was fun while it lasted.

Another time, Elvis began showing my sisters and me some karate moves in his bedroom. Rosemary decided to challenge him and asked, "What if you were on the beach and had only one arm, and someone kicked sand in your face?"

Elvis sat on the floor and Rosemary approached him, pretending to kick sand at him. Using one arm, Elvis grabbed her leg and, trying to be gentle, knocked her off her feet. Terry and I were lying across the bed, laughing at the two of them.

Rosemary stood back up, looked at Elvis, and asked, "Okay, what if you had no arms and only legs?" She came walking toward him again.

Using only his legs, Elvis had her back down on the floor in the blink of an eye. Elvis started laughing. Still, Rosemary kept putting his karate expertise to the test by proposing various challenging scenarios.

Elvis demonstrated several moves on Rosemary while Terry and I cheered the two of them on. At one point, they were both down on the floor when Rosemary managed to get Elvis in a headlock.

"I got him!" she shouted. Meanwhile, Elvis was beginning to twist her body into a pretzel.

Terry and I had been mainly rooting for Rosemary. Finally taking a break to rest, Elvis picked up a large glass filled with ice water from his night table and began leering at me.

"I dare you to throw it," I teased.

Continuing to stare at me, he said with a smirk, "Don't dare me," and before I had time to blink, I was covered in freezing water.

I went into the bathroom, dried off with a towel, and filled my hand with shaving cream. I kept my hand behind my back as I walked out.

Elvis was now facing my sisters. Walking up behind him, I said, "Elvis?"

As he turned around, I quickly smeared some shaving cream on his face and hauled out of there. I flew into the main room, passing the Ping-Pong table with Elvis in close pursuit. A few of the guys sitting in the room looked up in surprise as Elvis chased me around the table.

Laughing, Elvis finally gave up and walked back to his room. I waited a bit before going back into the bedroom, unsure if Elvis would have any other tricks up his sleeve. Lucky for me, all was safe upon my return.

Unfortunately, the trip was not all fun and laughter.

On the afternoon of March 9, Elvis saw a television report about twelve Hanafi Muslims taking over three buildings in Washington, D.C., and holding people hostage. I saw Elvis's deep love for our country as he became furious and talked about offering his plane to assist in some way. He even mentioned leaving Hawaii to go to Washington so he could speak with President Carter. I reasoned with him, along with Larry and Charlie, convincing him there was nothing he could do, and that we'd have to trust President Carter to sort things out. Eventually he calmed down, and fortunately the hostages were released a few days later.

Elvis had been drinking papaya juice excessively that day. He woke up shortly after going to bed, requesting more. He had consumed quite a bit of juice right before going to sleep, and my mind flashed to his problem with fluid retention and bloating.

Against my better instincts, I went into the kitchen to get him more papaya juice, but there wasn't any left. I came back and told him we had run out. Elvis then wanted me to wake an aide and send him out to get more. "Can it wait, Elvis?" I asked.

In a more normal situation, I would have been happy to see that he got some juice, but I felt it would be better for his health if Elvis curbed his intake. I was hoping he would just doze off again, but he became increasingly adamant about getting some more juice.

I remembered that Vernon had once asked Elvis if I did little things for him. I usually did, but I decided to resist this request for his own good. "Elvis, this much juice isn't healthy," I said.

I could tell he was angry by the way Elvis left the room without speaking and went into his cousin's bedroom, shutting the door.

I hadn't expected this reaction, and wondered what Elvis would tell Billy and Jo. Now I felt anger welling up inside me, too. Here I was, trying to do the right thing for him, but Elvis was behaving like a little boy. I stood firm and didn't follow him.

A little while later, Billy came into my room. "Ginger, Elvis wants to see you," he said.

I thought it was odd that Billy didn't bother to ask what was going on. I followed him back into his room and saw Elvis seated on the bed. Hoping he'd calmed down, I was prepared to tell him again that I was just trying to help. But, before I could say anything, Elvis looked at me and announced, "We're leaving Hawaii because of you."

I couldn't believe what I was hearing. Were we actually going to leave Hawaii over *papaya juice*?

I glanced at Billy, but he and his wife sat quietly, watching the drama unfold. I wondered what Elvis had said to them and what everyone would think. But I was determined not to back down. Meanwhile, Elvis was clearly bent on staying mad at me. He started saying some unkind things, insinuating that I didn't love him because of this. This shocked me; I was standing up to him because I *did* love him! His reaction hurt me deeply. I had been trying to do a good thing, and this wasn't the Elvis I loved. I was pretty sure now that the medication he had taken must be responsible for the inexplicable change in his personality.

My confusion and embarrassment were overshadowed by my anger and hurt over Elvis actually saying we'd leave Hawaii because of this. I walked out of the room while Elvis was still talking, shut the door, and ran down the hall to our room. I closed that door as well, hoping Elvis might return to normal if I gave him time to calm down.

I sat down on the bed. Moments later, I heard Billy's door fly open and heavy footsteps marching down the hall. Our bedroom door flew open, Elvis stormed into the room with a wild look in his eyes, and slapped me on the side of my rib cage. "No one ever walks out on me when I'm talking!" he said.

I started crying, more surprised by his furious action than hurt by the sting of his open hand. I was afraid to move on the bed. Who was this person? Where was the Elvis I loved?

When he saw how upset I was, Elvis quickly realized what he had done and bent down to put his arms around me, saying he was sorry. He told me we really weren't leaving, but that he had just said that.

Why? I wondered. Had Elvis just said that to scare me, and what was the purpose in that? I continued to cry in his arms. Although Elvis hadn't hit me hard, he had done the inconceivable: He had hit me. This was more traumatic emotionally than physically.

I could tell by his voice that Elvis was deeply remorseful for having struck me. Still, he didn't say what I needed to hear: "I understand you were only trying to help me." He had been used to getting his own way for so long, that I think Elvis honestly felt he knew what was best for his own health.

The dark mood that had transformed Elvis into someone I didn't recognize reminded me of the incident in Palm Springs over the yogurt. There, too, I'd only been trying to help him. If this was his reaction over yogurt and papaya juice, how could I ever say anything to him about his sleep medication?

I had never spoken to Elvis about the concern I had over that. When I had first become aware of the sleep packets being left for Elvis each night, I had questioned whether Elvis's insomnia was just in his mind. In my experience, I'd never known anyone who couldn't sleep. My view was confirmed when, one night, I had witnessed Elvis going to sleep without taking his nightly packet at Graceland. If Elvis could do that once, I believed he could do it again. With practice, I thought Elvis could learn to fall asleep unaided by sleep medicine over time, especially if he got out and exercised more. I began to question whether anybody had ever seriously tried to wean him off medication.

I wanted Elvis to try going without the pills, or to at least try cutting back on the dosage. This definitely wasn't the time to bring up that tender subject, though. I knew this wouldn't be easy, but I loved him deeply, and I wasn't going to let over-the-top reactions like these deter me from trying to help him.

I didn't say anything to my sisters about the juice incident. It was over and Elvis was in a better mood. I was disturbed, however, that his cousins had seen Elvis angry, yet had never tried to intervene or asked me what happened.

These people would become my family when Elvis and I were married. I wanted to feel close to them, but I was the newcomer. I wondered why they didn't go out of their way to approach me. I only had Elvis's best interests at heart and wanted them to know that. In this moment, however, I was simply too embarrassed to confide in them, so I let things slide.

On March 11, Ed Parker set up an evening for us at the Polynesian Cultural Center at Brigham Young University so we could enjoy a night of Hawaiian dances. Elvis had his hair styled and wore a gorgeous two-piece black-and-white outfit with Native American beadwork on the cuffs and at the waist. He looked so handsome, I wanted to take a picture, but I was out of film and so were my sisters.

When we arrived at the center, we discovered that word of Elvis making an appearance had spread fast. Fans were milling about outside the roofed amphitheater, eager to see him. The show was already in progress when we walked inside; thanks to the dim lighting, we were safely ushered to our seats.

However, as soon as I sat down beside Elvis, a few audience members looked our way. Slowly, other heads began turning to stare. Many people seemed more interested in seeing Elvis than they were in watching the show.

A man seated in front of us suddenly turned around, plopped his young daughter in Elvis's lap, and requested a photo. Elvis politely obliged.

As Elvis held on to the little girl, he leaned my way, shrugged his shoulders, and joked, "He's not getting her back."

I laughed and was glad that others in the audience who had also become aware of Elvis's presence were courteous and let him enjoy the show.

It was quite the spectacle, too! I'd never seen anything like it! There was a wide stage, tropical landscaping, waterfalls, and a spectacular mountain backdrop with volcanoes. Performers from all of the islands, in full costume with body and face paint, danced to the beat of drums and used fire, spears, and fans in their routines.

Close to intermission, we were escorted to a private room so Elvis wouldn't be disturbed. After visiting with a few people, we returned for the second half of the show, but left shortly before the finale to avoid the crowd. Still, as we were walking toward the car, we suddenly became enveloped by fans.

The driver opened the car door and Elvis was able to make his way inside along with my sisters, but I got caught in the group. I panicked as the car slowly began pulling forward. Luckily, the rear door was still open, and a guard was able to help me push through the crowd. I scrambled into the car. It had been an amazing night and I'd had a great time. I could tell Elvis had, too, since he talked about the show almost all the way back to the beach house.

Yet the next day, Elvis again seemed to experience another inexplicable mood swing. I was standing in the kitchen talking with Rosemary when his stepbrother David Stanley walked by and playfully punched me on the top of my arm.

"Keep your fucking hands off her!" a voice exclaimed.

Turning around in astonishment, I saw Elvis standing in the center of the hallway. Glaring at David, he angrily said, "You don't punch a lady. That's redneck shit!"

I was shocked by his fury. Where had that come from?

David was stunned, too. "I was only joking!" he yelled back at Elvis, then retreated.

Elvis returned to his room and I followed him. His prior good mood had completely evaporated. He started talking about "rednecks hitting ladies," and I tried to reassure him.

"Elvis, David was only being playful," I said.

But Elvis's mood wouldn't lift. "If David touches you again, I want to know," he said.

I left things there, wondering whether Elvis was acting like this because he felt bad about the earlier incident, when *he'd* been the one to hit me.

Elvis chose to mainly stay in his room that day and I read with him for a little while. Later, I went outside with Rosemary and Terry. At one point, we began talking to David and Ricky.

Shortly, someone came out and said Elvis wanted to see me. I returned to our room, where Elvis was seated on the bed. "What were you, Ricky, and David talking about?" he asked.

Our bedroom window faced the lawn where we'd all been gathered outside; now I realized Elvis must have been watching us. "Nothing in particular," I said.

Did he think we were talking about him? Or could something else be going on between Elvis and his stepbrothers that I didn't know about? I didn't dare ask what was going on; I was still feeling a little tentative around Elvis after the juice incident and didn't want to chance upsetting him in any way. I chose to change the subject.

Elvis never explained what he'd been worried about, but he continued to look at David in a strange way that day, as if he were trying to keep an eye on him.

Elvis and I went down to the beach the following afternoon. The wind kicked up, blowing sand in his eyes, and they got irritated. Discouraged and uncomfortable, Elvis wasn't really able to enjoy himself now, so he decided it was time for us to head home.

On March 13, we boarded the plane back to the mainland. Elvis carried the mother-of-pearl crucifix he had purchased, but he dropped it and the base broke off. His frustrated mood quickly lightened when we entered the plane and saw a photo of Elvis when he'd pounced on top of Rosemary taped to Elvis's bedroom door. We all got a chuckle out of that.

During our return flight, Elvis mainly stayed in the back of the plane with my sisters and me again. At one point, he reflected on the trip and talked about how his guest invitations had escalated in number beyond what he'd expected.

"Next time, I'm only taking about eight people," Elvis said, adding that Dr. Nichopoulos had told him he wouldn't come unless his wife and daughters came, too. "I'll never have that many again," he vowed.

Elvis also wasn't pleased because one of his aides had popped up and told him he was quitting when we got back. He said he had paid for his trip and the aide had decided to tell him this while he was trying to relax.

Still, I was happy we'd gone to Hawaii, not only because a dream of mine had come true, but because the trip had been good for Elvis overall. He had gone outside more and relaxed in a way I hadn't seen him do up until now. He'd also gotten to know my sisters better and really enjoyed their company.

Elvis was a wonderful and caring person 98 percent of the time. His bad mood swings were out of character, and I now fully attributed them to the prescribed medication he'd been taking. I wanted to take care of him. I knew there would be challenges ahead. Love could be hard and steep, shaking us at our roots, but I was sure we could make it through.

CHAPTER 20

When we landed in Memphis, my sisters went home and I returned to Graceland with Elvis. There, I was astonished to discover that the bathroom in his office had been redecorated in turquoise and white. Even the salon chair, which Elvis had told me belonged to his mother, had been reupholstered.

I couldn't believe Elvis had this done while we were away! This meant the world to me! It looked beautiful and we were both pleased by the results. It was nice having a room at Graceland decorated according to my taste. Elvis wasn't wasting time in taking steps to make me feel more at home here, and it was working.

Dr. Nichopoulos had tried to help Elvis with his eye problem before leaving Hawaii, but Elvis's eyes were still irritated from the sand, so Elvis asked his eye doctor to come to Graceland. That's when I was surprised to learn he had glaucoma. As Elvis lay in bed, the doctor examined his eyes and told me what a good patient Elvis had been in the past. Once, when Elvis was on tour, the doctor said, the pressure was building so fast in one of his eyes that he was called in and had to stick a syringe in his cornea to help relieve it.

"Elvis didn't even flinch," the doctor said.

I could tell Elvis was proud about this as he described how he'd put himself in a meditative state in order not to blink.

The doctor gave me instructions for helping Elvis care for his eyes. I stayed at Graceland, getting up through the night to administer eye cream and replace his bandages.

The doctor returned the next day to check Elvis's eyes and seemed pleased by the results. "They look much better," he told me. "You did a great job." I felt a mixture of relief for Elvis and pride that I was able to help.

Joe had given Elvis some of the photos he'd taken in Hawaii. Elvis's eyes were bothering him too much for him to look at the pictures then, but now we went through them together, reliving the good time we'd had. Elvis picked out one photograph of me looking over my shoulder and put it in a frame on the night table by his bed. I was touched that he wanted the picture there.

When he told me he was feeling better, I told Elvis I needed to go home for a bit, unpack, say hi to my family, and see Odyssey. Before I left, I kissed him and said, "Elvis, this trip meant so much. Thank you for taking me."

"You're welcome," he replied, and as souvenirs of our time together, Elvis gave me some of the photos Joe had taken and the mother of pearl cross he'd brought back.

I ran into Charlie on my way out the door, who said, "You know, the only reason we went to Hawaii was because of you."

"Thanks for letting me know, Charlie," I said. Having him point this out was a sweet ending to our holiday.

I'd felt closer than ever to Elvis since our trip. The redecorated bathroom did feel like *my* room, a gift from Elvis, welcoming me into his home. Elvis had his sanctuary and now I had mine. This bathroom was a place where I could keep my things, such as toiletries and some clothes.

In addition, now that I was the owner of some amazing jewelry, one day Elvis said, "You should have something nice to keep it in." He went into his bathroom and returned with a large, beautiful jewelry box. It was made of rich wood inlaid with copper and brass. Placing the box beside me on the bed, Elvis opened a couple of the red velvet-lined drawers, removed a few pieces of his own jewelry from them, and gave the box to me.

I kept it in my new bathroom at Graceland, feeling this was a place where my engagement ring and other valuable pieces would always be safe.

I usually dressed in the bathroom and applied my makeup there. I had always worn my eye makeup dark, and took care to wear it that way after once having Elvis comment, "Your eyes look different today," when I'd changed it a little.

Many times, I slept in my eye makeup. The first time I washed my face and Elvis saw me without the usual mascara and shadow, he teasingly called me Little Two because, according to him, without my makeup on, I looked like a two-year-old. Whenever Elvis saw me without eye makeup after that, I was Little Two. Otherwise, his old endearment, Chicken Neck, soon became interchanged with a new one, Gingerbread.

Not long afterward, Elvis asked me to bring him a picture taken of me when I was a child. I brought him a wallet-size school photo from first grade. Elvis inserted it into the corner of the framed picture of me in Hawaii, then placed it back on his night table where it would remain for the rest of our time together.

I also believe that Elvis felt closer to me too. He began to share more of himself, bringing me deeper into his world.

For instance, one night Elvis was in a reflective mood and said he wanted to show me his high school. I was eager to see it and happy that he wanted to share this piece of his past with me. We put on our leather jackets and helmets, climbed onto one of his Harley hogs, and headed toward the back gate.

It was our very first time out alone like this, without any friends, aides, or bodyguards, and it felt wonderful to have Elvis all to myself.

Riding toward downtown Memphis, we eventually turned onto a street and a large redbrick building came into view. Elvis turned his head and shouted through the face shield of his helmet, "Humes High School."

We cruised slowly by the school, then circled around and rode down a few more streets. At a housing project called Lauderdale Courts, Elvis slowed down again and then came to a stop.

"This is one of the places where I grew up," he said, again looking back at me.

As I looked at the older, nondescript, three-story brick building, thinking surely the apartments couldn't have been spacious when he was there, I found it hard to imagine Elvis living here at all. It looked too small for his larger-than-life persona.

We sat there for a few minutes, silently contemplating the housing project. Neither of us had really talked about our childhoods yet. We had been too busy dealing with the present and talking about our possible future together to delve into the past.

Staying so fully aware of his humble roots was the real reason, I felt, that Elvis was inspired to be so giving to others: He knew what it was like to do without.

As we slowly began pulling away from the curb, Elvis looked over his shoulder at me. "Man, you wouldn't believe how small my home in Tupelo was," he said with a laugh.

I held on to him a little tighter, hoping he would take me there one day.

Another night, Elvis asked, "Would you like to see the trophy room?"

"Yes," I said enthusiastically. I wasn't even aware that he had one at his home.

I followed him downstairs, where we passed through the living room and music room before entering a long room where framed gold records lined the walls and display cases were filled with trophies and awards.

Elvis took my hand as we slowly began walking down an aisle. Every now and then, he'd stop to point out various honors. The room was littered with gifts from fans, too. As we passed by a framed painting of the *Lisa Marie*, a gift from a fan, Elvis stopped, picked it up, and said, "You can have this."

It was a kind offer as I knew he was proud of the plane. Looking about the room at one point, curiously detached, he said, "You know, sometimes this seems like it's all someone else's."

As I stood beside him, surveying the broad scope of all he had done, highlighted here by records, trophies, and photographs, the enormity of his accomplishments hit me full force. And these markers were just the tip of the iceberg! No wonder it was difficult for him to fully fathom that he had experienced all of this.

At the back of the room, we paused in front of a full-size painting of a younger Elvis. He was portrayed against a gold sky, dressed all in white and standing among some clouds.

An artist in Las Vegas had painted it, Elvis said, marveling, "He basically took one look at me and drew it in detail. Man, he really captured my likeness, right down to the veins in my hands."

It was a beautiful painting, and after admiring it for a few more moments, Elvis nonchalantly said, "I want you to have this."

I was completely flabbergasted. This painting? Does he want me to take it right now?

"Thank you," I said with a surprised laugh, "but, Elvis, I don't think it will fit anywhere in my home."

"In your parents' new home," Elvis corrected me, seriously.

"Is it okay to leave it here for now," I asked, hoping he wouldn't be offended.

"That's fine," he said, with a soft smile.

Back upstairs, Elvis's generous mood expanded even more. Leading me into the dressing area of his bathroom, he gave me the most singular piece of jewelry I'd ever seen: his own large ram's head necklace in gold, inlaid with diamonds and emeralds.

"Always wear it with something black," he instructed.

It was around this time that Elvis decided I should have a bank account. He put Vernon in charge of opening one for me. Elvis put $5,000 into the account and I received a credit card. I had made a little money from working at the dress shop, but I was awestruck. This amount of money might have seemed small to some, but to me it was, quite literally, a fortune. I had never even owned personal checks or a credit card!

Elvis gave me more personal items whenever the mood struck him. His generosity was not just reserved for me though. I would later learn that Elvis gave away personal items to many that he knew and had often gifted everyone around him—doctors, nurses, maids, relatives, aides, friends—with things ranging from money, jewelry, and furs to cars and homes. At times he seemed to want to take care of the whole world.

Since Elvis's last tours, I had begun to see a pattern of him needing more help to go to sleep as a concert tour approached. He would take his usual sleep packet, then wake up shortly afterward, alert and asking for Tish Henley, the nurse who lived out back with her husband, to bring him additional medication, either pills or a shot of something to help him sleep.

I was troubled by this increased demand for medication. I felt giving more was a step in the wrong direction. However, Tish was a nurse and because of that, I put trust in her actions. My understanding was that she worked under the direction of Dr. Nichopoulos, so I had to assume that she was dispensing medication to Elvis only under the doctor's supervision. I could see where performing would be on Elvis's mind, perhaps making him increasingly anxious, but I wished there were some way I could encourage him to just try an alternative way to ease into sleep without relying on prescription drugs.

One morning, as Elvis called for Tish to bring him medication, I summoned up my nerve and told him, "Elvis, you don't really need that."

He looked at me and shook his head. "You don't understand," he replied. "I need it." I wondered—not for the first time—if Elvis had built up an immunity to whatever medication he'd been taking on a regular basis, and that's why he needed an increase in dosage. Whatever the case, I could only hope the medical professionals overseeing his care knew what they were doing.

The day before Elvis's next tour started, he brought me home so I could quickly pack a few things to take along. I hadn't purchased many clothes outside of the two times Elvis had sent me shopping during his Las Vegas engagement. Elvis had no idea that Terry was still loaning me some of her clothing. My mother said she would help me iron a couple of things; as she set up an ironing board in our foyer, I handed her one of Terry's garments.

While Elvis watched my mother iron, he said, "You gotta get Ginger ready. She's gonna marry me."

I blushed.

"I'm ironing as fast as I can," my mother teased, and pretended to iron faster.

Before long, with bodyguards in tow as usual, Elvis and I left for Graceland. A few minutes later, we passed some young men and women who had pulled over to the side of the road; they were obviously having car trouble.

Elvis slowed, put his window down, and asked if they needed any help.

"No," one of the women replied, then screamed as we pulled away and she recognized Elvis.

I looked back and got tickled when I saw her telling her friends. Each of them turned to look our way. This was one time I was sure they wished they'd accepted help from a stranger.

On March 23, we flew to Arizona for the start of Elvis's next tour. A couple of days later, Elvis had my brother flown in to Norman, Oklahoma, to learn the ropes as extra security. Elvis had been asking Mike about leaving his job with the fire department and coming to work for him. This was a big decision for my brother. But Elvis, as usual, was persistent and hard to turn down. Mike stayed only a couple of days, and I really didn't get a chance to spend any alone time with him, but I found myself hoping things would work out. It would be comforting to have a member of my own family on staff.

One of our stops on the tour was Louisiana, but after a few performances, Elvis told me he didn't feel well. I placed my palm to his forehead. This was the first time I'd ever seen Elvis truly look ill. He was perspiring and his head felt warm to me.

"I don't want to push myself," Elvis said, and asked me to get in touch with Dr. Nichopoulos.

Dr. Nichopoulos came to the room. He didn't tell me what was wrong, and Elvis was finally able to go to sleep. When he woke later, however, he still wasn't feeling well. Elvis told me he needed to speak with some people about his upcoming shows, so I went to my room.

Finally, after much discussion with various men in Elvis's entourage, it was decided that the tour would be canceled and Elvis would go into a hospital back home. I was very concerned about Elvis, but felt comforted by the thought that in a hospital they'd really be able to diagnose what was wrong and monitor his health.

We flew back to Memphis and went to Graceland. Elvis was going to check into Baptist Memorial Hospital. I wanted to go with him, but Elvis now said that he was feeling so bad, he'd rather have someone take me home while he went to the hospital.

This worried me even more, but he was insistent. "I'll call you from there," he promised.

Members of his entourage gathered around and they jumped into action, taking off with Elvis and leaving me at the proverbial curb.

At home, I didn't hear anything for hours. I decided to call Graceland and spoke with Aunt Delta, but she had no news. Elvis finally called me that night to say the hospital was running some tests.

He called me again the next day and said hello. He wasn't feeling any worse, thankfully, but when I said I'd like to come and see him, Elvis told me that right now he needed to go over business with some people.

I thought it was a little odd that Elvis wasn't asking me to visit with him. (Not until after Elvis's death, would I hear that when Elvis had taken ill in Baton Rouge, he was informed that three of his former bodyguards were going to publish a potentially damaging book filled with hurtful stories about him. Looking back, I strongly feel that Elvis had been discussing this book with others while he was in the hospital and didn't ask for me, because he didn't want me to know about it then. It wouldn't be until much later, that Elvis would mention the book to me.)

Elvis called the following day, too. This time he let me know he had an intestinal flu but was feeling better. "I want you to come to the hospital tomorrow and show my nurse your engagement ring," he said.

Before leaving Graceland to go home, I had tucked the ring back into my jewelry box for safekeeping. The next evening, my sister-in-law drove me over to get it. When I rang the front doorbell, Charlie answered. I stepped inside the foyer and, noticing movement in the kitchen doorway, I glanced that way and was surprised to see Lisa peeking her head out at me.

"Hi," I said.

Charlie smiled and said, "Priscilla's here, too. They're in town visiting. Would you like to meet her?"

"Sure," I said, caught totally off guard. I followed Charlie toward Dodger's bedroom. Suddenly I remembered how, when I was a child, I'd sometimes pass Graceland and imagine Elvis, Priscilla, and Lisa inside. How bizarre it was that I was here—and so was Priscilla!

I hastily reminded myself that Elvis had told me I was the "lady of the house" now, but it was still surreal to walk into Dodger's bedroom and find her in bed, with Priscilla sitting in a chair beside her.

"Hello," I greeted Dodger.

Then Charlie introduced me to Priscilla, a petite woman with chin-length hair.

I sat on a chair near the foot of the bed, and Priscilla and I began to talk. She was friendly and at ease.

I relaxed a little, figuring Priscilla must have seen Elvis with other women before me since their divorce. Maybe this situation felt more natural to her than it did to me. At any rate, she seemed like a nice person, and I was glad about that because becoming Elvis's wife would essentially mean Priscilla would be in my life, too.

At one point, we got into a conversation about dogs. I told her about Odyssey, my new Great Dane, and Priscilla said she had owned a couple of Great Danes in the past. They were great dogs, Priscilla said, very gentle.

"But don't get too attached to them," she warned. "They don't live very long."

Lisa had joined us in the room. She had been sitting on the floor, but now she stood up, walked over to me, and began playing with my hair. It was an awkward moment, to say the least.

Finally, Priscilla said, "Lisa, Ginger may not want you to do that."

I looked at Lisa and smiled. "It's all right," I said.

But Lisa obediently walked away and sat down on the floor again.

I suddenly remembered that Elvis was waiting for me; my thoughts returned to getting my ring. But how could I make a graceful exit? It hardly seemed like good manners to jump up and say, "Excuse me, but I have to go get my engagement ring."

At last, I decided to keep it simple. "I just stopped by to get something," I told Priscilla. "It was nice to meet you."

Then I said good-bye to Lisa and Dodger, rushed upstairs, retrieved my ring, and quickly left the house.

At the hospital, I was relieved to find Elvis looking better and in good spirits. He called his nurse into the room and proudly showed her my ring.

After the nurse left, he said, "Priscilla's in town."

"I know. I just met her," I said, and explained about stopping by Graceland to get my ring.

Elvis laughed. "I wish I could have seen that," he said. Then, after I'd told him that Priscilla and I had talked a little, he seemed to approve. "It's important that Priscilla and you are friendly for Lisa's sake," he said.

He would be leaving the hospital soon, Elvis added, and Priscilla and Lisa were coming to see him. Not ready for what could be another awkward encounter, I stayed just a short while longer and then left.

After Elvis left the hospital, he had a little over two weeks before his next tour began. Lisa remained at Graceland for a few days and, weather permitting, she was often outside, driving around in a pale blue golf cart with her name written on its side, a birthday gift from Elvis. Lisa would come into Elvis's bedroom sometimes, always curious to see what he and I were doing. You could see Elvis's joy when she was around.

During this visit with his daughter, Elvis took Lisa and me out for a ride on one of his three-wheelers for the first time. It was a cycle with one wheel in the front, two in the back, and a passenger seat. With Lisa sandwiched between us, we rode to the airport and looked at planes.

Lisa loved being at Graceland, and I was glad she and I had gotten to be around each other a little. When it was time for her to return to Los Angeles, Lisa didn't want to leave; she hid and the bodyguards had to look for her, eventually finding her near the meditation garden.

Elvis just wanted to spend the rest of the time before the tour relaxing. Late one night, he decided he wanted to take a small group of us to see the new Peter Sellers film, *The Pink Panther Strikes Again*. He rented a theater for the viewing and it was a wild feeling to walk in, knowing we had the entire theater to ourselves. Elvis and I took seats in the center of the auditorium, with the rest of the people in our group either sitting in the same row or behind us.

When everyone was settled in, Elvis looked over his shoulder toward the projectionist, and shouted, "Roll 'em!"

Before I knew it, we were all in hysterics. That film turned out to be one of my all-time favorite comedies.

But the jovial mood would be interrupted a few days later when Elvis and I were sitting in his bedroom talking when the commode in his bathroom began to make a noise. It was very early in the morning. As we talked, the noise continued. Elvis glanced toward the bathroom every few minutes, clearly becoming increasingly annoyed.

Before long, he quietly got up and left the room. He returned moments later with a machine gun in his hand. I thought I must be imagining things as Elvis walked right past me with the gun and went into the bathroom.

"Elvis, what are you doing?" I screamed.

He answered with a deafening barrage of gunfire, blasting his toilet to smithereens.

This was upsetting and completely unacceptable. I was more shocked than anything else by this action. I felt a cool stillness come over me.

Then I got angry, really angry. How could he think that this was okay?

Sometimes it seemed like Elvis was playing a game of "see what I can do" in order to watch people's reactions. His cousin Billy would later say in a book that he thought this was funny. It wasn't. I decided to leave before Elvis could exit the bathroom.

As I hastily descended the front stairs into the foyer, I glanced up and saw water running from the ceiling onto the chandelier. I walked out the front door and got into my car. My hands were shaking on the wheel as I drove home. I could only hope that, by leaving Graceland, I might be sending a message to Elvis that this sort of behavior wasn't right.

I had hoped to enter my parents' house quietly, without disturbing anyone, but as I pulled into the driveway, our dogs started barking and woke my mother. I never wanted to burden her, as she and my dad had enough going on with work and their marital problems, but I couldn't hide my feelings. I was too rattled.

My mother tried to comfort me as I told her what happened. I also explained the incidents in Palm Springs and Hawaii that had troubled me. I had kept these events from her before, but now everything came spilling out. She couldn't believe it and was clearly disheartened.

"I don't want you being in any situation where you could get hurt by someone else," she said, adding no matter who the person was, I came first.

I knew she wanted to protect me, but I explained how strongly I felt that Elvis would never really hurt me. At the same time, I had come home because I needed to clear my head and touch base with all the goodness in Elvis and everything that had drawn me to him.

My mother could see that I was trying to work things out. "Whatever you decide to do, I'll support you," she said at last.

We both left it at that and went to our rooms. I lay in bed for a little while, worrying that Elvis might come over. I wasn't ready to talk. He wouldn't like me walking out on him—I could predict that based on his reaction in Hawaii when I left while he was talking to me—but I couldn't just sit by and let him do something that I saw as terribly wrong.

I eventually fell asleep. When I woke up that afternoon, I went over the event again with Rosemary. I hadn't heard from Elvis. I didn't think my message about his behavior would sink in if I called him first—I definitely felt Elvis owed me an apology—so Rosemary and I went to see some friends.

By the time we returned home later that night, my mother said Elvis had called. When she told him Rosemary and I were out, he had asked to speak with Terry. She had told him Terry was on a college campus in another city, fulfilling a duty as Miss Tennessee, and they hung up. I waited for Elvis to call again, worried about how our conversation might go, but I heard nothing more from him that night.

The following day, Terry returned home. The minute she saw me, she asked, "What's going on with you and Elvis?"

Startled, I asked how she knew something was up.

"I was sitting in an auditorium last night when a state trooper came in and told me I had a phone call," she said. "I thought something terrible must have happened to someone, so I followed the state trooper outside."

The trooper led my sister across a field and into an administrative building with a couple of security guards. "One of them handed me a phone, and Elvis was on the line. He sounded angry, saying that he'd like me to come to Graceland so he could talk about you."

I couldn't believe what I was hearing! It sounded like Elvis was making this situation out to be my fault. He had no right to be angry at me. I wasn't the one who'd done something wrong!

"He wanted to send his plane for me," Terry continued, "but I told him I couldn't leave because of the event, plus I had driven Tony's mother up there with me. Elvis told me to let Tony's mother drive the car home, but I told him she had bad eyesight and it was an eight-hour drive."

Apparently, Elvis hadn't taken no for an answer easily. Terry said it was awkward, as she had to keep saying, "Elvis, I can't," in front of the security guards, who had remained in the room.

"When I got off the phone," Terry added, "the guards asked me if that was really Elvis." Terry said she was completely rattled by the call and couldn't wait to get home.

Did Elvis really not understand why I'd left? Did his stance that "no one walks out on Elvis" obscure his ability to see the issue at hand clearly?

I certainly didn't want to break up with him, but I sincerely wanted Elvis to understand why I had reacted the way I did. Hearing that Elvis had called Terry and sounded angry upset me. I decided not to call him just yet.

The following day, one of Elvis's aides called to ask me to come to Graceland. I thought things over. I wanted our relationship to work. I still felt Elvis owed me an apology. Then I remembered that he had tried to reach me that first night. Maybe he was trying to apologize after all, I thought, so I went to Graceland.

When I arrived, Elvis was seated in his bed with *The Prophet* lying open in his lap. I noticed that a new toilet had been installed in the bathroom. It looked as though nothing out of the ordinary had gone on here.

I sat down quietly beside him and waited, knowing *The Prophet* was one of the books he relied on for words of comfort and wisdom, especially about love.

Elvis turned to me and began quoting a passage from the book, saying, "You know, Ginger, 'When love beckons to you, follow him, Though his ways are hard and steep. And when his wings enfold you yield to him, Though the sword hidden among his pinions may wound you.'"

With love had come hurt, definitely, but Elvis had been going through his books to find an answer. I understood that he had chosen this passage to convey his emotions to me. Elvis and I were learning about love together. Whether through the lyrics of a song or words from a book, I knew this was Elvis's way of trying to have me understand him sometimes.

Nobody at the house—not the maids, Aunt Delta, Charlie, or the aides—ever asked me why Elvis shot his toilet, leading me to believe that Elvis must have said something to them. Either that, or they had simply witnessed incidents similar to this one before and were used to it by now.

CHAPTER 21

Elvis's tour was scheduled to begin on April 21. We would be on the road for almost two weeks. This was longer than what I'd experienced before, but, as always, I was excited about visiting cities I'd never seen. Our stops would include Greensboro, North Carolina; Detroit and Ann Arbor, Michigan; Toledo, Ohio; and Milwaukee, Wisconsin.

Every so often on this tour, Elvis would complain about feeling bloated, but otherwise he seemed to be in good spirits. His eyes continued to bother him after some shows; as usual, I placed a warm washcloth over them to help soothe the irritation.

Concerned about his audiences, many times while we were backstage, Elvis would ask someone to describe what the crowd was like before he went on. After one performance, he said to me, "Man, there were some people in the first three rows who looked like they were sleeping. What are they, dead?"

I knew he was very sensitive about making his fans happy, and I tried to reassure him. "Elvis, it was only a couple of people," I said. "I'm sure they loved the show."

Elvis varied the songs in each show, and you never knew what to expect; he would feed off of the audience's reaction and banter with people. He had more energy for some shows than others, but Elvis always put his heart and soul into delivering the best possible entertainment.

At the end of a performance in Milwaukee, however, there was a small mishap. Elvis exited the stage and, blinded by multiple camera flashes, he fell on the stairs and sprained his ankle. He was piqued when he got into the car and remained angry once back in his room. Dr. Nichopoulos wrapped Elvis's ankle (which unfortunately would cause him problems at future shows), and later when we were alone, he said, "People just aren't doing their jobs." Frustrated, he told me that a bodyguard named Dick "wasn't where he was supposed to be," and then he declared, "I'm getting rid of Dick, Joe, and a whole lot more!"

I knew Elvis was in a bad mood because of his ankle hurting him, but I knew there was another recent incident that caused him to express displeasure with a few in his staff: A girl had broken through the crowd and reached Elvis, purposely scratching his hand and making him bleed. Elvis had gotten angry and later complained to me about some in his entourage then too.

Finally settling down for the night and resting as comfortably as he could with his injured ankle, Elvis decided to invite my mother and sisters to come to Duluth, Minnesota. I knew the reason Elvis wanted my mother to join us: A few weeks before this tour, in a somber mood one day, I had confided to Elvis that my father had moved out of our house. I could tell by the look on his face then that this news had bothered him. Elvis had been continually asking me whether my parents were shopping for a new home. They hadn't been looking, but each time he'd brought the subject up, I'd just told him, "No, they haven't found anything they like." I didn't want to hurt his feelings. A house was obviously a huge gift, too big a present and my parents had expressed to me that they felt awkward about Elvis's offer on more than one occasion.

Although he was aware that my father had moved out, Elvis still had his mind set on buying a new home for my family and at the beginning of this tour, he had brought the subject up again, telling me, "I want to talk to your mother about it. I'm gonna invite her and your sisters to see some shows." I couldn't believe that in the middle of a tour, Elvis was thinking about my family.

My mother and Rosemary agreed to come, but Terry was unable to make it. He asked them to stop by Graceland to pick up a brace for his ankle, which a nurse would leave for them. Elvis chartered a Learjet out of Nashville to fly my mother, Rosemary, and a girlfriend of Ricky's out of Memphis.

My family arrived safely, and before the Duluth show, Elvis invited my mother and Rosemary into his room, where they gave him the ankle brace he had requested. Elvis asked how their flight was.

"Good," my mother answered. "At one point, the pilot told us we were flying at forty-seven thousand feet."

Elvis wasn't happy hearing this. He told my mother they never should have flown that high, because the plane could have popped rivets. "I won't use that company again," he said.

My mother and sister toured with us for a few days. Elvis invited them to ride in the limo with us, which displaced a few of the staff who usually traveled with him. I hoped this didn't bother anyone. Sometimes, members of his entourage had to take a shuttle bus from the airplane to the hotel, and once, when my family was directed onto the bus, Elvis quickly ditched the limo and we rode the bus, with Elvis squatting down in the aisle so he could talk with my mother.

When we'd returned to our hotel after Elvis's show in Chicago, he was ready to talk with my mother about looking at homes and the situation with my father. I left the room to get her and Rosemary, passing Colonel Parker as he entered the suite.

The colonel usually flew out ahead of us, landing in the next city to make sure everything was in order before Elvis performed. I still hadn't been around him enough to get a feel for who he really was. At one point, however, I had arrived in a city and entered our hotel suite, where I was surprised to see the colonel standing by a mobile cart, wearing a chef's hat and stirring a pot of soup.

There were times when Elvis expressed displeasure with his manager, feeling the colonel chose hotels too far away from the performance venues, and all because they had better food. Once, while we were riding to a show, Elvis asked, "Can't the colonel find anything closer?"

On another occasion, I had left the room so Elvis could talk privately with Colonel Parker. When I returned, Elvis was shaking his head in amazement. "I was sitting here telling him I had a sore throat, and all he was talking about was the next tour," he said.

I brought Rosemary and my mother into the suite and a few minutes later, Elvis and the colonel exited his bedroom. Elvis introduced my family to Colonel Parker, and when the colonel turned his back to walk away, Elvis gave a contemptuous wave of his hand, motioning him out of the suite.

The three of us followed Elvis back into his bedroom and he closed the door. "How are you doing?" my mother asked him.

Since his eyes had been bothering him a little, Elvis mentioned that, then invited her to sit beside him on the bed. Diving right in, he asked what she thought would be the best solution to her marital problems.

I knew this would be uncomfortable for her to discuss, but it would probably be good for her to talk with someone.

Telling Elvis now that she was completely drained emotionally, my mother said it looked like a divorce was the only solution.

"Is it the best solution, or the last alternative?" Elvis asked her.

"I'm afraid it's the best solution," she said.

Charlie knocked on the door, came in, and mentioned that Milo High was waiting at the airport to take Rosemary and my mother home so he could return again to pick up the colonel and take him where he needed to be.

Clearly unhappy about this interruption, however, Elvis shot Charlie a look and he left. Elvis then continued their conversation.

"If there's no chance of you working things out," Elvis told my mother, "I'd like you to see my lawyer, Beecher Smith, when you get home, and I'd like to pay for the divorce."

I remembered Beecher from the signing of Elvis's will. We were all stunned that Elvis wanted to get involved like this, but my mother thanked him graciously.

Before long, there was another knock on the door. Charlie stepped inside and reminded Elvis that Milo was waiting. It was obvious that Elvis was getting even more annoyed. As if trying to avoid any further interruption, he said, "Let's finish the conversation in Ginger's room."

We left his room and entered mine, where Elvis sat on the bed with my mother. He asked if she would still like to look for a new house. She thanked him, but said she was happy where she was.

Elvis pondered this for a minute, then told her, "Mrs. Alden, I know you won't be financially able to pay the house note and other expenses on your own. If you're happy in that house, I want to pay for it. You don't need a mortgage and your home will stay in your name."

I noticed my mother's eyes getting misty. Elvis then surprised us even more by adding, "I'd also like you to have a swimming pool and some landscaping done. You don't have any trees. You need trees."

Elvis was on a roll and we were swept up by his enthusiasm. Again, my mother thanked him.

Elvis asked what she thought my dad would want from the divorce, and my mother said our father would probably want his fair share of the equity in the house.

Now there was a knock on my door. When I opened it, Charlie was standing there.

Before he could speak, Elvis shouted, "Charlie, it's my damn plane, and I'll send it when I'm damn good and ready!"

Charlie made an about-face and left.

Putting his arm around my mother's shoulder, Elvis said then, "Don't worry. I'll see that my father takes care of everything."

Elvis's jeweler, Lowell, was along on the trip. Elvis called him into our suite at that point and gave my mom and Rosemary each a beautiful diamond ring. The two of them were flown home on his JetStar shortly afterward. The deep compassion and personal concern Elvis was showing for my mother's welfare deeply touched me to the core.

Elvis finished his last concert that April in Saginaw, Michigan. We flew back to Memphis then, where he would have a little over two weeks off until his next tour began on May 20.

The conversation with my mother was still on his mind. One day, Elvis told me he had spoken with his father to set things in motion regarding my mother's divorce and paying off our home. Elvis asked me to have my mother call Beecher Smith.

"Thank you," I said, and promised I would. I appreciated his offer to pay off my mother's mortgage, knowing how much it would mean to her to have that financial burden lifted, especially now that she was facing the harsh reality of making ends meet on her own.

Arriving at Graceland a few days later, I found Elvis finishing a conversation on his bedside phone. When he hung up, Elvis told me he'd been talking to Vernon, who had filed for a divorce from his wife, Dee. Elvis told me they had been trying to work out a settlement.

I was surprised to hear this; since Vernon was engaged to Sandy, I had naturally assumed he was already divorced. This was the first time I'd ever heard Elvis talk about his stepmother.

"My daddy used to come home from work and be tired, and Dee would have some entertainer or other people in the house," Elvis said, looking irritated.

I knew that Elvis was worried about his dad's health as well as the divorce. I placed my hand on his back, trying to calm him a little. "I hope everything works out okay."

"She better leave my daddy alone," Elvis said.

The specter of divorce was swirling around us: My parents, Vernon, and even one of Elvis's stepbrothers were all having marital problems. This was affecting both of us. Still, when it came to our own relationship, our love for each other continued to burn bright and our enthusiasm hadn't dimmed. Elvis still believed strongly in marriage and clearly wanted to get married again. I felt the same way: I wanted to be a wife and mother, and I believed if you were meant to be together and stay together, you would.

A short while later, Elvis got up from bed and began rummaging through a closet in his bedroom. He came across various hats and showed them to me, then pulled out a poster-size photo of himself taken when he was little. In the photo, he was standing between his parents, wearing overalls and a hat.

As he held the picture up to show me, Elvis stuck out his lower lip in a little-boy pout. "I was two and had a peanut in my mouth," he said.

"Now that's a 'Little Two,'" I teased, alluding to one of the nicknames he'd given me.

Elvis propped the picture on a chair, facing the bed, and asked, "Does this bother you?"

"No," I said. I wondered if the conversation about his dad had prompted him to seek out this particular photo. It would remain on the chair until the next day.

Now that the weather was warmer, Elvis would sometimes tell me we were going out on his motorcycle, but then we'd end up reading or watching television for a while. I didn't mind waiting; however, it got my hopes up. I'd remind him later and he would then say he was tired or just didn't feel like it, and I'd end up disappointed.

As this pattern repeated itself a few times, I began to think that Elvis just might not ever leave his house. He rarely left the upstairs floor. I remember one night, Elvis asked me, "Who's downstairs?"

"I saw Ricky downstairs with a girl," I replied.

"I don't want to go down, then," he said. Upstairs, Elvis was usually wearing something casual or his pajamas. He didn't feel comfortable going downstairs in front of strangers unless his hair was styled and he was dressed a certain way, and he was too polite to ask anyone to leave, so Elvis had effectively set up a world where he wasn't going downstairs in his own home.

He had everything he needed upstairs at Graceland: his office, organ, televisions, beds, Lisa's room, and bathrooms. Food, or anything else he might want, would appear at the touch of a button. What's more, being on the road for so many years had led Elvis to become accustomed to eating in bed or at a coffee table.

Did I wish Elvis went downstairs more, sat in the Jungle Room, ate at the dining table, or went outside more? Sometimes, sure, but I thought that would come in time. I was young and flexible, and wherever Elvis was, that's where I wanted to be.

Other times, Elvis would surprise me by deciding he wanted to go out and we would spontaneously go somewhere.

One night, Elvis said he wanted to show me the house in Tupelo where he was born. I got super excited about seeing the house. This would be another little piece of the puzzle of Elvis's life, and I was happy he wanted to share it with me.

As we passed time reading and watching television, I began worrying that Elvis would change his mind again. Fortunately, he didn't. Elvis eventually asked Billy Smith to get the motorcycles ready and invited him to come along with his wife.

The four of us left Graceland and headed toward Tupelo with bodyguards following. We had been riding on the highway for quite a while when Elvis took an exit before Hernando, Mississippi, and proceeded through a small town.

I looked back and noticed Billy and Jo were no longer behind us. I told Elvis, and we circled back around to look for them. They were standing by their motorcycle at the side of the highway. When we pulled up to them, we saw their motorcycle had an oil leak. Jo was splattered with motor oil.

Elvis suddenly decided not to continue. "We'll go another time," he said as we headed back to Graceland. I so wished Elvis had wanted to go on that night, and sadly, we never would get the chance to make it to Tupelo before Elvis passed away.

More and more I learned that Elvis liked pampering, as we all do. He occasionally asked me to shave him in bed or requested that I help him with his socks. His socks weren't always easy to get on. One night when I was trying to help him dress, I got down on the floor, rolled a sock in my hand, and began pulling it onto his foot. I had such a tough time that I started to laugh and Elvis did, too.

All the wishes that I make
Are made right from my heart,
But still, Sweetheart, they only tell
My love in just a part...
So as you read this Valentine
Here's what you'll have to do —
To each wish add a million more,
Each filled with love for you!

*Ginger
All My
Love
E —*

Left: One of four Valentine's Day cards Elvis surprised me with on tour in February of 1977. His special personal note to me is written inside.

Photo courtesy of Ginger Alden

Below: The Cadillac Seville Elvis gifted me with after his father didn't want it. I so loved this car!

Photo courtesy of Terry Alden

Elvis singing to my sister Rosemary on the beach in Hawaii.

Photo courtesy of Ginger Alden

My sister Terry, Elvis, and me having a great time while relaxing on the beach in Hawaii. *Photo courtesy of Rosemary Alden*

Left: An employee contact list from late April 1977. On this tour, Elvis had invited many people to see his shows, including my mother, my sister Rosemary, Elvis's cousins, and the wives and girlfriends of some of Elvis's family and staff.

Photo courtesy of Ginger Alden

Below: A hotel list on which Elvis wrote, "Come back here," shortly before I left a tour for a few days in May of 1977.

Photo courtesy of Ginger Alden

TCB — Taking Care of Business

May 1st
1124 Ginger

Elvis Presley Staff   City: Chicago, ILL.

1. Joe Esposito — 1114
2. Dick Grob — 1116
3. Sam Thompson — 1117 X
4. Charles Hodge — 1106
5. Lamar Fike — 1110
6. Al Strada — 1108
7. David Stanley — 1111 X
8. Dean Nichopoulos — 1107 X
9. Rick Stanley — 1104
10. Dr. Nick — 1126
11. ~~Ed Parker~~
12. Larry Geller — 1102
13. Mrs. Alden — Rosemary — 1103
14. Billy Smith — Jo — 1109
15. Lowell Hays — 1105
16.

Security — 1127
Wardrobe — 1125

Room To Room Dial Room Number
Room Service Dial "7370" until 4:00 am

Remarks: Advise Security Room - 1127 - For House Keeping. All Nite Movies = Cinema Keys in Rooms

ELVIS PRESLEY ENTERPRISES • 3764 ELVIS PRESLEY BLVD. • MEMPHIS, TENNESSEE 38116

Mobile   Show— —Sheraton Inn
               301 Government St., Hwy.
               (205) 438-3431

Providence   Hilton Inn
               1150 Narragansett Blvd.
               Cranston, R.I.
               (401) 467-8800

Augusta   Sheraton Inn
               363 Maine Mall Road, Exit 7
               Portland (South), Me. 04106
               (207) 775-6161

Rochester   Show— Hilton Inn on Campus
               175 Jefferson Rd.
               (716) 436-0520

Binghamton   Binghamton Treadway Hotel
               8 Hawley Street
               (607) 722-1212

Philadelphia   The Baltimore Hilton   *← COME BACK HERE*
Baltimore   The Baltimore Hilton

Jacksonville   Jacksonville Hilton
               565 South Main St.
               Jacksonville
               (904) 398-3561

Baton Rouge   Show— — — —Baton Rouge Hilton   *Tuesday night*
               5500 Hilton Ave.
               (504) 923-2323

Macon   Macon Hilton   *Wednesday night*
               180 First St.
               (912) 746-1461

Elvis leaving our hotel, with me in front followed by Joe Esposito and Sam Thompson. We were heading for the Macon Coliseum in Georgia on June 1, 1977.

Photo courtesy of Keith Alverson

My magnificent diamond TLC necklace that Elvis had made for me. It stood for *tender loving care* . . .

Photo courtesy of Ginger Alden

Lisa Presley and my niece Amber in the summer of 1977 in the music room of my parents' home in Memphis. Lisa enjoyed playing around on the piano. *Photo courtesy of Ginger Alden*

Me and my Great Dane, Odyssey, in July of 1977 at Audubon Park in Memphis. He was my "gentle giant." *Photo courtesy of Terry Alden*

Elvis's ninth-degree black belt karate certificate, which he picked out and gave to me for no special reason while we were walking through his trophy room one day. He told me he didn't want to try for the rank of tenth degree because "there was nowhere to go after that." *Photo courtesy of Ginger Alden*

Elvis and me leaving the Market Square Arena in Indianapolis, Indiana, on June 26, 1977. This was the last concert Elvis would perform on tour.

Photo courtesy of Keith Alverson

> GOD GAVE ME TO YOU!
> HE GAVE YOU TO ME

Elvis's beautiful words that he wrote to me on the back of a photo while visiting my parents' home on August 6, 1977.

Photo courtesy of Ginger Alden

Elvis, Lisa, and me returning to Graceland on August 12, 1977, after a private screening of the movie *The Spy Who Loved Me*.

Photo courtesy of Shantay Wood

I've thanked our God for choosing me
To share in a part of your life
Though our time together was very short
I would soon have been your wife

I treasure every moment we've spent together
And I'll always remember your ways
I only wish I could have met you sooner
When you were singing in your earlier days

But God must have planned it all along
And chose this time for us to meet
Maybe we both had to learn about life
So that we could fill each others needs

And if the moment ever comes
that I can see you once again
I'll walk up very gingerly
And gently take your hand

I'll look deep into your eyes
No words will need to be spoken
Though we'll have been apart for quite sometime
Our bond of love will never have been broken

I'll gaze at you so proudly
Thinking of all thats left undone
We can start from the beginning
For our lives will have just begun

Then I'll say a prayer to our God
And thank him once again
For giving me eternal life
with my love & my best friend.

A poem I wrote not long after Elvis passed away.   *Photo courtesy of Ginger Alden*

"Here, let me do it," he said, finally managing to pull it on.

I saw pampering as trying to do little things for Elvis that would not only feel nice but could be good for him at the same time. I brought him dried fruit, thinking that would be a healthy snack. Sometimes, Elvis picked at it, which was a step in the right direction.

On occasion, I had mentioned wanting to play racquetball or go horseback riding with him, but he'd made the same excuses he sometimes gave if I asked about riding his motorcycle: He just "didn't want to do it right now" or felt too tired.

Undeterred, I kept trying. I knew Graceland had a swimming pool on one side of the house, but in all our months together, I had yet to see it up close. Thinking this might be a way to get Elvis out, one night I mentioned that I'd love to see his pool.

"I'll show it to you," he said.

Yes! We stepped outside the back door of Graceland. Luckily, it was a nice spring evening. Elvis took my hand and led me down a walkway. We soon came to a kidney-shaped swimming pool, but Elvis continued right past it and took me to an area he called his "meditation garden."

"I had this built a few years back," he said.

"This is so beautiful, Elvis," I observed, looking around.

It was a lovely, peaceful place, surrounded by a curved brick wall with stained glass panels inset into its arched openings. In the garden's center, water splashed in a circular fountain pool enclosed by an ornate wrought-iron fence.

Elvis walked me over to some chairs by the pool, where the two of us sat down amid the tranquil surroundings.

After a few minutes, Elvis broke the silence. "I'd really like to perform in Europe. Can you imagine if I went to England? I'd have to sing from a cage. I'd need more security than the president!"

It had never dawned on me before that Elvis hadn't ever performed in another country. I thought of him as so well traveled, and he was so beloved worldwide that it seemed impossible he'd never sung in Europe. I had been gazing at the pool; now I looked up and caught Elvis looking over at me.

"You know," he said softly, "my daddy told me that, since we met, it was the first time he saw the little boy he put overalls on back in East Tupelo."

I saw the warmth in his eyes and felt overcome, knowing this was Elvis's way of saying his father approved of us.

"My mother always told me to marry a brown-eyed girl," he went on. "She said they'd be more faithful."

This was the first time Elvis really talked about Gladys Presley with me. I was glad to hear him bring her up; I was eager to learn more about Elvis's past, particularly his childhood.

"I really wish I could have met her," I said, hoping to encourage him to talk more about his mother.

"She would have liked you," Elvis said, then fell silent again for a moment before adding, "I really want to have more children. I'd like us to have a little boy."

"A boy would be great," I agreed. My brother was quite a bit older than me, so I was used to girls, having sisters and nieces; I'd always wondered what it would be like to have a little boy around. I was mainly happy to know that Elvis wanted children with me as much as I wanted to have a child with him.

Elvis brought up a name he liked then, mentioning Jesse for a boy. I remembered this was the name that had been given to his twin brother.

"How about Grace Lynn for a girl's name?" I ventured.

He liked that name, too. "When the time is right, God will let me know," he said with a soft smile, as if wanting to reassure me once again.

We returned to the house a little while later, where Elvis said, "I'd like to change some things. Has your brother said anything to you about working for me?"

I told Elvis that leaving the fire department was a difficult decision for my brother to make right now. I explained that Mike had two daughters to take care of and a pension. I knew he couldn't just jump ship, because the decision would affect his whole family.

"Tell him the offer stands and he'll be taken care of," Elvis said.

Our tranquil days and nights were occasionally interrupted by Elvis's mood swings. One night, Elvis and I were watching television in Lisa's bedroom when a program came on that Elvis didn't care for. He started making comments about it, then suddenly left the room. He returned with a gun and shot the television.

Why didn't he just change the channel? I thought in exasperation.

Quickly looking over at me, as if to say oops, Elvis started laughing and cursing about the program. At least he recognized that this was something I wasn't comfortable with. Still, I wondered what I should do now.

Walking out on Elvis last time hadn't produced the desired result, so I decided to stay. If this was a test, I was hanging in there.

On another occasion down the road, he shot the phone in Lisa's room when it buzzed and disturbed him. Again, I didn't leave. But I did begin to think there must be a shed somewhere out back, stockpiled with television sets and telephones.

I didn't like this behavior, but I loved Elvis. The big question was how I could find a way to make him see that he shouldn't do this sort of thing.

Luckily, the phone-shooting incident would be the last one that happened while we were together. As time went on, I began to think that maybe I'd gotten through to him after all.

From the start of our relationship, I had willingly given up my job, my hobbies, and spending time with family and friends to accommodate

Elvis's schedule and desires. I had loved being caught up in Elvis's magical, whirlwind world, and I was passionate about building our new life together at Graceland. Now, as our relationship continued to grow and strengthen, I began feeling more comfortable and able to express myself and I wanted to incorporate my own passions into our life together. Elvis had shown how he felt about me in his way and now I hoped to use my talent to help him see even more how he was in my heart and mind.

Elvis and I had read so much about numerology that I was now intrigued by the possibility of numbers correlating to certain events in our lives. I also liked the idea that certain colors or gemstones could be lucky for us.

I wanted to design a necklace Elvis could wear onstage, one that would incorporate our numbers, four and eight. Elvis loved the idea, so I began a few sketches, keeping them at Graceland to work on periodically. It felt great to be doing something artistic; I hadn't had time to do much drawing, and I still loved it.

Having always been interested in karate, I asked Elvis to teach me some beginning steps and stances. He was happy to oblige me one night. I pestered him a little as he was teaching me. I wanted to learn fancier, more advanced moves, but Elvis kept telling me to start at the beginning.

We finally stopped to rest at one point. He sat on the bed and I put my feet up against the bottoms of his.

The next thing I knew, I was on the floor. I think his strength actually shocked him, because Elvis burst out laughing. "Are you all right?" he asked.

I had to laugh, too, as I stood up and rubbed my hip. "Yes."

With a knowing look, Elvis said, "Ginger, always start at the beginning. Be patient and learn."

Impressed by this simple display of skill, I decided to take his advice. I also felt it was time to get to know his family some more, as they would be my family too one day, so I began extending myself to them, starting with Dodger.

Elvis loved his grandmother. I always followed him in to say a quick hello to Dodger whenever the two of us were entering or leaving Graceland together. One time after we'd stopped in to see her for a few minutes, he said, "We should visit with her more."

One afternoon, Elvis was asleep and I decided to visit Dodger on my own. I went to her room and knocked on her door. When Dodger invited me in, I found her seated in bed.

"I just wanted to say hello," I said.

Right away, Dodger's conversation turned to her grandson. "I'm so proud of Elvis," she said. "You know, Gladys was a strong mother. She worried about Elvis. When he was small, she saw him and another little boy fighting, and Gladys ran out with a broom to chase the other boy away. Gladys even had Red West up against the wall with a kitchen knife once, for saying something about Elvis."

I wasn't familiar with this name at the time, so I politely nodded and encouraged her to go on. Dodger told me that Gladys sometimes cooked fish in the house; Elvis hated the smell of it and that's why he hated fish now. I had learned this earlier on tour, too, when an aide asked what I wanted for dinner and I told him fried shrimp. As the bodyguard, Sam, brought Elvis and me our food that evening, he had said to me, "Good luck eating that in front of Elvis."

Elvis didn't say a word when I first began to eat, but then he asked me to prop the container's top up so he couldn't see my food. When I told Sam this later, he said, "I can't believe you ate that in front of him."

It was nice talking with Dodger. She was sweet, opinionated, and funny. Best of all, she seemed as eager for me to marry Elvis as I was. Dodger told me that she loved me and hoped Elvis and I would have a little boy. "I was tired of seeing that blond stuff come down the stairs," she said.

I wasn't sure who she was talking about, but Dodger was the first person to really make me feel like part of the family.

I mustered up the courage that same day to go out back and visit Vernon, too. When I walked into his office, he was at his desk and Patsy Gambill was at hers.

"Hello," I said, and we exchanged a few pleasantries. I was there for just a few minutes, because Vernon looked busy and I didn't want to interrupt him. It wasn't a long visit, but at least it was a start.

CHAPTER 22

By now it was the middle of May and getting close to the next tour. As before, Elvis seemed anxious about his upcoming performances. He started again asking for more medication to help him get back to sleep whenever he woke up.

For the first time, I learned from his nurse, Tish, that she sometimes gave him placebos. This meant Elvis had unknowingly been going to sleep at times without as much help, which I found comforting to hear. Once again, I wondered if Elvis's dependency on medication to fall asleep was more in his head.

On the other hand, I also saw that Elvis was sometimes wakeful after taking a packet. It was difficult for me to know whether his insomnia was so chronic that the medication didn't work when they gave him a regular dosage, or whether he'd just been given a placebo then. This was something I definitely wasn't qualified to judge.

I had another concern as well. I wondered if this medication could be harmful to Elvis in the long run. A few times, it seemed clear to me that it had affected his mood and behavior in negative ways.

Sometimes a nurse named Marian Cocke also visited and would dispense medications to Elvis. It wasn't clear to me why since Tish was living on the grounds. I would learn after Elvis passed away, that she was a private-duty nurse and friendly with Dr. Nichopoulos, who continued to stop by Graceland to check on Elvis as well and sometimes administered medications to Elvis himself. On occasion, there would be give-and-take between the two men, the result of Elvis expressing what he wanted for sleep and what Dr. Nichopoulos thought he should have. There were times when the doctor told Elvis he didn't need any more, which I agreed with.

I continued to wonder how, with nurses and Dr. Nichopoulos tending to him both at home and on tour, Elvis had gotten to a point in his life where he was so dependent on this sleep medication. Because I had once seen Elvis forget to take a packet and fall asleep, I thought it would have been great for his doctor to do an experiment and just not give Elvis any medication for a night or two. I would have helped him with that.

But this never happened in my presence. Dr. Nichopoulos seemed to be trying to manage the situation, rather than create a final confrontation or intervention.

Once, shortly after Dr. Nichopoulos had left Graceland, Elvis mentioned to me that the doctor owed him a lot of money. He didn't go into any detail at the time, as if it was just another thing he wanted me to know. However, a thought crossed my mind then: Was this why Dr. Nichopoulos had not drawn a line in the sand when it came to curtailing Elvis's sleep medication? Was he afraid of losing his job with Elvis?

The next tour started on May 20 in Knoxville, Tennessee, and would end on June 2 in Mobile, Alabama. At one point during the tour,

Elvis and I were sitting in a car on our way to an airport to travel to the next city. A song I liked came on the radio, and I softly began to sing along.

One of the lyrics was, "Make love to me tonight." As I sang this, Elvis tapped me on the leg and motioned toward our driver. Apparently he was afraid the driver might overhear me.

Embarrassed, I stopped singing. Did Elvis think singing that song made me look less than proper? I was aware of the irony here. For someone whose image was based on sex appeal, Elvis was surprisingly conservative and protective of how others saw me. Perhaps this was also the image of me he preferred to hold on to for himself: as young, innocent, and inexperienced in many ways, which I certainly was. He was old-fashioned that way, despite the rock-'n'-roll and Hollywood life he had personally experienced.

Elvis had come of age in the 1950s and it was now the spring of 1977. I was just out of my teens. Despite being somewhat of a tomboy, I was not a feminist. I identified more as a southern belle who liked car doors being opened for me and other chivalrous, gentlemanly gestures. About the only feminist advance that directly touched my life was being able to wear pants in high school. I simply hadn't paid much attention to politics at that time, and although Elvis watched the news, he didn't typically talk about politics either.

Despite being older than I was, Elvis was still strikingly handsome in his very early forties. But he was human, like we all are, and I suspected he was sensitive at times. I really thought it was unfair how tabloids sometimes printed unflattering photos of Elvis taken from certain angles while he was onstage. My suspicions that he might feel sensitive about his looks were confirmed when Billy Smith once told me not to ever show Elvis any unflattering photos of himself. I would never do that, but I wondered if he were speaking from experience.

One particular night caused me to wonder what it must be like for Elvis to be constantly faced with his younger self in movies and magazines. He had arrived at my house, where he wanted to go straight to Rosemary's room despite the late hour.

"Let's get Rosemary up!" he said with his usual boyish enthusiasm, walking down the hall and flipping on the light in her room. She woke and blinked hard as Elvis took a seat on her bed.

Elvis started talking to her and then lay down on his stomach, asking me to massage his back. While I did this, he noticed some albums sitting on the floor beside Rosemary's bed and started flipping through them.

When he came across one of his own albums, *Elvis: The Sun Sessions*, he stopped and pulled it from the stack. The cover was illustrated with a picture of a young Elvis standing on his toes, in mid-movement, microphone in one hand and a guitar hanging from a strap around his neck.

I wondered what was going through his mind as Elvis carefully studied the album for a few moments. Shortly, I got my answer: "I like that," he said, then placed it back among the others.

Elvis didn't look drastically different to me at forty-two than he had back when he was my age. He was simply older. But it was still hard to believe I was with the same person as that singer rocking out on the cover of the album. It was almost as if there were three different men: that young Elvis on the album cover, the movie star Elvis who'd done all of those films, and now the serious, spiritually curious adult Elvis who was here on my sister's bed, sharing his life with me.

Elvis was fully aware that he wasn't twenty years old anymore. A couple of times he made comments to me in reference to that. After one show, for instance, he felt the audience hadn't been very responsive.

"Everyone wants to see the 'old' Elvis," he said.

On the other hand, he also went on to tell me he actually thought his voice was stronger now than it had ever been. I agreed. I'd heard many of his earlier recordings, and I certainly thought Elvis's voice had grown richer. His voice was at its peak.

I rarely knew if Elvis was going to introduce me during his shows. He knew I was shy about having the spotlight on me, but he got a kick out of doing it anyway.

I usually sat onstage behind his soundmen; however, one time, I had to sit farther away. Elvis introduced me and wanted me to come up onstage. It was a long walk, but no sooner had I reached the top of the steps onto the stage, when Elvis immediately asked me to go sit down again. The crowd got a laugh out of that.

In our hotel room afterward, I said, "I'll get you for that," and started to tickle him. This was the first time I had ever done this, and I was delighted to discover that Elvis was ticklish. I loved to hear him laugh.

About a week into the tour, we were in Elvis's room after his show in Binghamton, New York, when I started thinking about how, in the midst of my new life with Elvis, the combined force of his personality and my own feelings for him had swept me along on this emotional riptide. Elvis had become my total focus. I had become so consumed by being with him, and by taking care of him, that my own needs and identity had been partly steamrolled by trying to keep up with his fast-paced life and be the best partner I could be for him. I loved him and wanted to be with him, but I also was starting to feel a little lost.

I understood the pressure Elvis was under, and I was prepared to put any thoughts of my own career aside to support him. However, Elvis had his interests and passions, and I began pondering how I could integrate some of mine, like art, into our life together. I especially missed painting.

The breakup of my parents' marriage was also weighing on my mind. I knew my mother and father would probably be better off living separately, yet I felt a deep underlying sadness, sure this would be definite. I just wished things could be different for them.

That particular night in Binghamton, I experienced a complex convergence of emotions brought on by my own feelings of loss, coupled with my ongoing anxiety about Elvis's dependency on sleep medication and the effects the drugs seemed to sometimes have on his personality. I really wanted to help him. Everything suddenly hit me like a freight train and I began to cry. I just needed to, if only to relieve the emotional pressure.

When he saw my tears, Elvis thought I must be upset with him. "You're not happy with me," he ventured.

I shook my head. How could I begin to explain? Then words came rushing out. "Elvis, I love you," I said. "It's not that. It's my parents, my art, it's all these things."

Finally, perhaps because I was in such a raw, vulnerable state, I added, "I also worry about you and your medications sometimes."

Elvis was quiet. I knew he didn't like being confronted about any of his habits. This time was no different. Still, his response shocked me to the core. "I think you should go home for a few days," he said.

This really hurt. It also seemed unfair. I had just been trying to reach out to him, to really communicate honestly with him about my feelings. I didn't want to leave at first, but then I reconsidered. Maybe Elvis was right, and it would be good for me to go home and sort through my thoughts and get some rest.

Elvis picked up a tour schedule from his night table, wrote something on it, and handed it to me. When I looked, he had written "Come back here" and drawn an arrow beside "Baltimore, Maryland."

I left Binghamton and flew home to Memphis, still uncertain about my decision to leave and feeling emotionally shaken. Now I was embarrassed as well. What would those around Elvis think about me leaving so abruptly?

I tried putting on a brave face when I showed up at home. "I'm just taking a little break," I told my family. "I needed to rest, and Elvis wants me to return to the tour in a few days."

I didn't try to explain more than that. My emotional turmoil was too difficult, too complex, and too private, to explain.

Fortunately, my family was as supportive as always. They didn't press, and I didn't go into detail.

Once I was home and things were quieter, it was easier to sort through my emotions. Elvis may not have been focused on my personal interests, I realized, but when I had told him about my grandfather's health and the problems my parents were having, he had been sensitive about what was going on in my life. In fact, Elvis had jumped into action and done everything he could to make things better. I began thinking about his many responsibilities, especially when he went on tour. Now I felt guilty and upset about not holding things together better. I could only hope that Elvis knew, at least on some deep level, that I'd brought up the medication because I cared so much about him and his well-being.

I thought Elvis would call me, but the next day went by without a word from him. The following day there was still no call. Now I had to wonder whether we were breaking up. I stayed at home and rested. I felt absolutely miserable.

Finally, he called me on the third day. "I miss you," Elvis said, adding that he wanted me back on the tour. I was happy to hear his voice and told him I missed him, too. Elvis immediately began arranging my return.

The next morning, a car pulled up in front of my house. I assumed it was one of Elvis's aides sent to bring me to the airport. But, as I walked out the front door, I saw that Elvis was sitting in the backseat.

I was stunned! I couldn't believe he'd left his tour to pick me up.

It wasn't exactly an intimate moment, though. A bodyguard, Billy Smith, and Larry Geller were also in the car. I felt embarrassed as I joined them. The last thing I'd wanted was to put anyone out, or to create an inconvenience for Elvis.

Elvis smiled at me, but he was quiet. I couldn't say anything, either, with everyone else in the car, so I leaned my head against his shoulder, wanting him to know with this small gesture how happy I was to be with him again. In response, Elvis took my hand and held it as we headed to the airport.

Once aboard the *Lisa Marie*, Elvis and I went into his bedroom and talked a little. "I know you're upset about your parents," Elvis said, "and I want you to listen to me, Gingerbread. I'm gonna help with that."

I remembered how he'd told me the night I left that he thought I was unhappy with him. I carefully thought through how to express my true concerns.

Finally, I said, "Elvis, you mentioned that you thought I was unhappy with you. I love you, but it's how the medication makes you act sometimes that I don't like."

Putting his hand up to his head, Elvis began thumping his temple with his forefinger. "Ginger, you don't understand me," he said.

"Elvis, I'm trying to," I replied.

I could tell Elvis was finished talking about this, because he changed the subject. "If you like art," he said, "we'll do something about it. We'll find you a place where you can do your art."

I suspected Elvis meant a room at Graceland. This moved me deeply, because it meant he had been listening to me after all. I thought maybe a little of what I was saying was sinking in. That was the important thing. We were making progress.

Any conversation about medication would have to be approached carefully and in time. I knew I couldn't change things in one day, but I was determined to keep trying.

Elvis performed in a few more shows after that. Once, when he was seated at the piano and singing "Unchained Melody," a few audience members threw some coins onstage. This infuriated Elvis. He thought people were trying to hurt him.

I tried my best to calm him down afterward. "Elvis, people pay to see you," I said, "and when you sit down, they can't see you as well. Your audiences love you. You could probably walk onstage and just stand there for an hour, not singing, and people wouldn't complain. They want to see you that bad."

Vernon, however, was more blunt. He once told Elvis, "Son, they don't pay to see you sit down."

We returned to Memphis, where we would stay for a couple of weeks until Elvis's next tour. Elvis asked Larry and his backup singer, Kathy Westmoreland, to remain in town. Unbeknownst to them, he had decided to give each of them a brand-new Lincoln Continental.

I was at Graceland on June 4 when Elvis invited them to come over that evening. With Billy Smith and Ricky in on this surprise, Elvis presented Kathy and Larry with their new cars.

Elvis was in a great mood. He had indulged in the kind of grand gesture that he so loved doing and looked content. Before long, Charlie came outside, too, to see what was going on.

As Kathy and I looked over her car, Elvis asked me to take a test ride with her. I didn't know Kathy but she seemed like a nice woman. We circled around the neighborhood and made small talk.

Back at Graceland, everyone was gone by the time we returned except for Billy. He was standing on the porch with a solemn look, holding the jug of water that Elvis had with him when I left. I got out of the car, sensing something was wrong.

Billy handed me the water, asked me to take it up to Elvis, and walked away. Why was Billy acting so mysterious? Suddenly feeling anxious, I nearly ran upstairs.

Elvis wasn't in his office, so I walked into the bedroom and then looked toward the bathroom. I saw Elvis inside looking pensive, sitting in the black chair with one leg crossed over the other, shaking his foot. As I stepped into the bathroom doorway, I saw Charlie. He was perched on the toilet seat with his back to me. Neither of them was speaking.

I walked around Charlie to see his face and gasped in horror. His nose was all bloodied and swollen! "What happened?" I asked.

With a nervous laugh, Elvis said, "Well, Charlie was drinkin' and mouthin' off about me givin' cars to Kathy and Larry, and sayin' somethin' about him gettin' a Rolls-Royce and prices, and was embarrassin' me. I told him to shut up. He was spoilin' the moment." Shrugging his shoulders, Elvis added, "He asked me to hit him, so I hit him."

I looked at Charlie, trying to process this. It was obvious he had been drinking. Now he laughed stiffly, as if everything was okay and he could pass the incident off as inconsequential.

The two of them joked around for a few moments, but the mood in the room hung heavily over the two of them. Charlie left soon after that.

I could tell Elvis felt terrible about what had happened. Shaking his head, he said, "Charlie shouldn't have done that." He kept repeating this over and over, acting very disappointed with Charlie. They were both in the wrong, I thought.

Charlie had to have known that big, gift-giving moments were important to Elvis. Of course, Elvis should never have punched him. How could he have hit his good friend?

For something like this to happen, I began wondering if things had been building up between Elvis and Charlie. I continued to listen to Elvis and tried to calm him down.

"Charlie will come back around," I said, but Charlie didn't reappear and Elvis wasn't about to go downstairs and seek him out.

We finally went to sleep in the morning and woke in the afternoon. Charlie didn't come around to see Elvis the next day, either. Elvis was really down, and he started talking to me about taking a trip to Las Vegas.

We had just come back from a tour and I felt Elvis was simply trying to run away from what had happened. I told Billy this in private when I saw him next. He said I shouldn't go to Las Vegas with Elvis, because Elvis "would probably get something he didn't need."

What did he mean by that? I was confused.

I didn't press Billy with questions at the time, but in retrospect, I wish I had.

I didn't want Elvis to go to Las Vegas, so I boldly told him he shouldn't run away from the problem. "Charlie will get over it, Elvis," I said. "We should stay in Memphis." He looked glum, grew quiet, and didn't say any more about going to Vegas. I continued trying to cheer him up and, luckily, before long, Elvis acted like he was in a better mood.

In the morning, I returned home. Later, however, when I called Graceland, I was told that Elvis wasn't there. I was puzzled. Did he actually go to Las Vegas after all?

Unable to reach him, I became concerned. In the middle of the night, Elvis called me at home. I suspected he was phoning me from Las Vegas. From his heavy sounding voice, it sounded like he'd taken some sleep medication. "I miss you," he said.

"I miss you, too," I told him. "Where are you?" There was silence on the phone. He didn't say. I knew that, in his condition, we couldn't really have any sort of conversation. We spoke briefly, said we loved each other, then said good night. My heart sank as we hung up. I prayed Elvis was all right and would come home soon.

The following afternoon, someone called from Graceland to say Elvis wanted to see me. I thought it was odd they didn't put him on the phone. This concerned me and I was on edge. What had happened?

I rushed over, and when I entered Elvis's room, I was greeted by the sight of Elvis lying in bed on his side, facing me with his eyes closed and hooked up to an IV. Scared, my heart sank again. I had never seen Elvis like this before.

Charlie, Billy, and a few others were standing around. Dr. Nichopoulos was sitting in a chair.

"What happened?" I asked.

Charlie told me that Elvis had gone to Las Vegas and taken too much medication.

I had one burning question. *Why?*

It crushed me to see him like this. Everyone stood about the room, quiet. Gradually, Dr. Nichopoulos and the guys began slowly exiting the room. I lay down beside Elvis. How could he have let the incident with Charlie do this to him? I wanted so badly to understand what had been going through his mind.

I stared up at the ceiling, brokenhearted, and my eyes welled up. Suddenly, I felt Elvis move on the bed beside me. I looked over as he began rolling over onto his back.

Turning his head my way, Elvis slowly opened his eyes. He didn't say a word, but with an unsteady hand, he took his finger and wiped a tear from my eye.

I took his hand.

I tried to smile at him, but it was difficult. All I could think about, over and over again, was how Elvis was always surrounded by people, so how could someone have let this happen?

The questions swirled in my mind as confusion and anger blurred my vision. Billy seemed to have known that Elvis might do something like this. Who went to Las Vegas with Elvis? Elvis would never have gone on his own. Did others have prior experience with this sort of behavior from Elvis? If so, why didn't they stop him if they thought it would be a bad thing? What had Dr. Nichopoulos been thinking when he saw Elvis like this?

It took me a long time to fall asleep. When the two of us woke up the next day, I was relieved to see Elvis acting more like his old self. Whatever had been troubling him, he seemed determined to put it behind him, behaving as if all was well. Charlie was back around and so I chose to let things return to normal, but there was a lot left unsaid between us.

In retrospect, I can't help but feel that Elvis's plunge into that kind of extreme depression for those few days was exacerbated by Elvis's knowledge of the scathingly negative book coming out, written by his former bodyguards Dave Hebler and Red and Sonny West.

Elvis soon returned to his usual upbeat mood after this incident. One day, I was getting ready to go home to check on Odyssey when he said, "You can drive my Stutz if you want."

This would be cool, I thought, but when I put my hands on the steering wheel, I had sudden misgivings. If ever there was a time when I wouldn't want to put dents in a car, it was this one!

I drove the Stutz home as cautiously as possible. I played with Odyssey for a while and then decided to take Terry with me in the Stutz over to see our friend Cindy.

As we pulled into her driveway, Cindy stepped outside. When Terry and I got out to meet her, a man from the press suddenly approached us, wanting to take my picture beside the car.

I hadn't noticed anyone following us, but then it dawned on me that of course someone would notice the Stutz. It certainly wasn't the kind of automobile one saw every day. Most people would suspect it belonged to Elvis.

I didn't want to publicly flaunt Elvis's car and declined to pose for the photographer. He decided to put Cindy in the picture. The photo appeared in our local paper the next day along with a small write-up referring to me as Elvis's "friend," taking the car for a spin.

Not long after that, Elvis told me CBS planned to do a special on him. They would be filming some of his performances during his next tour. Elvis wanted me to have some new outfits to wear and sent me to Los Angeles to go shopping with Rosemary. I was excited to finally see Los Angeles. Elvis put Joe in charge of setting things up. We stayed at the Westwood Marquis Hotel with our own limousine and driver at our beck and call.

Rosemary and I stopped by Joe's apartment while we visited L.A., where he showed us some photo albums with pictures of Elvis taken through the years. I realized that Joe had known Elvis for a long time. He also had some older photos of Elvis and Priscilla on his walls. I knew Joe's girlfriend, Shirley, was friends with Priscilla and now I figured Joe must be, too.

Elvis had forgotten to give me money before we left, so Joe called him. Elvis wired the money to a local Western Union office. When Joe saw that Elvis had wired $2,000, he laughed.

"That would only pay for one of Linda's outfits," he said.

Linda must have had expensive tastes, I thought. Two thousand dollars was more than enough money to buy clothes for me.

We were in L.A. for just two days, but Rosemary and I made the most of it, not only shopping but visiting Universal Studios and sightseeing around the city. Our adventure got even more interesting when we departed on an American Airlines flight and discovered that the singers Kenny Rogers and Brenda Lee were both on board as well as the actor David Huddleston.

I remembered David from the film *Blazing Saddles*. He had fun walking around and telling jokes to Rosemary and me. Rosemary egged him on and asked him to repeat some of his funniest lines from the film.

Kenny Rogers was a friendly, down-to-earth man dressed in jeans and a sport coat. He sat in front of us, and I told him that Elvis and I had recently enjoyed watching him on television, singing "Sweet Music Man," a song Elvis loved. Kenny generously gave me a cassette tape recording of his yet-to-be-released album, which contained the song.

Brenda Lee was friendly as well. While she and I were talking, Brenda noticed a stain on my top and said she had a new product from Japan designed to clean fabrics. She went back to her seat, then returned to ease herself between Rosemary and me, where she began applying the product to my top and trying to rub out the spot.

As I watched Brenda earnestly do her best to help clean my outfit, I wondered if she, Kenny, or David would have even spoken to me a year ago. I knew that was unlikely. Being with Elvis had made this possible. Once again, he had introduced me to a new and exciting facet of his celebrity world—even when he wasn't with me.

By the time I returned to Graceland, Lisa was in town. It was good to see her, and she seemed happy to have my company as well, even calling me "Gingerbread" after hearing Elvis use my nickname. Elvis had yet to tell Lisa about our engagement. He had earlier talked with me about this and said that he wanted to wait until the right time, a time when he felt comfortable telling her. This would represent a significant change in his daughter's life, and he wanted the announcement handled properly. He had asked me not to share the news with her yet, either. This was something I had understood completely.

Lisa was usually out and about on the grounds of Graceland, playing with friends or family members, or riding around on her golf cart. One day, she invited me to ride with her. I got on and she took off fast, bouncing around the grounds and chasing the horses, stirring up dust in our wake. It was great fun, and I looked forward to spending more time with her in the future.

One afternoon, I was sitting at the foot of Elvis's bed and talking with him while he stood at his bathroom sink, dressed in pajamas and a robe, and smoking a cigar. The window was raised a little in his bathroom; suddenly, I saw him turn, move quickly toward the window, and look out.

He then raced out of the bathroom past me, grabbing a machine gun as I shouted, "Elvis, what is it?"

I quickly followed him downstairs as Elvis ran out the front door. He stopped on the porch and looked around. "I heard screaming and saw someone with a gun chasing Lisa and the other girls," he said breathlessly.

I froze beside him, frightened, scanning the grounds.

Then I noticed his cousin's kids and their friends playing off to one side of the house. One of the teenagers had a plastic gun and was chasing the others.

I told Elvis this and, as relief swept over him, he started to laugh. I did, too. I knew the fear of intruders was always with him, and I was glad this time nothing was amiss.

Elvis stood on the porch with me for a few minutes, his robe gently blowing in the wind, a cigar between his lips and a machine gun in his hand, as we caught our breath. Then I noticed one of the pink tour jeeps, filled with fans, slowly making its way up the driveway.

"Elvis, the jeep is coming," I said.

He turned around and quickly headed back inside. Following him, I closed the door, knowing as the jeep passed by, they now had a postcard-tranquil vision of the mansion.

CHAPTER 23

Elvis's next tour would start on June 17. My sister Terry was relinquishing the Miss Tennessee crown at that time, and the director of the state pageant had asked her to invite Elvis. When she mentioned this to him, he thanked her but declined, saying he didn't want to detract from the pageant. He had been unaware that his own tour was starting on that date anyway, since others handled his schedule and travel arrangements.

I knew I wouldn't have another chance to see Terry in her crown, so I asked Elvis if it would be all right if I missed the first day of his tour to attend my sister's ceremony. He understood that I wanted to support her and arranged for me to join him after the pageant.

While Elvis flew to Springfield, Missouri, for the start of his ten-day tour, I traveled to Jackson, Tennessee, with my family. We watched Terry give up her crown, and it was a bittersweet moment.

Afterward, I flew into Kansas City, Missouri, on a Learjet, which Elvis had chartered for me, to join the tour.

The CBS special would be Elvis's first since his *Aloha from Hawaii* satellite show, and filming began on June 19 in Omaha, Nebraska.

Al Schultz, the husband of comedian Vicki Lawrence, had been hired to do Elvis's makeup for the CBS special. I watched Al apply it in the dressing area of Elvis's bathroom before departing the *Lisa Marie*. Of course, I had never seen Elvis in base makeup needed for television, and when he stepped out, I thought it looked a little caked on, pasty and thick. Elvis looked much better without it. I really didn't know much about television and stage makeup. Maybe this much makeup was necessary for the camera.

Elvis was in a good mood, but I could tell he was quite nervous. By the time the show started, however, his movements were slow and he seemed hazy at times. I guessed that the doctor must have prescribed Elvis something to help calm him down, which would explain why Elvis was acting so sluggish. I rooted for him, as always, but it wasn't one of his best performances.

The following show in Lincoln, Nebraska, was better. Elvis was in complete control. Filming picked up again the next night inside the Rushmore Plaza Civic Center in Rapid City, South Dakota.

Vernon and Sandy were along on this tour. In South Dakota, we were ushered into a backstage dressing room. The three of us sat on a couch, watching while Elvis was filmed accepting a plaque from the mayor. The plaque was being given to him in honor of this being the first concert ever held in the city's new auditorium.

Elvis normally didn't like to wait backstage long. I could tell he was hot in his jumpsuit by the way he'd started to perspire. A young Native American girl then presented Elvis with a medallion of life from the Sioux Nation while we were all waiting for the show to begin.

In the distance, I could hear the crowd chanting as they eagerly awaited Elvis, but his focus was on the young girl. His face lit up. He had such a soft spot for children. Elvis kept complimenting the girl, trying to put her at ease, and gave her a kiss.

When Joe told Elvis it was time to get ready for the show, I could tell Elvis felt like Joe was rushing him, which he didn't like. "When I've got something to do," he said, "I'll be there when I get there."

Elvis could have simply walked away after getting his award, but he stood there, continuing to focus on the Native American girl. He wanted to see that she was given something in return, and finally asked an aide to make sure she received one of his scarves.

Elvis's show went well that night. At one point, he walked to the side of the stage and introduced his father. He mentioned how he had missed Vernon not being able to be on tour because he'd been sick for a while.

Elvis then began walking toward me. I noticed a gleam in his eye and got nervous. Raising his arm, he pointed his finger at me.

"I'd like you . . . I'd like you to say hello to my girlfriend, Ginger," he announced. "Ginger, stand up, honey."

Shyly, I stood up, blushing furiously amid the clapping and whistling. Elvis quickly said, "Sit down, Ginger. That's enough for her."

A wonderful feeling swept over me. He had introduced me to the world!

Elvis then broke into the song, "Hurt," and I silently began pulling for him, as there were certain notes he liked to reach in various songs. He hit his notes that night and I thought he did a magnificent job.

After Elvis's death, there would be some fans who would question why he didn't take this opportunity to introduce me as his fiancée during this time, despite my engagement ring, but I understood. First and foremost, Lisa didn't know about our engagement yet, and he wanted her to be prepared. Elvis had made some people close to him aware of it back in January, but that was the private Elvis.

In addition, Elvis was a professional entertainer. He knew our announcement would have huge publicity consequences, and being very protective of me and our relationship, I knew he wasn't ready to have the press focus on me even more. I didn't think twice about any of this that night. I was simply thrilled that he'd introduced me on camera.

Occasionally, the crowd was particularly rowdy, and I always worried that a fan might get hurt. I'm sure some did, especially those who pushed to the front of the auditoriums to grab one of Elvis's scarves, but I was never really afraid for my own safety. I was, however, worried that an especially enthusiastic fan might accidentally hurt Elvis, since I'd seen him get scratched before. One time, near the end of a performance, someone threw something onto the stage and the object struck Elvis in the head.

Stunned, Elvis immediately went into a defensive karate stance. "What is it? What is it?" he shouted toward those of us who were seated onstage and to his security.

Everything happened so quickly, I wasn't sure if the audience even realized he was upset.

I then heard some voices yelling, "Frisbee!"

After the show, I raced to the limousine and climbed into it. A few minutes later I saw Elvis, enveloped by his entourage, moving quickly toward the car. He had just reached the limo when I heard a loud thud that made me jump.

Elvis had hit the car window with his fist. The limo doors flew open and everyone quickly piled inside as Elvis fumed, "That damn Frisbee was so close to my eye, and when it hit, it hit hard, man. I almost walked offstage."

Elvis and the guys began discussing what had happened, and I learned that the security guards had found a teenage boy who threw the Frisbee. The boy had attached a note inside it.

Felton, one of the soundmen, had told Elvis that the boy apologized, but it would take Elvis a while to calm down inside the car.

Although it was an innocent act on the boy's part, I knew how concerned Elvis was about safety, and understood how something like this really scared him. Once again I was reminded of how vulnerable Elvis was despite all of his security, and of how aware he was of that, too.

After a show in Des Moines, Iowa, we flew into Madison, Wisconsin, and landed in the early morning hours. Elvis, Vernon, Sandy, and I took a limousine with a few staff members from the airport to a hotel.

As we stopped at a red light, we all suddenly noticed what looked like a fight breaking out at a nearby Skylane Standard gas station. Two young men were picking on another man. Elvis lowered the window and watched for a moment.

Before any of us could stop him, Elvis opened the door and jumped out of the car. The bodyguards followed in close pursuit. Elvis had yet to change; still wearing his stage suit, he walked smack into the middle of the fight, assumed a karate stance, and said something to the young men.

I watched anxiously along with Vernon and Sandy. Not surprisingly, the men looked completely baffled to see none other than Elvis Presley standing in front of them! In a minute, everyone was smiling and shaking hands.

When Elvis rejoined us in the car, he was still keyed up and talked about the fight he'd prevented. Soon, though, he went on to talk about other things, as if he had just done his good deed for the day. Elvis knew he could affect people, and I think he truly felt his best when he was helping others.

Elvis decided he'd like my family to see his last couple of shows, so he flew them in to join us in Cincinnati, Ohio. Terry was busy with our friend Cindy and couldn't make the flight. When my mother and Rosemary arrived and Elvis saw just the two of them, he asked where Terry was.

"She couldn't come," I told him, and explained why.

Elvis wasn't pleased by this. Due to Terry's commitments as Miss Tennessee, he hadn't been able to get to know her as well as he had Rosemary. He called Terry at home and said, "Get your girlfriend and I'll have a plane bring you."

He chartered a Learjet out of Nashville to pick up my sister and Cindy in time for them to see his show. I was touched that seeing my family meant so much to him. But I wasn't surprised: Family, I knew, meant a lot to Elvis.

We were staying at the Netherland Hilton. That evening, a few hours before Elvis's show, his mood plummeted because the air conditioner in his room wasn't working. He wasn't happy with the food he'd ordered, either.

A little while later, I went into my room to get ready, and my mother and Rosemary came in to visit with me. I was setting my hair and talking to them from the bathroom when the bedroom door suddenly flew open.

"Where's Ginger?" Elvis demanded.

Quickly stepping from the bathroom, I asked, "What's going on?"

Elvis was gone. My mother and Rosemary looked stunned. "I don't know, but Elvis looked quite upset," my mother said.

I heard the voices of people running down the hall. Someone shouted, "Which way did he go?"

I peered into the hallway and saw the bodyguards running. Obviously, Elvis had somehow escaped them. But why? What was he trying to do, and why had he been looking for me?

I sat in my room for a little while, worrying. Before long, the phone rang. It was one of the bodyguards. "Elvis wants to see you," he said. Apparently, Elvis had left the Hilton and checked into a nearby hotel.

I went downstairs, where I ran into one of Elvis's fans. He asked me to pose for a photo. I was then escorted to the new hotel.

When I saw Elvis, he said happily, "We have air-conditioning now."

I hated thinking that he'd gotten himself so worked up before a performance, and I was relieved to see that he seemed to have calmed down and was in a better mood. However, because the new hotel didn't have enough room for all of us, Elvis announced that he wanted to return to Memphis after his Cincinnati show.

During the performance that night, I left my chair behind the soundmen to race quickly to the restroom with Rosemary. When we returned, we tried reentering through the door we had exited, but it had locked behind us.

I could hear Elvis start to introduce his band and began to get nervous. What if Elvis wanted to introduce me to the audience, but this time I wasn't there? I was panicked, thinking this might throw him, sure that he would be concerned about what had happened to me if he suddenly saw that I was missing.

Luckily, Rosemary and I found an unlocked door and I made it back to my chair without Elvis noticing. I was glad I did, too, because Elvis went on that night to introduce his father, me, and my family, as well as a British fan club.

On our flight back to Memphis, Rosemary told Elvis about us getting locked out. He was relaxed after the show and just thought it was funny.

"I would have stopped the G-damn show and looked for you," he declared.

After a brief stay in Memphis, Elvis decided to bring more of his family on tour with us, and Patsy and Jo Smith boarded the plane. I hadn't been around Patsy much because she was typically working out back whenever I was at Graceland, and I had rarely seen her in the house. However, later my mother said Patsy had knelt down in front of her on the plane, telling her she was glad to meet her, because she had heard so much about her. This was nice to hear.

During Elvis's show in Indianapolis, he introduced his father and then me, saying, "I'd like you to say hello to my girlfriend, Ginger. She is something to stare at. That's it. That's enough, Ginger!"

Introducing Terry as Miss Tennessee, he went on to present the rest of my family as well, saying, "and her mother and her sister Rosemary. And, Rosemary, ya know, you just stay put," he joked, referring to us being locked out during his previous performance. "They're a very lovely family and I love them," Elvis added.

He introduced some of his family that night as well, calling Jo his "assassin," and saying, "Patsy works for my dad and she's as nutty as a fruitcake."

Once back on the *Lisa Marie*, my mother said Patsy had chatted with her on the shuttle bus. And, when she stepped from it to board the plane, Patsy had walked beside my mother, putting an arm around her.

Once again, I was touched by these small gestures of warmth and acceptance. It was nice to think that some of Elvis's family was beginning to recognize us as part of his life now.

Back in Memphis, thinking of my mother once again, Elvis brought up the subject of her home. He wanted to speak with my mom, so I called her at work and handed him the phone.

"Mrs. Alden, I want you to call my father and take your house notes, payment books, or whatever you have on the house to him. He will take care of it for you," he said.

After speaking with Elvis, my mother later called Vernon. He reiterated what Elvis had said, and asked her to bring her payment book and any papers on our home over to his house the following day.

The next evening, Vernon was visiting with Elvis in Lisa's room when I arrived at Graceland. As I walked in, Vernon said, "Your mother just brought me her payment books. She doesn't have to worry about her mortgage anymore."

I thanked both Elvis and Mr. Presley. I knew a great burden had been lifted from my mother's shoulders, and it felt wonderful. I could never pay Elvis back financially for this kind of expansiveness, but my family and I would be forever grateful.

CHAPTER 24

My favorite time of day had always been early evening, just as the sun started to set. Now, with the warmer weather, Elvis and I sometimes sat on the front porch at Graceland, where he usually brought a cigar and a jug of water outside with him.

The view over Graceland's rolling front lawn was beautiful. Elvis and I both loved how peaceful it was. Sometimes we didn't talk at all, just listened to the sounds of nature.

One evening, as we were sitting quietly on the porch, Elvis took notice of the crickets. "Listen," he said. "They're singing in unison."

It occurred to me that, when Elvis talked about music as the universal language, he wasn't just referring to humans. He heard music everywhere, in all levels of life. Because music had been a big part of my life, too, early on, watching Elvis sing and hearing him talk about music made me wish I hadn't been too self-conscious to continue singing.

Once, Elvis asked if I knew the song, "Since I Met You Baby." As we sat in bed together, we began singing it and harmonizing together. I didn't know all of the words, but I loved it when Elvis said we sounded good together. If singing with Elvis couldn't help me get over my fear of doing this in front of people, probably nothing could!

Another night, Elvis asked Billy and Jo to come to his bedroom. He'd been talking with me about a new song of his, "Way Down." He had recorded it in October 1976 and it would be the last song he would ever record. When Billy and Jo came in, he put the record on the stereo.

Still seated in bed, Elvis began to sing along with it. When it was time to sing the words, "way down," Elvis wanted each of us to take a turn, pointing to Jo, Billy, and me in turn. When it was time, he pretended to hit the low notes that J. D. Sumner reached in the song.

We all chimed in, and I had a lot of fun. I felt a little more like part of Elvis's family that night, singing and cutting up with his cousins.

When I arrived at Graceland one day shortly after that, Elvis said, "I was talkin' with my daddy, and he asked me, 'Isn't Ginger gonna use that credit card?'"

I thought Vernon would be happy that I didn't. I had started to notice Vernon coming over more when I was there; once, when Vernon's attention was on something else in the room, Elvis tapped my arm and motioned for me to watch him, as he had done once with Lisa.

After his father left, Elvis asked, "Did you notice that it's almost as if my daddy hates to leave the room when we're together? It's gonna do my daddy's heart good to see us married," he said.

I was excited that Elvis felt this way and hoped he was right.

Elvis hadn't really gone out anywhere since we'd been off tour. He talked about riding his motorcycle or the three-wheelers, but he had canceled whatever plans he'd made at the last minute.

One afternoon, I was at home when my mother decided to have a backyard barbeque. I got excited, thinking this would be a great thing for Elvis to do. I hoped it would encourage him to get out and vary his routine for a change.

When I called and invited him, however, Elvis declined. I felt stymied. This was discouraging.

Shortly afterward, my father called and my parents got into a heated argument. My mother was upset afterward, afraid that my father might show up at the house. She wasn't ready to see him. She decided she'd go to a hotel for the night and, since I wasn't happy about Elvis not wanting to come over, I went with her. So much for the barbeque.

That night, my mother and I talked about my dad for hours and I didn't get any sleep. The phone in our hotel rang around 5 A.M. It was Elvis's aide, Dean, saying he'd gotten the number from Rosemary. He put Elvis on the phone.

I told Elvis where I was and why my mother needed me there. Then our conversation turned back to the barbeque. I tried to explain to Elvis that I really wanted to get him out more.

"Ginger, you have to understand, I can't do what normal people do," he said.

I was confused by this statement. Elvis had been to my house before. Why was this so different? Had he thought our barbeque was going to involve meeting a whole bunch of people? This barbeque had been for just my immediate family. Maybe I hadn't been clear about that; I explained it to him again over the phone.

"Oh, well, I like hamburgers," Elvis said easily. "Maybe next time." He asked me to come to Graceland then and bring my mother.

Dawn was breaking when we arrived. I was surprised when I went upstairs and found Elvis sound asleep. It was as if he felt comforted, knowing we were on our way.

It was a beautiful morning, so I decided to take a walk with my mother around the grounds behind Graceland, and ended up taking her to the racquetball court. I had yet to see it myself. We took a quick peek inside the court, then went back to the house.

Because Elvis was still asleep and my mother and I hadn't had any rest, I told her to go into Lisa's bedroom. Meanwhile, I lay down beside Elvis. Before I knew it, I was out like a light.

When I woke that afternoon, Elvis asked where my mother was. "Lisa's room," I said sleepily.

Elvis got up, went down the hall, and brought my mother back into his room. Always respectful of her, he apologized about the barbeque. My mother told him she understood, and they had a nice visit. I felt happy, satisfied that at least they were spending some time together, even if it wasn't the time I'd hoped for.

In a solemn mood one night, Elvis brought up the book that his three former bodyguards had written about him. I had no idea who they were.

"Just because I'm a public figure," he said adamantly, explaining why the guards had written the book. "Everyone has done good things and bad, but most of it's untrue anyway."

Elvis looked at me quite seriously then. "I want to make it clear. It's not the content, but the principle of the thing that hurts me."

"I helped make Dave Hebler a seventh-degree black belt," he said, shaking his head. "Red got on an elevator once and punched a guy. I think that went on a lot. The guy was going to sue me," he added. "I had lots of lawsuits. I did a lot for these people and their families. I bought them homes, helped put their kids through school. The fact that they would turn and do this to me . . ." Elvis paused, noticeably upset.

Then his mood lifted. "I know the general public will stand behind me," he said. "I'm gonna let it pass and not say anything." He fell silent for another moment, then became more contemplative. "You've got to kill it and get it behind you. If something ever bothers you, Ginger, you've got to kill it and get it behind you."

"Don't worry," I said, trying to soothe him. "Most people will see through what's in the book, and your fans will stand behind you."

I would learn only shortly after Elvis died, that Vernon had fired these men before Elvis and I ever met. At the time, I hoped only to reassure Elvis, and I thought it helped because things returned to normal. Elvis seemed to have arrived at a place in his mind where he had figured out how to handle this serious betrayal by people who had worked for him. From that day on, I would never hear another word from him about the book.

As often as Elvis refused to go out, he would suddenly decide he was in the mood to go out more again. Sometimes we'd take a ride on his three-wheelers and Elvis would even let me drive one, which I loved to do.

Elvis would usually race his three-wheeler down to the Southland Mall parking lot, buzz around some hedges, come back to Graceland, drive fast by the pool, and jump the walkway to the racquetball court.

One night, after letting me ride one of his three-wheelers, Elvis generously offered to give it to me to keep at our home. I shook my head, bemused. Like the huge self-portrait Elvis had once given me, I had no space big enough to keep it. I told him I would leave it at Graceland.

Elvis loved driving fast sometimes whether he was on a three-wheeler, a motorcycle, or in a car. Once, I was heading home from Graceland, riding in my Cadillac on Mt. Moriah Road with Elvis at the wheel. As we approached a stoplight, it turned yellow. Elvis gunned the accelerator to make it through the intersection.

Looking back, I saw the bodyguards stuck at the red light. Elvis drove on, unaware, and for the next few minutes, I thought about how nice it felt to be alone with him. I understood he needed extra protection because of his celebrity, but I did wish there could be more times like this, when it seemed like there were just the two of us on the road.

Whenever Lisa was at Graceland, her company brought out Elvis's playful side. Elvis and I were sitting on the front porch one afternoon when Lisa buzzed by in her golf cart, asking the two of us to ride with her. Elvis got behind the wheel and, with me at his side and Lisa in back, took off.

Still wearing his pajamas and a robe, a cigar clenched between his teeth, Elvis barreled close to the gates, jumped a few curbs, then buzzed up the driveway and tore out the back entrance. We passed a church, then raced through the back gate, where Elvis stopped by his office to talk with his dad, then got back on and sped away with us again. I cherished times like this, because Elvis was so clearly relaxed and enjoying himself.

While Lisa was with us, I reminded Elvis that my niece Amber was close to Lisa's age. I was happy when Elvis suggested bringing Amber to Graceland so the two girls could meet. Happily, the two of them hit it off, and Lisa started inviting Amber to play and for sleepovers. This helped me feel like our two families were starting to blend at last, and led me to know Lisa a little better.

Besides playing with Amber or tearing around on her golf cart or Elvis's three-wheelers, Lisa loved to sing. Sometimes, I'd find her sitting on the stairway at Graceland with Amber, singing Fleetwood Mac tunes like "Dreams." She also loved to play the piano; some of the few times Elvis sat downstairs at Graceland, was to watch Lisa at the keyboard.

I played piano a little by ear myself. Occasionally, Elvis wanted Lisa and me to play together on the organ in his office while he listened. Once, Lisa was talking on the phone with her mother and asked me to play something on the organ. She held the phone my way, telling Priscilla to listen. Embarrassed by my so-so ability, but wanting to please Lisa, I chose something short.

One afternoon I arrived at Graceland to find Elvis in his room, seated in bed. He shook his head in wonder at me and said, "Lisa came into my room earlier, walked up to me, and asked, 'Daddy, you love Ginger more than you love Linda, don't you?' I told her, 'Yes, but now don't forget that Linda was nice to you, she took you places and did a lot of things for you.' She said, 'I know, I'm just happy.'" Elvis made a walking movement with his fingers, and added, "She skipped out of the room."

It was nice of Elvis not to want Lisa to think less of Linda just because he was with me, I thought, and I could see how relieved he was that Lisa approved of me. I was glad, too. I'd been hoping that many of the people around Elvis, especially his family, would come to accept me, but no one was more important in this regard than Lisa.

I had yet to tell anyone outside my family and close friends about our engagement and Elvis had still yet to tell Lisa. I wore my engagement ring most of the time at Graceland, rarely taking it off but to wash my face. However, because the ring was so valuable, sometimes I felt safer, when going home, to leave it in the jewelry box Elvis had given me.

Several days later, however, I happened to be in Lisa's room when she came up to me and asked if her daddy and I were going to get married.

My answer nearly got caught in my throat, thinking someone must have told her about our engagement. "I hope so," I told her, completely caught off guard. I knew how much Elvis wanted to tell her at the "right time," and I didn't want to jump the gun.

Right away, she called me her "second mommy." Lisa's innocent, pure acceptance of me made me feel really good. Later, I learned that the reason Lisa had asked me about our marriage was because she'd been playing in my bathroom with one of her friends when I was away and she'd seen my engagement ring in my jewelry box. Her friend had been the one who'd explained to her what the ring meant.

As a father, I knew Elvis had been anxious about telling her, but I also knew that Lisa knowing about our engagement, and accepting it, would surely make things easier for Elvis as it had now for me. I went into the bedroom and told him about what had just happened with Lisa. His look, a mixture of surprise and relief, seemed to say, "Okay . . . the cat's out of the bag now, I'll talk to Lisa . . . here we go."

Shortly after that, Lisa joined us. Calling me Mommy, she giggled, and then said that she was going to call me Mommy even in front of her mother.

Elvis and I exchanged looks that said exactly the same thing: "*That will go over well.*" I didn't like to think about how Priscilla might respond to this, and I'm sure Elvis didn't either. But at least our concern about what effect this would have on Lisa had been completely unnecessary. Lisa clearly seemed fine about the idea of us getting married.

There was a fairly new amusement park in Memphis called Libertyland, and one day I decided it would be fun to take Lisa and Amber there.

"Can Lisa go?" I asked Elvis.

He said it was fine and didn't mention anything about having a bodyguard with us. I assumed this was because he felt more relaxed about security in our hometown.

Terry was away, but I invited my mother and Rosemary to come along, as they had yet to meet Lisa. We drove to Graceland from our house to get her. Lisa was ready and waiting for us, sitting on the front porch and wearing a swimsuit, flip-flops, and a shirt wrapped around her waist.

After parking at Libertyland, we were walking toward the entrance when a couple stopped us. "Is that Lisa Presley?" they asked.

I was startled. It still amazed me that Lisa was so easily recognized by the public. We had a great time on the rides, and on the way home, we stopped at a local 7-Eleven store.

Lisa and Amber jumped out of the car before I did, but then Lisa stopped. She had to have an older person with her, she said, and I was relieved to see that she'd already developed a sense of caution that most kids her age lacked. She was always going to need to protect herself in ways most of us never have to think about.

A few days later, I was leaving Graceland to go home when Lisa asked if she could come with me to see Amber. I took her with me and the two of them played a little.

When she saw Odyssey, my Great Dane, Lisa decided on the spot that she wanted a puppy. I hesitated. I knew this would be a big undertaking, especially because Lisa was at Graceland only part-time.

"You'll have to ask your father first," I said.

"It's okay," she said. "I don't have to ask him."

I was a little taken aback, but amused by her attempt to sway me. "Well, the stores are closed right now anyway."

She gave me a look of bewilderment, and no wonder: When Elvis shopped, people opened stores especially for him.

"We still have to ask your father," I repeated.

She smiled, but I could tell my words didn't sit too well with her. She then took a nearby pen and a piece of paper, writing "come on," and a few choice words of protest.

I began tickling her and she started to laugh. Everything was good again. Later, when I took Lisa back to Graceland, she seemed to have forgotten all about wanting a puppy and never mentioned it to Elvis.

The more time I spent with Lisa, the more aware I became that Lisa knew full well what a special place she held in the world as Elvis's daughter. She had the qualities of a leader and generally took charge whenever she was playing with other children, including Amber.

Once, one of the children Lisa had been playing with came up and told Elvis that Lisa had called his nurse, Tish, an inappropriate name. Elvis immediately asked Lisa to see him in his bedroom.

As he gently began reprimanding her, Lisa started to cry, and Elvis looked hurt. I didn't know who was more upset by the scolding—Lisa or Elvis.

CHAPTER 25

As the summer progressed, Elvis continued to spend his time relaxing at Graceland and every so often, at my parents' home. During one of his unannounced visits to our house, Elvis stepped into our foyer and our poodle, which he'd nicknamed Mud Face because of the dog's markings, began humping his leg.

With Mud Face clinging to him, Elvis started laughing and proceeded to walk into our den. "Get off me, Mud Face," he snapped, still smiling, "or I'll knock your dick stiff."

My mother and a friend of hers were sitting in the den. I was used to Elvis's off-color language by now, which he typically curtailed a bit in front of my mom, but now they both stared at him.

"Elvis, this is the minister's wife," my mother said.

With a sheepish smile, he immediately apologized.

My mother laughed. "I was joking," she said.

Relief swept over his face. Elvis visited with us for a while and was nice enough to go into the music room to play the piano and sing for us.

A few nights later, Elvis wanted to take me into his trophy room again. There was so much to see, and I was sure there would be even more new things now. He gave me a teddy bear from one of the shelves and a framed black-and-white photo of himself taken when he was younger. As we were looking at a color photo taken of him on the set of the movie *Charro!*, I casually mentioned that I liked westerns, which I'd often watched with my dad, and Elvis gave me that photograph as well.

"You know," Elvis said as we continued through the room, "if anything ever happens to me, I want you and Lisa to take people on tours through the trophy room."

I didn't think much about the statement at the time. It was just an offhand remark. Elvis was a young man. In all the time I knew him, he never talked about death or seemed to act like he was worried that he might not have a long life. That night, I knew he was referring to a time in the distant future, and that this was Elvis's way of saying that he saw us having a life together. It touched me that he wanted to involve me as one of the guardians of his legacy.

Before leaving the trophy room, Elvis also gave me his ninth-degree black belt karate certificate. It had been presented to him on his birthday and was signed by Ed Parker.

Another night that summer, the two of us were sitting in Elvis's bed when he got up to use the restroom, suddenly turned around, and announced, "I'd like us to have our picture taken professionally."

I smiled, thinking this would be great. My family and I had always respected Elvis's privacy and refrained from photographing him, other than the few snapshots I'd taken in Hawaii. I had very few pictures of the two of us together.

"I'd really like that, too," I replied.

Elvis smiled back and said, "I need to lose some weight," then continued into the bathroom.

I was surprised. This was the first time I'd ever heard Elvis mention anything directly to me about his weight.

When you're with someone almost every day, you don't really notice that person's weight fluctuations. Although, on occasion, I did notice that Elvis appeared to look a little thinner after a show from losing fluid by perspiring. Because Elvis struggled with fluid retention and occasionally got cortisone shots for pain, I had never looked at him as being that overweight. There were just some days when he seemed a bit bloated. If he wanted to lose some weight, I wanted to help him. I knew it would be better for his health in the long run if he probably did lose a few pounds.

Later that night, Elvis had some ice cream sent up to the room. As I looked at the small mountains of ice cream in the bowl, I wondered, *What about losing weight?* I knew the maids were unaware that he wanted to shed a few pounds and I felt compelled to say something here.

"Elvis, you just said you wanted to lose weight," I pointed out. "You don't need to eat that ice cream."

Without saying a word, he threw the bowl against the wall and then glared at me with anger. This hurt me, and although I felt my anger rising, too, I kept my cool, got down on the floor, and began cleaning up. As difficult as that moment was, I was still glad I'd chosen to speak up rather than remain silent. I looked at the ice cream on the floor as another small win, if only because now Elvis couldn't eat it.

Elvis sulked for a bit, and continued to remain quiet as I called one of the maids to come upstairs and help finish cleaning up. I could only imagine what she thought. I remained quiet as well for a little while after the maid left, and Elvis finally said that he was sorry. I accepted his apology. I knew it was hard for him to admit to any weakness. Because he'd said he was sorry, I did think that, deep down at least, he recognized I had spoken up because I was trying to do something good for him out of love.

By the middle of July, the weather had turned very hot. Elvis began talking about how my mother's home was now taken care of and how the next step would be to put in a pool and some landscaping. He asked me to invite my mother and Rosemary over so that he could discuss this, but didn't want me to tell them his plan yet.

Elvis was in a lighthearted, fun mood that day, which led him to want to play a small joke on the two of them. He asked Al Strada to run out to McDonald's for some gift certificates.

When my mother and Rosemary arrived, Elvis invited them up to his office and gave them a hug. They took a seat on one of the couches in the room.

I followed Elvis over to his desk. He sat down and we began waiting for Al. Meanwhile, trying to create suspense, Elvis occasionally whispered a few things to me. I could barely suppress a giggle because I could tell by their faces that my mom and sister were wondering what in the world was going on.

It took Al a long time. Elvis was growing impatient when Al finally returned. "Where were you?" Elvis demanded.

"I got a speeding ticket," Al confessed. He handed Elvis the certificates.

Of course my mother and Rosemary couldn't see what they were. Elvis made a big show of writing "fifty cents" on each gift certificate, then asked Rosemary and my mother to stand up. He walked toward them, hiding the certificates behind his back.

"Hold out your hands," he said solemnly.

When they complied, Elvis placed a certificate, facedown, in each of their palms. The certificates looked like checks.

When my mother and Rosemary turned over the certificates, they burst out laughing.

Elvis got the biggest kick out of his joke. After a few minutes, though, he said, "Those are just the French fries. Here are your Big Macs." He then handed a generous check to my mother and another one to Rosemary.

Overwhelmed, they hugged and thanked him. My jaw dropped. Elvis hadn't let me in on this part of the joke. He must have written the checks out beforehand because I never saw him do it.

Reassuring my mother that she wouldn't have any more financial worries now, Elvis told her that her home had been taken care of and all he had left to do was put in the pool and landscaping. "I want to set up a bank account for you, too, so that you won't have to work full-time," he said.

Then, looking at Rosemary, Elvis added, "I'm going to have Joe put you on the payroll, to accompany Ginger on tours, to assist her."

The three of us were stunned into silence. What could we say to this?

Shortly after that, Elvis mentioned that he thought his throat might be getting a little sore.

My mother said, "Let me feel your forehead," and he leaned toward her. Putting her palm up to his forehead, she said, "You do feel a little warm."

From his smile, I could tell he appreciated my mother's sincere attention and concern. I sure hoped he wasn't getting sick.

The phone buzzed. Elvis answered it, then said, "Let's go downstairs."

We followed him, wondering what he had up his sleeve now.

Sure enough, Elvis wasn't finished astounding us with his generosity. Parked next to the porch was a brand-new green TR-6 convertible. "This is for you, Ginger," he said. "I bought the last one in Memphis."

I have a new car? I was blown away and ecstatic. Looking inside, though, I saw that the car had a manual transmission. Then I was concerned. My father had once tried teaching me how to drive a manual, but I was no expert.

Determined to master my new car despite this obstacle, I gave Elvis a hug and jumped into the driver's seat, asking Rosemary to join me for a spin. I began inching my way down the driveway, lurching, braking, and praying.

Looking back a few minutes later, I saw Elvis standing beside my mother on the porch, the two of them laughing. I made it out the back entrance and then lurched to a stop, momentarily baffled. I was unable to figure out how to make the car go forward or in reverse.

A fan suddenly jumped out of nowhere and snapped our picture. I was fine with having my picture taken, but embarrassed about having anyone see me jerk up and down the road in this new car. One thing was for sure: I wasn't about to make a hasty getaway.

When we returned to the house, it was starting to get dark. Lisa was at Graceland and had been riding around on her golf cart. She zoomed over and stopped when she saw us, asking my mother and Rosemary to join her. They climbed into the cart and I laughed as she took off with my mother and sister, whose faces betrayed more than a hint of fear.

While they were gone, I told Elvis how much I appreciated the money he'd given my mother and sister and the new car, too, but reminded him that he didn't need to keep buying me things to show he cared. He already had my heart. Worried about his throat, I asked him how it felt and he said he felt better. I was glad.

Before long, my mother and Rosemary joined us again. They were laughing and said they'd had quite the experience, chasing the horses around out back on Lisa's golf cart. Elvis then decided he wanted to show us a tape about President Kennedy's assassination, which he said the comedian Mort Sahl had given him.

"Mort didn't want it because he told me he was getting death threats," Elvis said. I was intrigued and remembered Elvis once mentioning Kennedy's assassination to me, after coming back from our "first date" to Las Vegas.

That night, Elvis showed us a tape that contained still shots of what looked like a gunman in a bush by the grassy knoll in Dallas, Texas. He started telling us about something called the Gemstone File, a conspiracy theory surrounding Kennedy's death. I was fascinated as Elvis talked about this theory. He was convinced that Lee Harvey Oswald didn't act alone on that tragic day. I found myself wondering if what Elvis said was true.

Elvis continued to present me with one surprise after another that July. Late one night he suddenly announced that he wanted to go look at wedding dresses. I got excited as Elvis phoned Billy Smith, told him what we wanted to do, and asked him to come up.

Elvis and I were sitting on the bed in his room. When Billy walked in, Elvis pointed his finger at him and started talking to him about our wedding. "This is the big one, Billy. After this, there won't be another. This time it's gonna be right, man. It's gonna blow some people away."

He asked Billy to get Jo, too. I never saw Elvis change clothes so quickly. Then the four or us climbed into Elvis's Stutz and cruised the mostly empty streets. I was nearly trembling with excitement after hearing Elvis talk so openly about our marriage. Had he finally had a sign that the time was right to set a date?

Before long, we drove over to Union Avenue, where Jo thought there was a bridal shop. We passed a boutique and, when he noticed some bridal gowns in the window, Elvis pulled over.

He and I got out while Billy and Jo opted to stay in the car. "Which ones do you like?" Elvis asked as we stood in front of the window and admired the gowns.

We talked about the dresses, trying to get some ideas for a design. Afterward, we drove around a bit more, hoping to see some more gowns in store windows. Unable to find any more, we returned to Graceland before long. We said good night to Billy and Jo, then went upstairs, where Elvis's good mood expanded as he continued to talk about our wedding.

"I'd like to have the ceremony performed in a nondenominational church," he said, "a church shaped like a pyramid. Charlie told me something about a church shaped like a pyramid down by the river. What do you think?" he asked.

Remembering that Elvis thought pyramids contained a special energy, I thought the church sounded magical. "That sounds really nice, Elvis," I replied. My heart was pounding hard. This was for real! Elvis had a church picked out! He'd even talked to someone else about it!

Elvis mentioned another church on Summer Avenue, then said, "We could have our reception in Vail, Colorado, or at Graceland."

I had never been to Vail. "That would be amazing," I said. "I'd love to go to Vail."

He asked me to start making out an invitation list for the wedding. I found a pen and paper and began writing down the names of some friends and family members. Still a little giddy from the conversation, my mind was spinning. It wasn't easy to think of everyone in that state of mind, so I put the paper in the drawer of my night table to return to later.

All along, Elvis had been saying that God would come through and tell him when the time was right for us to marry. His deep spirituality made him feel that God was working through him, and I appreciated his belief. This night had been a revelation, a time filled with promise and excitement as we planned our future together. I went to bed early that morning, happily thinking that at last Elvis felt the right time for us to marry was drawing near.

I'd been spending so much time at Graceland or touring with Elvis for the past eight months that I hadn't really seen much of my friends. One day, though, I decided to take my friend Debbie over to Graceland. She had a comical side and was a lot of fun.

When Debbie said she'd love to meet Elvis in person, I shook my head. "He's asleep," I said.

She wanted to see him so badly, though, that I finally relented and led her upstairs. Debbie quietly tiptoed into his room and went right up to the bed.

Elvis was facing the opposite way. As my friend leaned over to peer at him, I suddenly remembered his gun, lying on the floor next to the bed.

"Be careful," I whispered. "If he wakes up, it'll scare him, and no telling what would happen."

We retreated downstairs, where we ran into Lisa. She wanted to take us for a ride on her golf cart. The two of us held on for dear life as Lisa sped merrily around the grounds and through the pastures of Graceland.

Another afternoon, one of my dearest friends, Peggy, asked me if I'd go with her one night to listen to some music at a nearby club. I hadn't seen her in quite a while, so I was happy to go.

When I told Elvis about my plan, he said, "I don't mind if you go, but don't stay out too late."

Peggy and I both had a cocktail at the club. Afterward, I brought her to Graceland to meet Elvis. It wasn't late, but when we walked upstairs, Elvis was sitting in bed, dressed as usual in pajamas and a robe. I suddenly worried about how he'd feel, having a friend of mine see him this casually dressed, but after I introduced them, Elvis politely said, "Any friend of Ginger's is a friend of mine."

Peggy sat down in the chair across from his bed and I sat beside him. "You smell like a brewery," Elvis said, looking at me.

My face flushed red with embarrassment. I'd only had one drink earlier and felt I hadn't done anything wrong.

For a split second, Peggy had an expression that telegraphed, "Oops, hope he's not mad at me." But she hastily tried to smooth things over. "Congratulations on your engagement," she said.

"Thank you," Elvis said.

Peggy had taken karate classes at Memphis State University, so she started talking with Elvis about his own interest in karate. They had a good conversation, and I relaxed.

Elvis played the organ for her a little later. By then it was late, so trying to act more like "the lady of the house," I decided to invite Peggy to sleep over. We put her in one of the rooms downstairs. I felt content, knowing she was there. Peggy was the first friend I'd ever had stay overnight at Graceland.

I wasn't totally on Elvis's sleep schedule and sometimes woke before he did. One day, while Elvis was still sleeping, I decided to venture to the pool behind Graceland and take a swim by myself, just for something to do. I hadn't been in the water very long when the guard Harold walked by.

Looking at me, he asked, "Excuse me, who are you?"

"I'm Ginger," I said.

Harold laughed and apologized. "You look much shorter in the water."

I laughed, too, but I was a little puzzled. Did I look taller, sitting in the car?

I'd spent so much time with Elvis that I'd only ever seen the guards Vester and Harold while I was driving in and out of the gates. I'd hoped to get to know everyone who lived and worked at Graceland better by now, but it wasn't always easy, since I spent most of my time upstairs with Elvis. Certainly when I became Elvis's wife and lived at Graceland, though, that would change. I looked forward to knowing them all better.

At Graceland, I usually left my Seville parked out front. One afternoon, Elvis and I were returning from a drive in his Stutz when I saw Dean washing my car. I knew Elvis must have asked him to do this, and I was surprised, as once again it was only dusty. I took good care of my cars. However, I was starting to understand how Elvis kept his cars looking so pristine: It was easy when others were washing them for you. Now Elvis was doing the same for me with my car.

Dean didn't say anything as Elvis and I walked by. I knew Elvis was paying him, but by the look on Dean's face, I knew he wasn't enjoying this particular chore. I hoped he wouldn't resent me for Elvis having him do this. Dean was another person I would have to get to know better over time, I decided.

One day, Elvis and I were reading through some spiritual books when he brought up a script he hoped to do as a film. "It's called *The Mission*," he said.

Elvis didn't talk in detail about the plot, but my curiosity was aroused. As he continued talking about the script, I understood that Elvis saw it as an extension of what he had been trying to do with his music. The movie would have a spiritual theme and would parallel the books he had been studying. Elvis even mentioned that there were small parts for Terry, Rosemary, and me. He thought he had a copy of the script in the attic and I followed him there to try to find it. The attic was filled with racks of clothing, as well as some trunks and boxes. Elvis began looking through a box, but he was unsure of where the script was, so we returned to his bedroom before too long.

"Would you like to make more movies?" I asked.

Elvis frowned a little. "I'd really like to do a serious one," he said, "another one without singing." I had not seen all of Elvis's films. "Which one didn't you sing in?" I asked.

"*Charro!*," he replied.

I hoped that one day he would look for this script again, and that his dream to do this would come true.

Another night, I was in my bathroom at Graceland when the phone on the wall above the toilet rang. It was Elvis, asking me to come into his bedroom.

I slid the folding door aside, walked into the bedroom, and saw Charlie, his hands covered in blood, hovering over Elvis as he relaxed in bed.

"What happened?" I gasped.

"Charlie's been drinking and smashed his hands through a glass window, somewhere, for some reason," Elvis said, shaking his head. "He's cut his knuckles."

I realized that Elvis wanted me to see this, but I had no idea why. I had come to see Charlie as a jack-of-all-trades who would do anything for Elvis, from coloring his hair to helping out onstage. What would possess him to punch out a window? I wondered, and shuddered a little, remembering the incident where Charlie had been drinking and asked Elvis to hit him.

Without saying a word, Charlie turned, went out the door, and started downstairs. Suddenly, we heard a thud.

Elvis quickly got up and I followed him to the stair landing. Charlie was lying in the foyer, laughing. Looking down at Charlie, Elvis said, "Charlie, get up. You look like a worm."

Two aides heard the commotion and quickly came to assist Charlie to his feet. "I'm sick of this shit," Elvis told me, and spun on his heel to return to the bedroom.

As I followed him, I figured the nurse, Tish, would most likely be getting a late-night visit from Charlie.

Elvis took a seat on his bed and picked up a book. "There's gonna be changes around here, Gingerbread," he said.

I sensed he wasn't just talking about redecorating Graceland this time.

I'd been at Graceland a few days straight by then. The next morning, I told Elvis that I needed to go home to get more clothes and check on Odyssey. Luckily, my mom and sisters helped me out by taking care of my dog whenever I needed them to, but I wanted to take my share of the responsibility for him.

"I don't want you to go," Elvis said. "I'll be alone."

He'd never said this to me before. Knowing that so many others lived and worked at Graceland, I had to wonder how Elvis could feel alone. "Elvis, you have more people around you here than I have at home," I said.

"They're not my friends," Elvis said, surprising me with his candor. "Do you think if it weren't for their paychecks, they'd still be around?"

I wondered who he meant. Was he doubting the loyalty of some of the people around him as true friends? I knew there were times he'd been displeased about various things and he'd also thought some people weren't doing their jobs on tour and even at home. Elvis had even mentioned firing a few. He once complained to me that some aides weren't where they were supposed to be and then called Billy Smith up, asking him to speak with them. Going downstairs later, I saw Billy reprimanding a few of the guys at the dining room table.

I wanted to allay his mood, so I decided to stay one more night. The next day, Elvis didn't protest as I started to leave. However, when I went downstairs and out to my car, I was shocked to see that the air in all four of my tires had been let out.

I went back upstairs and found Elvis hiding on the floor by my side of the bed, laughing. "I was trying to get you to stay," he said.

Shaking my head, I gave him a light kiss on the cheek. This was now turning into a humorous battle of wills. I was ready to play. *Well, watch this,* I thought.

I got into my car, drove slowly through the gates, and made it to the nearest gas station. I thought of Elvis hiding and laughing. As an attendant put air into my tires, I couldn't help but smile.

By now it was August, and with my parents' divorce moving forward, as part of the agreement, Elvis's lawyer had asked my father to sign a quit claim deed turning our home over to my mother. True to his promise, Elvis paid my father his equity in the house so the property could belong solely to my mother. None of us knew how we could ever thank Elvis enough for such a magnanimous gesture.

On August 3, I was at Graceland when my mother called to let us know that a huge truck carrying two large pin oak trees had pulled up to our home. The trees were planted on each side of our front walk. A couple of days later, landscapers arrived to plant three more trees and five crepe myrtle shrubs.

Elvis wanted to see our new landscaping. On August 6, he and I left Graceland and went to my house with Charlie. When we arrived, Elvis stood on our front walk for a few minutes, proudly surveying the new greenery.

Afterward, we visited with my mother and sisters at the house for a while. "Now, Mrs. Alden, your mortgage is taken care of and the trees are in," Elvis said at one point. "All you need is the pool installed, and they should be starting it soon."

Elvis was in a great mood. Before long, he said to Charlie, "Let's do a little singing," and we followed them into our music room.

Charlie sat down at the piano and Elvis began singing "How Great Thou Art" with such power, it felt like the roof would blow off. "Listen to this," he said a few times, wanting my family to witness how he could hit certain difficult high and low notes. Afterward, he sang "Unchained Melody," and it cut right through me.

The spell was broken when my brother's two-and-a-half-year-old daughter, Allison, who had been napping in another room, began to cry.

Elvis heard her and walked down the hall to my mother's room. I followed him and saw Allison lying on the bed, sobbing. Elvis walked up to her, bent over, and kissed her on the forehead.

My mother came in then. She picked Allison up and carried her into the den, where she sat on the sofa with Allison in her lap. Elvis took a seat beside them. He began tickling Allison, trying to make her laugh. Then, making some funny motions with his hands, he playfully said, "Whoop woo, whoop woo, Daddy!"

Allison finally started laughing. Elvis continued this game for a few minutes, clearly getting a kick out of making my niece smile. A warm feeling came over me as I watched this and imagined having a child with him, thinking how wonderful it would be.

Later, we went into Rosemary's room, where we sat with Rosemary on her bed and talked about numerology and life. Elvis was so busy thinking and talking that he quickly asked Rosemary for a pen and paper.

She handed him a couple of sheets of yellow stationery from a pad nearby. Elvis wrote some numbers and letters down on them, trying to explain things to us as he went along.

As always, Elvis was enjoying the process of looking for words inside words, and finding a special significance in certain things. He shared some of his discoveries about numbers with us, and what he thought it meant if the numbers were in a certain order. For instance, using the mark of the beast, three sixes, Elvis added the numbers together, which totaled nine, and explained this number symbolized war and destruction. Meanwhile, the number seven was a "God-like" number, Elvis said, because within it was contained the word "Eve."

Elvis entertained the idea that numbers influenced one's life, and I was fascinated, as always, to hear what was going on inside his head.

Later, I brought in a photo album that included some pageant pictures of me. As we were looking through the photographs, Elvis took one out, flipped it over, and wrote, "God gave me to you, God gave you to me," on the back of the photograph. It would be one of the many special things forever dear in my heart.

CHAPTER 26

As much as Elvis loved being at home, a few days later he announced, "I've been off too long." I knew it was in his blood to perform and one of the things that made him the happiest.

His fans obviously wanted to see him as much as he wanted to see them. There were usually fans at the Graceland gates, and people tried to follow him anywhere he went if they happened to spot Elvis out and about. I never heard Elvis complain about this or turn down an autograph.

However, early one evening, the two of us went outside to sit on the front porch. The guards had left the front gates open, unaware that Elvis and I had come out, and a small crowd was gathered at the foot of the driveway.

Suddenly, a few fans began inching their way closer up the driveway toward us. I glanced over at Elvis, who was dressed in his robe and pajamas. He looked at the advancing fans without a word, then stood up and moved his chair behind one of the columns. A few minutes later, he took his jug of water and cigar and abruptly stood up.

"Let's go back inside," he said.

Elvis had been caught in an internal tug-of-war between his instinct to embrace his fans and his own need for privacy. Had the gates been closed, I'm sure Elvis would have stayed out longer on that warm summer evening but he accepted this as part of his life and I accepted this as part of my life with him.

Another evening, Elvis said he wanted to take Lisa and me to Libertyland. I was thrilled, especially because Amber was also at Graceland that night and I knew how much the two girls loved the amusement park. They grew quite excited when I told them our plan.

An hour went by, then another. It was getting late. I took the girls into my bathroom to help them get ready, where I styled Lisa's hair in a bun and the three of us got dressed. We were all anxious to leave and have fun.

When I walked out of the bathroom to look for Elvis, however, I found him still in his pajamas and in bed. "I've decided not to go," he said.

I felt really frustrated. Elvis had canceled our plans to go out at the last minute many times, simply because he had just changed his mind. I had been disappointed by this unpredictable behavior before, but this time I was more upset. Going to the amusement park would be a good thing for him to do, and I knew how much the girls were looking forward to it.

Remembering something Elvis had once said to me, I decided to challenge him. "Elvis, I thought you once told me that you could do anything," I said, then silently waited for his reaction.

"Get George Klein on the phone," he said.

Victory! We contacted George. My spirits quickly sank, though, as I heard Elvis's end of the conversation and realized George was telling him the workers at Libertyland had either gone home or were preparing to close up the park.

They talked for a few more minutes, then Elvis hung up. George called back a little later, however, to say the employees would stay late and keep the park open. Victory again!

Suddenly, Elvis was in an upbeat mood. He asked me to invite my sisters and made a few calls to ask other friends and family to join us. Elvis even told me Rosemary could bring her date for the evening and Terry could include our friend Cindy.

When my sisters and their friends arrived at Graceland, Elvis got dressed in his loose blue jumpsuit and black stage belt. We went downstairs, joined some of the guys, and decided we needed more cars. A small group of us cut across the backyard to Vernon's house so we could use some of the cars parked there.

At Libertyland, Elvis and I spent well over an hour on the Zippin Pippin roller coaster. We sat in the front car, which was scary but I loved it. Elvis rode with his hands raised high in the air. A few times he even pretended he was going to stand up as the coaster sped around its loops and hills. Periodically, the ride stopped so anyone could get off or switch partners, but Elvis and I stayed on.

We later rode the dodgem cars and Elvis played a couple of arcade games, winning a few stuffed animals for Lisa as well as a stuffed pink panther and a big yellow bird for me.

Rosemary and her date unfortunately had to leave early. She thanked Elvis and gave him a hug. Dawn was breaking by the time the rest of us decided to head back. Elvis remained in great spirits, along with everyone else, as we returned to Graceland. The two of us said good night to everyone and Elvis and I retired upstairs. It had been a wonderful night.

Terry and Cindy remained at the house, visiting with some of the guys, and the two of them eventually fell asleep downstairs in the TV room. Having been on tour with us before, Cindy had gotten friendly with David, and he invited her to join us on the next tour. I was pleased to hear this. My two worlds were finally beginning to merge as one.

A couple of days later, my mother was shocked to receive word that she was behind on her July and August house note payments. She called Beecher Smith, Elvis's attorney, for assistance, because she had given him all of the paperwork dealing with her home as Elvis had requested.

Beecher apologized and said he'd been so busy, he had forgotten to take care of everything. Right after that, he sent a letter to my mother's mortgage company, stating that it was an oversight and asking for the full payment amount owed on the home, and whether there would be a prepayment penalty for paying off the mortgage entirely in one lump sum. My mother was relieved to have Beecher sort things out for her so quickly.

On August 12, Elvis decided he wanted to see a movie and rented the United Artists Southbrook 4 theater. He took me, Lisa, and a small group of friends to see the latest James Bond flick, *The Spy Who Loved Me*.

A few days later, I noticed more activity around Graceland as members of Elvis's entourage began preparing for his next tour, which would take us to Portland, Maine. Elvis really wanted Rosemary and my brother to come along, so I asked them and was thrilled when my brother said he could take some vacation time and both of them agreed to join us.

Elvis had mentioned needing to lose some weight before this tour, and I was pleased to see that, for the first time, he was showing more awareness of his diet. On August 15, he began having only small amounts of yogurt and drinking a lot of water.

Lisa was still with us, but she would be leaving the next day to return to Los Angeles and get ready for the new school year, so Elvis wanted to spend time with her. It was a cloudy day. Between periods of drizzle, the three of us, along with my niece Amber, took a short ride around on her golf cart in the afternoon.

That evening, Elvis and I watched television. My stomach began to cramp and I realized my time of the month was starting. My periods were often bad, especially during the first few days. Hoping Elvis would understand, I ventured, "Could I join your tour in a day or two?" Embarrassed, I went on to explain why, even though I knew Elvis would want me with him.

He gave me a displeased look. "I'd like you to go," Elvis said, then waited a beat. "See how you feel."

Later Elvis made some calls, trying to arrange for a private screening of the new movie *MacArthur* at a local theater. At one point, Elvis told me he thought a piece of tooth had broken off. He wanted to have it checked and filled. He showed me a small glass box with some temporary crowns in it that he carried on tour, in case he chipped a tooth while traveling.

Elvis set up an appointment with a dentist named Dr. Hoffman. He asked Billy Smith to come over and, along with Charlie, we left Graceland in the Stutz around 10:30 P.M. We arrived at the dentist's office, where Elvis gestured at me, saying, "Isn't she ugly?"

Smiling, Dr. Hoffman replied, "Yes."

Elvis later reappeared from the dentist's room, the problem fixed. Dr. Hoffman then took some X-rays of my teeth. Meanwhile, Charlie said he'd made a phone call to Graceland to find out if anyone had managed to set up a screening of *MacArthur*, but discovered the projectionist wouldn't be around that late.

We returned to Graceland around 12:30 A.M., and I followed Elvis upstairs to his bedroom. Elvis mentioned that he needed to speak with a couple of the guys for a few minutes, so I went into Lisa's room. I wanted to see if Lisa and Amber had gone to bed. They were nowhere in sight. Even the kids operated on "Elvis time," so I figured they were downstairs playing.

A short time later, Elvis asked me to come back to the room. He was now alone. We watched a little television, then Elvis called downstairs to have the bed made.

Mary, one of the maids, came upstairs to do the bed, so Elvis and I moved into Lisa's room. I lay on the couch while he turned on the television and sat down in the chair across from it, where he lit up a cigar. When he mentioned wanting to play racquetball later, I got excited. This would be my first time seeing him play, and I thought it might help relax him before his tour.

We'd been watching TV for a little bit when, without any warning, Elvis suddenly turned it off. His eyes quickly cut away from the television screen to my face.

"I've been thinking a lot about getting married lately," he said, fiddling with the cigar in his mouth and studying me, waiting to see my reaction.

"Really?" I was caught completely off guard.

"Really," Elvis said, smiling.

Again, he talked about having our wedding ceremony take place in a nondenominational church, like the pyramid-shaped church Charlie had told him about. "I would like certain people there," he said, "public officials and friends. And there should be so many police officers to guard the church, so no news media can get to us. I don't want this to be a three-ring circus," he declared.

Elvis paused for a minute. Then, using his hands to show me a measure of length, he said, "The limousines should be so many inches longer than a normal-length limo and in blue."

As I nodded, my excitement mounting, he continued, meticulously going over every detail. "I've thought about your gown. The dress should have a high collar and I would like it to have small rosebuds with gold threads through it. I'm gonna have someone work on it in Los Angeles."

"You don't have my measurements," I said, thinking practically for a moment.

Elvis gave me a look, as if to say he knew exactly what those measurements would be. Once again I was swept along by his ability to make anything happen. The vision of what the dress would look like and the reality of the wedding drew more sharply into focus. I couldn't believe Elvis had already given this much thought to everything! On the other hand, wasn't this the way Elvis had done everything with me from the start?

"You should wear clear, glass-looking slippers and a tiara in your hair," he said. I loved these ideas. Then he brought up bridesmaid dresses. "I think pink would be good. What color would you like?"

"Lavender would be pretty," I said.

Elvis smiled and shook his head. "This has got to be the wedding of the century." He sat quietly for a moment, then added, "We should pick a date. I've been thinking about my birthday, your birthday, or Christmas. What do you think?"

I didn't hesitate. "Christmas would be nice," I said.

He nodded, giving me another soft smile. "That will be our gift to God."

I felt as Elvis did, that God wanted us to be together and would be pleased to see us married on such a special day. I was so happy, I stood up, walked over to Elvis, and kissed him full on the lips.

He returned my kiss, then said, "I'd like to announce our engagement to the audience at the end of the tour in Memphis. We'll put it in the local paper too, under the regular engagement section, nothin' fancy."

I smiled. Here was Elvis, going with his own version of the wow factor once more. He turned the television back on and we settled down again to watch it.

A little while later, Elvis left the room, saying he had to talk business with some of the guys. I figured this must have something to do with his upcoming tour.

After he'd finished his meetings, I asked Elvis if he still wanted to play racquetball, knowing some exercise would be good for him. He told me he did.

It was after 4 A.M. Elvis called downstairs and asked Billy and Jo Smith to meet us. I hated the idea of waking them. By now, however, I'd learned that, when Elvis called, most people jumped.

Elvis changed into a warm-up suit and loaned me one to wear that wasn't overly large. I was still on a high from our conversation about the wedding, and eager to be going outside to move around. We met up with Billy and Jo and the four of us walked down to the racquetball court.

Other than peeking inside the racquetball court once with my mother, this was my first time seeing it. Elvis wanted to show me around before we played. The court was as lavish as most of Graceland, with a custom bath and spa, dressing room, bar, pinball machine, jukebox, and workout area with weight equipment. There was even a piano.

Elvis quickly took me up to the roof, too, and showed me an outdoor jogging track. It was still dark out. There was precipitation in the air, but that didn't seem to disturb him. His gaze swept over the property, then Elvis pointed to a nearby area and said if I wanted to paint again, he'd build an art studio for me there.

I couldn't believe this night could get any better, but it had. I had no idea Elvis would offer something like this! What really touched me was that he hadn't forgotten our last conversation about me wanting to reconnect with art and not lose the things that had been important to me before I met him.

"Thank you," was all I could muster, inadequate as I felt it was.

Back downstairs, we rejoined Billy and Jo. I went onto the court with Jo but I had never played racquetball before. I tried to give it a go but unfortunately didn't feel like moving around much because my cramps had returned. We weren't out there long and then Elvis and Billy walked onto the court while Jo and I sat behind a nearby glass partition. The two of them began to hit the ball around and then Elvis started cutting up. He was laughing, being silly, and having a good time. Pretending to hit himself on the leg with his racquet sometimes, Elvis kept turning around, making funny faces to see if Jo and I were watching.

Elvis soon got tired, though, and he left the court to come over and sit down beside me. We then watched Billy and Jo play for a bit. When they came off the court, Elvis went over to the piano and started to play, singing "Unchained Melody" and then "Blue Eyes Crying in the Rain." When he finished at the piano, he walked over to one of the stationary bikes and peddled for about ten minutes.

About 6 A.M., Elvis and I went back to the house. Billy came upstairs, too, because Elvis wanted him to help dry his hair. Elvis and I peeked in on Lisa and Amber, and I was glad to see the girls were both in bed and fast asleep.

Elvis and Billy then went into Elvis's bathroom. I went into mine, changed into my sleepwear, then came out and lay on the bed.

I listened to the hum of the hairdryer in the bathroom for a bit. Shortly after that, Billy left and Elvis walked out, having changed into blue pajamas. Around 6:45, Elvis called downstairs, asking for whoever was on duty to bring up a packet of medication to help him sleep.

I was still suffering from sharp menstrual cramps. Seeing that I was in such discomfort, Elvis called Tish to bring me something to relieve the pain. He again asked if I was going to come with him at the beginning of the tour. I hated to disappoint him, but knowing how I was going to feel for the first few days, I told him I'd like to wait just one day, if not two, until I felt better.

I hoped Elvis would understand. He sat quietly for a few moments, thinking things over. "I want you to buy something special for when we announce our engagement during the show in Memphis then," he said.

I smiled. This was good. He understood.

"All right," I said, relieved.

Tish sent up a Tylenol with codeine for me. Right after that, Ricky appeared with Elvis's morning sleep packet and we both took our medications. Elvis wanted to show me a couple of new books he'd been given recently, so the two of us settled in bed and began looking at one of them. The book's title was *A Scientific Search for the Face of Jesus* and described the Shroud of Turin, which had supposedly been wrapped around Jesus after he was taken down from the Cross. Elvis and I were both intrigued.

As we flipped through the book, Elvis showed me some photos of what the author claimed was the face of Jesus impressed on a shroud. Then, putting that book aside, Elvis showed me another one by Betty Bethards called *Sex and Psychic Energy*. This book highlighted ways to tune into your partner's energy, your inner self, and your chakras. Elvis pointed out a few illustrations.

We didn't look at the book very long because we were both growing drowsy from the medications and soon fell asleep. Sometime later, I was awakened by movement on the bed. I was still groggy from my medication, but I was aware of Elvis calling downstairs and asking for another packet to help him sleep.

I glanced at the clock. It was eight o'clock in the morning but I wasn't surprised that Elvis was having trouble resting. By now, I was used to seeing him keyed up before a tour, and he'd been off a long time before this one.

Still, when he hung up, I asked Elvis what the problem was. "I just can't sleep," he said.

He sounded pretty alert, which surprised me. I wondered if there had been placebos in the medication packet he'd taken earlier.

Ricky brought up another packet shortly and then left. I hoped Elvis would finally be able to rest. We both settled down in bed again, and I quickly fell back to sleep.

In a little while, feeling some movement again, I opened my eyes. It was now close to 9 A.M. and Elvis was sitting on the side of the bed with his back to me. I moved over to him and put my hand on his back. "What's the matter?" I asked.

Elvis said he still couldn't sleep. In a few minutes, he stood up and told me he was going to read. He picked up the book on psychic energy and headed toward the bathroom. Once again, I wondered if the contents of his medication packets had been altered because Elvis seemed pretty much unaffected by whatever he'd taken.

"Don't fall asleep," I said, remembering the bed in his dressing area.

Elvis stopped before going in, looked at me with a little boy pout, then smiled and gave me a little wave. "Okay, I won't," he reassured me, and continued into his bathroom.

Between the Tylenol with codeine and the fact that I'd had no rest since the day before, I once again fell into a deep sleep.

Just after 2 P.M., I awoke with cramps. Elvis wasn't in bed. I was curious where he was but unable to look right away as my period had begun and I was beginning to bleed heavily. I got up and rushed to my bathroom to take care of this. While using the toilet, I picked up the phone on the wall above it and called my friend Cindy, knowing she'd expect to see me on the plane when everyone left for the tour. I told her I was thinking about coming in a day late because of the discomfort I was experiencing with my period.

I then quickly called my mother at work. "Where are you?" she asked.

When I told her I was at Graceland, she asked why I wasn't home packing. "I've been thinking about coming in a day late," I said.

She reminded me that my brother and sister were going.

I hesitated. I'd completely forgotten about this. I knew Elvis had really wanted me on tour from the start. Even though I knew I wouldn't be feeling good, I changed my mind. "Okay, I guess I'll go," I said, then told my mother I needed to hang up, I wanted to find Elvis and tell him.

"Where is he?" my mother asked.

"I don't know," I said. "I'm going to go check on him."

I quickly finished up in the bathroom, then walked into Elvis's bedroom in search of him. I glanced at the clock and saw it was close to 2:20. The bathroom door was cracked open a little.

I knocked on the door and said, "Elvis?"

There was no answer. Slowly opening the door, I peered in and saw Elvis on the floor off to the left. I stood paralyzed as I took in the scene.

Elvis looked as if his entire body had completely frozen in a seated position while using the commode and then had fallen forward, in that fixed position, directly in front of it. His legs were bent, the upper part of his chest and shoulders touched the ground, and his head was slightly turned to the left with his cheek resting on the floor. His arms lay on the ground, close to his sides, back toward his legs, palms facing upward.

It was clear that, from the time whatever hit him to the moment he had landed on the floor, Elvis hadn't moved. A blow dryer was lying on the floor, almost touching the top of his head. Billy must have left it there when he'd finished drying Elvis's hair. The psychic energy book had been placed on the arm of the chair. The chair sat against the wall, under his window, facing the counter. The book lay open, undisturbed.

I rushed over, bent down beside him and said, "Elvis?" A horrible fear shot through me.

His pajama top had slid forward a little because of his inclined position. I touched his lower back. His skin felt cool. Saying, "Elvis!" again, I gently turned his face toward me.

A hint of air expelled from his nose. The tip of his tongue was clenched between his teeth and his face was blotchy, with purple discoloration. I gently raised one eyelid. His eye was staring straight ahead and bloodred.

Frantic now, I quickly reached for the phone by the toilet and called downstairs. The maid Nancy answered.

In denial of what I was seeing, my only thought was, *Don't alarm anybody, Ginger. He's going to be okay.* But I heard the tremor in my voice as I asked Nancy which aide was on duty.

She hesitated a moment, then said, "Al Strada."

"Send him up right away," I said.

Al rushed to the top of the stairs. I met him in the hallway and cried, "I think something's really wrong with Elvis!"

We ran into the bathroom. When Al saw Elvis, he mentioned something about a blood pressure kit and rushed to Elvis's night table, with me on his heels. Bending down, he opened a door. When we glanced inside the cupboard and saw it was empty, we raced back to Elvis.

Al immediately called downstairs, and I realized Joe was in the house when Al asked for him. Moments later, Joe appeared in the doorway of the bathroom. Not wanting to be in the way, I knelt off to one side as he and Al turned Elvis over onto his back.

Elvis's legs remained in a bent position, his feet not touching the floor. Al and Joe lifted him a little more toward the center of the bathroom and laid him in front of the counter.

I moved in closer as Joe lightly began to slap Elvis's face. "Elvis, breathe!" he repeated urgently, while Al pressed on Elvis's chest. Al and I joined in, begging Elvis to breathe.

Then Joe mentioned calling Dr. Nichopoulos. He stood up and went over to the phone on the wall. Glancing back at Elvis, Joe first called for an ambulance instead. He then tried Dr. Nichopoulos but didn't reach him.

Al got on the phone, spoke with someone who I assumed was from Dr. Nichopoulos's office and hung up, telling Joe that the person in the office was trying to locate the doctor by calling his pager. Joe tried calling the doctor again. Dr. Nichopoulos finally answered the page, then Joe phoned Vernon at his office. Charlie entered the room and joined in our pleas for Elvis to breathe.

Vernon arrived minutes later, accompanied by Sandy and Patsy. "Oh God, son, don't die!" he pleaded. He looked as if he might collapse, and someone moved the book from the chair by the window and placed the chair by Elvis's head for Vernon.

He sat down and shouted, "Breathe!" with the rest of us as Sandy tried giving Elvis mouth-to-mouth resuscitation.

Joe and Charlie had tried to pry open Elvis's mouth, but it was clenched too tightly shut. Feeling completely helpless, I could only watch and pray. I felt as if I were trapped in a nightmare.

It seemed like a long time, but I'm sure it was just minutes later when I heard a commotion on the stairs. Looking over my shoulder, I saw a couple of paramedics and quickly moved out of their way, backing into Elvis's bedroom.

The paramedics began CPR on Elvis as Lisa suddenly appeared in the bedroom doorway. "What's wrong with my daddy?" she asked.

Instinctively, I moved to protect her. I didn't want her to see her father like this. "Nothing, Lisa," I said, turning her away.

As I started to shut the bedroom door, Lisa said, "Something's wrong and I'm going to find out." She took off down the hall toward the entrance to Elvis's dressing area. Racing to the bathroom door, I spotted Al standing down that way and shouted to him, "Lisa's trying to get in!"

Al quickly shut and locked the door. I knew they would be taking Elvis to a hospital soon; thinking I'd be riding in the ambulance with him, I rushed to my bathroom and hastily dressed in the clothes I'd worn the previous evening. Afterward, I hurried toward Elvis's bathroom just in time to see the paramedics and the other men lift Elvis onto a stretcher.

I moved out of their way as they started toward the stairway, with Vernon and the others following close behind. As I watched the paramedics carry Elvis downstairs and out the front door, the reality of what was happening suddenly hit me. I began to cry as the ambulance sped away. I suddenly felt very alone and needed to talk with someone.

I returned to my bathroom and dialed my mother's number with shaking fingers. The minute my mother heard the quaver in my voice, she said, "What's wrong?"

Gripped by anxiety, I said, "I think something has happened to Elvis."

"Maybe it's not that bad," she said, trying to calm me down.

"Mom, they've taken him in an ambulance and it looks bad." I broke down.

"I'll be there as soon as I can," she said, still trying to reassure me.

I hung up the phone, relieved that my mother was coming. I found myself wishing more than anything that I really had been trapped in a bad dream, but there had been a crack in the universe and a cold reality was creeping over me.

CHAPTER 27

It was shortly after 4 P.M. when I turned from the window in the living room. I would later learn that this was the time Elvis's death was announced publicly.

Amber was approaching me. "Where's Lisa?" I asked, feeling a mixture of grief and concern about Lisa being alone.

Amber told me Lisa was in another room with some family members. A few other relatives of Elvis's were sitting on the stairway, so I took Amber over there and we sat on the front steps, too.

I had never felt so completely lost. I saw George Klein walk over to the table by the stairs and try making a phone call. As he hung up and stepped into the middle of the foyer, I walked down the stairs and hugged him.

George embraced me in return and we both broke down. "He loved you so much," he said.

I understood George had lost his dear friend, and I could only hope he knew just how much his comment meant to me.

Lisa walked up to me then. Wanting to comfort her, I brought her upstairs with Amber, where I sat beside Lisa on the couch in her room and put my arms around her. I struggled through my own fog of grief in search of the right words to say to this little girl who'd just lost her father.

"You know your daddy loved you, Lisa," I managed. "He was a wonderful father and he's gone to heaven, but he will always be watching over you." She sat quietly beside me. I wondered if Lisa could possibly grasp any of this.

Before long, a team of men arrived from the police department and led me into Elvis's office, where they asked me a few questions. After they'd gone, I turned everything over in my mind. *What had happened to Elvis?*

It was impossible to get a grip on the situation. I was too flooded with emotion. I returned downstairs and sat at the dining room table with Amber, knowing that by now my family must have heard the news, along with the rest of the world. I hadn't been able to call them, and they hadn't managed to reach me, either, because the phone lines were jammed and so was the street outside Graceland.

Everyone in the house was grieving. I was surrounded by all these people, and yet I felt alone. The only people who could really change that for me at the time were in my own family, and waiting for them was difficult. Eventually someone told me my sister Terry had managed to get through and was on the phone.

I took the call in the hall by the stairs, breaking down again. I could tell Terry had been crying, too, as she said, "I'm sorry." She let me know that our mother, Rosemary, and my sister-in-law were on their way.

After the call I retreated to the dining room again. Everyone at Graceland was crying, disbelieving, offering or receiving comfort at various times. Just after five, my family made it through the front door. We hugged each other and they began offering their condolences to Vernon and other members among Elvis's friends and family.

A while later, Aunt Delta approached me. She gently asked if I had anything upstairs that I wanted to get, as they needed to close it off and lock it. I asked her if I could borrow a suitcase and she loaned me one. Rosemary said she'd go with me and Delta walked upstairs with the two of us.

Upon entering Elvis's office, I glanced toward his bedroom. I had slept wearing my engagement ring and the TLC necklace Elvis had given me. Now I considered my photos on his night table, the necklace I'd tried designing for him but had yet to finish, and the wedding list in his room. Seized by an overwhelming desire to stay linked to Graceland, I left all of those things there.

In my bathroom, I gathered a few items, placed them inside the suitcase, and picked up my jewelry box. I took one last look at Elvis's bedroom before following Delta back downstairs.

Elvis's funeral arrangements were beginning to be discussed among some of the people gathered there. Someone told us we would be called when they were completed. Things were moving quickly, and they didn't seem to need me or to consult with me on what those plans would be. The pain that I was feeling was like nothing I'd ever experienced before. I felt I needed a private haven to try to process what really was unfathomable, that Elvis was dead.

This was the beginning of my grieving process. The only safe place I could think to do this was at home, where I'd be surrounded by my family.

I said good-bye to Vernon, Sandy, Dodger, Lisa, and others. It was more difficult to leave Lisa because I'd grown closer to her, but I felt she would be all right as she was surrounded by her family.

My emotional pain was so great, it took every ounce of energy I had to make it through the front door. I had to focus on just putting one foot in front of the other. The police parted the crowd gathered at the gates of Graceland to let us through.

Even back at home and alone with my family, I couldn't shake the feeling that I was trapped in a nightmare. My father returned to the house in an effort to lend me his support and told me how sorry he was.

Later, my mother told me that, right after I'd called her at work, she had to put her head down on her desk. Another employee asked if she needed to go to the nurses' station. "I told him I didn't think I could make it there," my mother said, and told her colleague that Elvis was in the hospital, but not to say anything. She then went to her supervisor and said she had to leave.

My sister-in-law had been worried about Amber, naturally, so my mother had headed home to pick her up on the way to Graceland. On her way home, my mother had heard on the radio that Elvis was dead.

The traffic was so congested on their way to Graceland that, when they came to a red light at the corner of Elvis Presley Boulevard and Winchester Road, my sister-in-law, Carolyn, had jumped out of the car and stopped traffic with her hands so my mother could make the turn. They had then driven the few blocks to Graceland in the turning lane with the emergency flashers on.

At the gates to Graceland, Carolyn had yelled to a nearby police officer, "This is Ginger's mother!" to make him clear a path. That was the only way they'd made it through Graceland's gates to pick up Amber and me.

Every television channel carried the news of Elvis's death, but I couldn't watch the reports. At one point, someone told me that Joe Esposito had been interviewed; they'd heard him say he was the one who found Elvis.

What? I couldn't believe it! Little did I know that the untruths were just beginning.

That evening, someone called our house to say there would be a private viewing of Elvis's body at Graceland at eleven the next morning, on Wednesday, August 17. I dreaded this. I wasn't sure if I could see Elvis this way.

Later that night, the Shelby County medical examiner ruled Elvis's cause of death as cardiac arrhythmia with severe cardiovascular disease present. How was this possible? He was only forty-two! After hearing the news, I asked my mother to lie in bed with me. I couldn't stand the thought of being alone.

Yet, oddly, that night I felt Elvis's presence in the room with me. A comforting, peaceful sensation enveloped me. Maybe I wasn't alone after all, I thought. Maybe Elvis was still watching over me.

It was a sleepless night for all of us. My parents had to take the phone off the hook because we were being barraged by reporters calling from all over the world.

There were moments during that night when I found myself wishing I hadn't been the one to find Elvis. But, as difficult as it had been, had I not been there and only heard of his death, I felt it would have been harder for me to take in the news of him passing away.

A massive crowd had gathered in front of Graceland by the time my family and I arrived for the viewing the next morning. Some people looked like they must have slept all night by the gates.

As I stepped through the front door, I found it was still nearly impossible to imagine that Elvis was gone. A little over twenty-four hours ago, I had been upstairs with him right in this house, planning our future together. There was a surreal element to almost everything unfolding in front of me.

I saw Lisa walking about, mingling with various people as she went to and from the kitchen. I greeted her, Vernon, and a few others, then went into Dodger's room and gave her a hug. She had always been nice to me and this was so hard.

Priscilla Presley had arrived with her own family. Of course she would be here because she was Lisa's mother. Yet, as I watched Priscilla greet a few people—some of whom I had never met before—I felt strangely displaced. Elvis had been trying to get it through my head that, as the future Mrs. Presley, I was the lady of the house, but now that role seemed farther from reality than ever, and I found myself withdrawing from those gathered.

When I saw Joe a little later, he didn't approach me with any explanation as to why he'd said he was the one who had found Elvis. This wasn't the time or place to ask him about his version of events, but knowing Joe had done that felt like a small but painful betrayal.

The furniture in the living room had been removed and replaced by folding chairs, adding to the surreal nature of the experience. Some chairs were arranged against the right wall, facing the fireplace, while others were in rows lined up in the center and facing the music room. My family and I took seats in some center chairs; from there, I glanced around the room at the various floral arrangements.

Flowers were continually arriving and being brought into the room. My family and I had sent some earlier. Now, I wondered which arrangement was mine. My flowers were as lost as I was.

Before long, I noticed Priscilla and her family enter and seat themselves against the wall facing us. A little while later, a copper casket was brought into the house and placed at the entrance to the music room. It was around noon by now. When the lid was opened, it was hard for me to look. Charlie stood at the head of the casket, greeting viewers as they paid their respects to Elvis. I waited awhile, steeling my resolve, then finally walked to the front.

Elvis was dressed in a white suit with a pale blue shirt and white tie. It seemed odd. I'd never seen him in a suit. As crazy as it might have looked to some, I thought it would have been more appropriate if he'd been dressed in one of his jumpsuits, or even in his pajamas and robe. Absurdly, I thought he would have felt more comfortable that way. Also, where was his gun? Where were his jug of water and cigar?

While I was standing there, Lisa came up to the casket and stood next to me. I smiled at her and she gently touched Elvis's hair. I lightly stroked the side of his face.

From his post near the head of the casket, Charlie said, "He looks good, doesn't he?"

I managed to look up at Charlie and nod.

In a mystical, knowing way, Charlie spoke again. "Ginger, he hasn't gone anywhere," he said softly. "He's just on another plane right now."

I felt comforted by Charlie's words. *Where are you, Elvis?*

I couldn't help but hear Elvis's voice in response, saying the same words he had whispered in my ear in the back of the church at my grandfather's funeral: "Son, you're on your own." Only this time the words sent a chill through me and cut me like a knife.

I returned to my seat, but every so often, I got up again to look at Elvis. Strangely, what had been so difficult for me to do in the beginning now brought me peace. Elvis looked like he was just sleeping.

While I was seated in my chair between visits to the casket, an unfamiliar woman tapped me on the shoulder. "Priscilla would like to see you," she said.

Surprised, I followed her around the corner. We entered the foyer and I saw Priscilla standing next to the front stairs. "Hello," she said, and introduced me to the woman who'd come for me, Joan Esposito, who I would later learn was Joe's ex-wife.

I was even more stunned when Priscilla drew me into a hug. "Ginger, I know how much Elvis loved you," she said.

"Thank you," I said, embracing her in return. I suddenly had the most incredible feeling of acceptance, as Priscilla acknowledged what Elvis and I had together. "Would you like to meet my family?"

"Not right now," she said, "but I'd like to later."

I walked back into the living room and sat down, relaying to my family what had just happened. When Priscilla entered the room again later, I got up and introduced my mother to her and her parents.

After a time, everyone was informed that there would be a public viewing at three that afternoon. I really thought it was a wonderful idea that his fans would be given the opportunity to pay their respects, too. I was sure that was a cue for most of us to leave, so I decided to return home before it began. As I was leaving, I was told the funeral would be the next afternoon, August 18, at two.

Of course, Elvis's death made worldwide headlines. Everything Elvis had ever done became the substance of stories run in every media outlet imaginable.

I had known Elvis was a big star, of course, but after we fell in love and became intimately involved, I had mostly stopped paying attention to his celebrity and had begun to see Elvis the man, rather than Elvis the famous entertainer. Now I realized that the scope of his fame was beyond what I or anyone else could imagine. The shock, loss, and interest surrounding the news of his death wasn't something I had seen since the deaths of the Kennedys and Martin Luther King Jr.

Even knowing this, losing Elvis was nothing like that for me. I was experiencing grief on the most fundamental and intimately personal level. I had lost the man who had turned my life upside down and had become my friend, teacher, protector, and lover—the man I had loved deeply and planned to marry.

I was no longer the same young woman I'd been that first night I accompanied my sisters to Graceland. My whole being—physically, emotionally, and spiritually—had become intertwined with Elvis. To me, his death was no news story. This was my life being torn apart.

Yet, my house continued to be flooded with phone calls from voracious reporters who insisted they needed to get a story *now*. No matter what I was going through personally, they all saw me at the center of the story. I took cover in my bedroom in a futile attempt to hide.

At one point, my mother came into the bedroom, looking exasperated. She said that two men, from two separate tabloids, were on our front porch and almost getting into a fistfight over who deserved an interview with me. The hungry lions Elvis had warned me about were right outside my door, and this time, Elvis couldn't fly over in his car to protect me. I felt so sorry she was having to deal with this.

I certainly had no plans to give any interview and was hurt that they were even out there. Then my mother told me that one of the men had said Linda Thompson was giving him an interview, and that Linda was saying she might have saved Elvis if they'd stayed together.

This hurt and I was horrified. How could anyone say such a thing? And how cold, self-serving, and egotistical it would be if she did! From what I'd seen, no one could have claimed to have saved Elvis that day.

The reporter told my mother that, if I didn't give an interview, they were going to print Linda's story. I was furious. Elvis had stopped seeing Linda and she certainly wasn't there on the day he died. To me, it had seemed that Elvis had died instantly. Not even the world's greatest heart specialist could make a statement like hers!

I asked my mother to turn the reporters away. One of the men told my mother he'd be back in a little while to see if I would change my mind. I felt terrible. In the midst of this horrible tragedy, I suddenly had this going on? I thought and thought about things, slowly becoming more conflicted and anguished over whether to give an interview. My mother and I were way out of our depth and I was extremely upset. My family and I had no experience with this sort of thing.

Feeling like I had a tiger by the tail, my tears slowly turned into anger again. This was what I was up against now. Some kind of story was going to be put out there, and I couldn't let Linda say something like this without a response. When the reporter returned, I agreed to give the tabloid an interview at an upcoming date.

I slept fitfully. The next morning, everything hit me hard. Extremely depressed, I got up and went into our kitchen. My mother was making breakfast and I sat down at our breakfast table, put my head down on my arms, and began crying inconsolably.

Later, turning on the television, I learned that two teenaged girls had been killed and another injured when a drunk driver ran his car into a crowd gathered on Elvis Presley Boulevard. This tragedy only added to the horror of it all. It seemed like the entire world was spinning out of control.

That afternoon, I slipped into a black dress and headed for Graceland with my family and our friend Cindy. We arrived a little before the funeral services were scheduled to begin. A few people were already inside and we exchanged hugs and hellos.

All of the folding chairs that had been in the living room now faced Elvis's casket, which was again positioned at the entrance to the music room. My family and I sat in the dining room, watching people arrive.

Before long, I recognized the actress, Ann-Margret, who had been romantically linked with Elvis years earlier in Hollywood, when they had appeared in a few films together. She was there with her husband, Roger Smith. I also noticed the actor George Hamilton, who had been friends with Elvis, and Colonel Parker, who was wearing a baseball cap and puffing on a cigar. Dr. Ghanem, Elvis's doctor in Las Vegas, was there as well.

Close to 2 P.M., we entered the living room. Never one to call attention to myself or to try to put myself front and center, I decided to sit about six rows back from Elvis's casket. Aunt Delta, Dodger, Vernon, and Sandy sat on the front row. Priscilla and her family took seats behind them.

After a while, Lisa appeared by our row, came over to me and sat in my lap, seeking her own kind of closeness and comfort. I put my arms around her and she visited with us, talking with Amber and Sandy's daughter.

The services soon began with a eulogy from the comic Jackie Kahane. Rex Humbard, a television evangelist, spoke, and then the Reverend Bradley led the sermon. Kathy Westmoreland, the Stamps Quartet, and a few others sang.

It was a beautiful ceremony. Afterward, each row of people was instructed to file past Elvis's casket. As I walked toward the front, I struggled to hold back tears.

I had made it a point to never say good-bye to Elvis when leaving Graceland in the time we had together. Now, looking at him for the last time, I forced myself to whisper good-bye under my breath.

I turned to Vernon, Sandy, Dodger, and Aunt Delta, hugging them, then returned to my seat. When the service was over, Joe approached my family and me, instructing us that we would be riding in the fifth limousine behind the hearse. I wanted to think that Joe was just trying to do his best to get everyone to the mausoleum and putting them in whichever car he could, but, when Elvis was here, he had always moved others around to keep me at his side. Now that seemed forgotten. It was a small slight, but it stung. It seemed I had become insignificant, the exact opposite of how Elvis made me feel.

When I walked out of Graceland, I saw multiple white limousines lining the driveway and would later learn there were sixteen in total. Our limousine driver opened the doors to our car. I got into the front with my mother, while the rest of my family and Cindy climbed in back.

We sat, waiting for all the limousines to fill. Then Vernon, Sandy, Lisa, and Priscilla walked out and got into the first limousine. Before long, the pallbearers, George Klein, Gene Smith, Jerry Schilling,

Charlie Hodge, Lamar Fike, Joe Esposito, Billy Smith, and Dr. Nichopoulos, exited the house, carrying Elvis's casket.

As the men took a few steps toward the hearse, suddenly a huge branch broke from a tree and landed in the yard not far from them. I shuddered, thinking how eerie that should happen at this moment.

The procession slowly made its way down the driveway with a police motorcade flanking the hearse. As the hearse passed through the gates, nearby police officers saluted.

Turning onto Elvis Presley Boulevard, we began the three-mile journey toward Forest Hill Cemetery. Elvis would be laid to rest inside a crypt there, in the mausoleum. The scene before me played like some bizarre television reel, with tens of thousands of fans lining both sides of the boulevard, many of them openly crying.

This got to me, and I turned my focus to the floor of the limousine. When I glanced up again, for some reason, my attention suddenly focused on one woman in the crowd as she quickly snapped a photo and then put her camera down. Then it hit me as we passed her. It was Caroline Kennedy. I couldn't believe that, with the multitude of people lining the street, I had looked up right at that moment and she was part of the crowd, no different from any of the others, it seemed. And yet, at that moment, we were actually connected through experiencing a historic death: Caroline and her father, and me and my fiancé. Hundreds of flower arrangements, in all shapes and sizes, covered the lawn at the mausoleum. The hearse came to a stop, and my family and I waited in our car while the pallbearers removed the casket and carried it inside.

When I entered the mausoleum, every seat looked filled in the small area. Vernon, Lisa, Priscilla, and a few members of Elvis's immediate family had been secured seats. I looked around as others came in. Like me, they, too, had to stand wherever they could.

Again, I felt invisible.

A nice man kindly stood and graciously offered me his seat. The ceremony was brief, with the Reverend Bradley saying a few words. Afterward I followed the others outside. I didn't realize that Vernon and a few others had remained. No one had told me what to do.

Everyone waited outside until Vernon had exited. I had an empty feeling as we drove away and returned to Graceland, where food and beverages had been set up in the kitchen.

Who could eat now? I wondered. Then I saw Priscilla walk through the kitchen, as well as Linda Thompson. A fragment of a story Elvis had once told me suddenly flashed in my mind. The story was about a man who passes away and then watches from heaven as the numerous women he left behind gather at his funeral. I couldn't help but think Elvis must be getting a kick out of seeing this.

I walked into the dining room and saw Vernon seated at the table. He motioned for me to come over and I went and sat beside him.

Vernon showed me a photo someone had recently given him that had supposedly been taken at the time of Elvis's death. The picture showed what looked like a figure, wearing a white robe, standing among the clouds. The face in the photo was indistinguishable and Vernon seemed to be pondering the significance of the picture, as if it held some hidden spiritual meaning. I knew how he felt. I, too, wanted to believe in something to make sense of this tragedy.

By the time my family and I arrived home from Graceland after the funeral, a reporter from one of the local papers, the *Commercial Appeal*, was camped out on our front porch. He wanted to know if I would grant him an interview.

After hearing that Joe had said he was the one who had found Elvis and after being treated as if I were just another mourner throughout the course of the day, I was alarmed that the truth would be twisted. As shattered as I felt, I decided to speak with the reporter for a few minutes so that history would not be rewritten by others who had their own agenda. Afterward, the reporter asked whether I had a picture of Elvis and me together. Thinking of the nice picture Elvis had given me, the one taken in Hawaii with the two of us smiling, I gave it to him.

A few days later, my interview was printed in the *Commercial Appeal*. Joe, Vernon, and a few others had also given interviews. Vernon acknowledged my engagement to Elvis, and Joe said that I had been the one to find Elvis in the bathroom. Their statements momentarily relieved my unease. Their honesty was a small comfort, but it was important to me.

On August 21, Elvis's will was filed with the Shelby County Probate Court in Memphis. He had named Lisa, Vernon, and Dodger as his beneficiaries, with Vernon named executor of the estate, along with the National Bank of Commerce and Joseph Hanks, their accountant.

People later would ask me if I'd expected to be included in Elvis's will, but that had never entered my mind. Yes, I had witnessed him sign it, but it looked like a will from 1976 that Elvis was re-signing in 1977 with the new date just before he hurried off on a vacation with me. Why would he have altered his will to include me before we were even married?

Elvis and I were both young and enjoying each other. We thought about life, not death.

The same day the will was read, Vernon called my home and said he wanted my mother and me to come to Graceland so he could talk with us. I was nervous driving over. I was still a little intimidated by Vernon. On top of that, it would feel strange to walk back into Graceland, knowing Elvis was gone.

One of the maids greeted us at the front door. Inside, Vernon was seated at the dining room table. He leaned over, trying to look at me from the head chair.

"These damn chairs," he grumbled as my mother and I joined him. "Linda Thompson picked these out, and they're so high you can't see over the back of them."

Once we were seated, Vernon took a deep breath and looked directly at me. "Ginger, I know how much Elvis loved you," he said. "I know he wanted more children and you to be their mother."

My eyes stung and I was having difficulty swallowing, much less speaking. I nodded, appreciating his acknowledgment of my bond with Elvis.

Vernon glanced down for a long pause before he continued. "I'm sorry, but I'm gonna have to ask you for your credit card back," he said then.

I certainly didn't mind handing the card over. Still, I wanted to make sure that Vernon remembered I'd hardly used it. I had always been wary of spending Elvis's money freely. That wasn't how I was brought up.

"Mr. Presley," I said when I found my voice, "you know I mainly used this card for identification when writing a check."

"I know, Ginger," he said, "but Linda went out and charged a lot when Elvis broke off with her."

Enough said. I quietly handed over my credit card.

"I know the Cadillac Seville you have is still in Elvis's name," Vernon said once he'd tucked away the card, "but I'll go ahead and have the title transferred over to you."

"Thank you," I said, startled. Having driven the car all these months, I hadn't given a thought about it still being in Elvis's name.

"The contract has already been signed to have the pool put in at your home," Vernon continued, "and we'll get that under way as soon as possible."

After another pause, he turned his focus to my mother. "Mrs. Alden, I know I'm goin' against Elvis's plans and wishes," he said. "We didn't get the mortgage paid, so I'll have my attorney Beecher Smith send the papers and payment book on your house back to you. I'm sorry, but at the moment of Elvis's death, my power of attorney was stripped away."

I was shocked. I could tell by the look on my mother's face that she was, too. She looked as if a bomb had been dropped.

"You are behind on two payments and you'll have to make those up," Vernon added flatly.

My mother sounded near tears. "But, Mr. Presley, there is no way I can keep up the house notes by myself and pay the mortgage company to catch up."

"Well, when we get the pool in, maybe, Mrs. Alden, you can sell it and get more money for it," Vernon said.

Vernon had just admitted that Elvis wanted the home paid for. As I looked at my mother sitting there, my heart broke a second time, this time for her.

I was still trying to process what was happening here when Joe appeared from the kitchen, said a quick hello, then told Vernon they needed to hurry, as there was more business to be done.

It hit me that I had been here for a few minutes, yet not once had any of us talked about how much we all missed Elvis and how terrible it felt to be at Graceland without him being there.

I felt like I'd been strapped onto some sort of conveyer belt and Joe was moving things along. If this was "taking care of business," it wasn't being taken care of in the right way this time.

In a state of twisted emotions—loss, confusion, anger—I stood up in a daze as my mother and I said our good-byes to Vernon and Joe, walked out to the car, and drove away from Graceland. The hopes, dreams, and plans Elvis had been sharing with me up until five nights ago had vanished. It was being made clear to me by many around him that I was on my own.

My mother and I were silent on the ride home from Graceland. I looked over at her from time to time, my eyes getting misty. Elvis had been talking about buying a new home for my family since January, and had promised my mother that he would help her. I couldn't believe that something he'd wanted to do so badly, something that we all thought had been taken care of—including Elvis—hadn't been done at all.

Looking at the predicament my mother was in now, I wanted to ask God why, on top of me losing Elvis, was this happening to her?

Since my father had been paid his equity in the house, she held the mortgage and he was paying his own rent on an apartment. This meant that making the house note payments as well as paying her other bills would be a terrible financial burden on my mother. At the same time, she didn't want to sell the house. We had to live somewhere.

The next day, my mother called the collections department to explain her situation. She wrote a letter and sent in a payment, concerned about foreclosure. A nice man who worked there told her if there was anything he could do, he'd be glad to try. He was kind enough to waive the late fee charges. The mortgage company was going to let her pay partial payments for a few months, until she caught up.

My depression deepened as the days slowly passed. I cried often and wouldn't leave the house. My mother slept with me some nights as our family continued trying to process the tragedy.

We received odd calls during this time. One lady told my mother she was Gladys Presley and would watch over Lisa and me. Going from one extreme to the other, I even got a death threat. My mother did her best to protect me, fielding calls or refusing to answer the phone altogether.

I began to heed Elvis's lessons and started meditating as I searched for answers to the many questions I had about my life. Why had Elvis and I met? What was the meaning of what I'd experienced with him? And why would I experience this amazing relationship, only to have it disappear almost as quickly as it had materialized?

The book written by some of Elvis's former bodyguards had been released earlier that summer, but I made a conscious decision not to read it. I was in serious mourning, and these were people I didn't know, talking about a time before I met Elvis. All I knew about the book was that it had wounded him, and that was enough reason not to touch it.

Ed Parker called to see how I was, which I deeply appreciated, and sometime later, George Klein took me out to lunch. During our meeting, George told me that, about three weeks before Elvis passed away, he had thanked George for introducing us.

This made me feel good. "Thank you," I said. I needed to hear that. It was a glimmer of light during a very dark time.

On August 26, I saw in our local paper that Vernon had moved Gladys Presley's body to the mausoleum to reside next to her son's. I knew Elvis had been very close to his mother while she was alive, so I was glad that the two of them were in the same resting place. I hoped it brought Vernon some measure of comfort and closure after Elvis's death, too.

On August 29, there was an attempt to steal Elvis's body from the mausoleum. I was saddened by the bold move. Who in the world would do such a horrible, insensitive thing? Shortly afterward, Vernon petitioned the Memphis Shelby County Board of Adjustment to have the bodies of both Elvis and his mother brought to Graceland for burial.

That same week, my mother received her payment cards back from Beecher Smith, along with a letter stating that, had Elvis lived, the balance on our home would have been paid.

CHAPTER 28

The days following Elvis's death blended into one another. The few times I left the house, I wore sunglasses and even tucked my hair into a turban to disguise my appearance. I could barely function.

Sitting in our den one morning, I heard a commotion outside. Large cranes had pulled up to our curb. *Oh my God, the pool!* Part of the gift Elvis had intended to give my family had just arrived. They began work and, by Labor Day, the job was complete.

Vernon called my home again, this time inviting me to his house on Dolan Street. He'd dropped such a bombshell on us last time, I was nervous about seeing him alone. I asked my mother to accompany me.

When we arrived, I could see Vernon was visibly disturbed. He took a seat in a chair while my mother and I sat on a couch and began talking about the morning Elvis died. In a pleading voice, he asked, "Ginger, do you remember seeing anyone upstairs who had no business being up there? Ginger, please try to remember."

I was stunned. Was he trying to imply that someone could have been involved in Elvis's death? This was the first time that thought had ever occurred to me. But I could only shake my head. "I was asleep, Mr. Presley," I replied.

"Did you hear anything?" he pressed.

"No," I said.

Vernon was quiet for a moment, then said, "If I only knew."

If he only knew what? I realized that I'd never had a chance to speak with him about his son's death. I was still struggling to understand the events myself, but I carefully recounted my memories of that horrible morning as best I could.

When I was finished, Vernon said he'd been told that David Stanley had rushed a friend off the property that day for some unknown reason. Vernon even mentioned something about a suspicious shot that could have been given to Elvis without the drug showing up in Elvis's bloodstream.

This sounded crazy to me. Who would do such a thing, and why? Was Vernon, in his own cloud of grief, grasping at straws? It was clear that he was a grieving father searching for answers and someone to blame.

I silently reflected on what I'd seen in the bathroom. I still felt Elvis's heart had just stopped.

"I didn't realize how important Elvis was until he died," Vernon was saying, shaking his head.

It was an odd statement for Vernon to make, but maybe, like me, he hadn't been prepared for the magnitude of the worldwide outpouring of support. In any case, it was obvious that Vernon was as tormented as I was about Elvis dying so suddenly. To both of us, it seemed inconceivable that Elvis could just be taken from us at such a young age when he still had so much to live for and was actively planning his future.

Vernon then changed the subject. "I don't know what to do about Charlie," he said. "I need Charlie like I need a bunch of weeds in my yard."

From that, I figured Charlie was still residing at Graceland. Vernon also went on to say that he had tried for a long time to get Elvis to fire Sonny and Red West, the bodyguards who'd written the negative book on Elvis.

Vernon said he'd told Elvis, "Can't you see they're hanging on for what they can get?"

In response, Elvis had replied, "Daddy, I see beyond that. You see their wants, I see their needs."

Vernon added, "I dropped it then."

Vernon obviously wanted to open up to us. My mother and I let him, but we could only listen. We had no answers for him.

As we left Vernon's house, the conversation left me slightly unsettled. I felt it was preposterous to think that someone had purposely done something to Elvis, but now I wondered, *Could someone have accidentally given Elvis something that would have contributed to his death?*

Whatever the answer to that question might be, I understood Vernon's desperation to explain the incomprehensible. At a time like this, all you could do sometimes is keep asking why.

In early September, the interview I had granted the tabloid came out. The cover of the issue featured a photo of Elvis in his casket.

I was horrified by this invasion of privacy and mortified that my story was associated with such a picture. *Who could have taken that photo?* As for the article, the word *sensationalism* came to mind, and that was an understatement. My story was not fully told, and there were quotes attributed to me that I did not say.

I was getting a crash lesson in the ways of the press. It would later come to light that a cousin of Elvis's had been paid to take the photo of Elvis in his casket. The threatened Linda Thompson interview was not in the issue but would appear shortly afterward in another.

Not long after that, I decided I wanted to visit the mausoleum again. Rosemary and I took a ride over to the cemetery. It was a desolate place now that all the flowers were gone from the lawn; only a single large wreath had been placed on the locked door.

Even so, as Rosemary and I stood there together, it made us feel inexplicably closer to Elvis. My own faith and our discussions of spiritual possibilities now flooded my thoughts. Whether out of need or real truth, I momentarily felt as if his spirit was all around us.

I began having strange dreams after Elvis died and would wake many times during the night. Each time I woke, I thought Elvis was still alive. Then reality would sink in and drag me down again.

In one dream, Elvis was wearing a turban. He and I were inside a hotel, walking down a long hall, while a party was going on. People were standing in doorways, laughing and partying. Then some of them began turning to look at us in surprise, as if asking, "Is Elvis alive?"

In another dream, I was with a much younger Elvis at a carnival. We were holding hands and running, looking in some shop windows.

I even dreamed that Elvis walked into his bedroom, naked, while I was sitting on the bed. It was after his autopsy and he was stitched down his stomach, legs, and arms. I was frightened as he sat beside me, but Elvis said, "Everything is going to be all right."

In an even more terrifying dream, Elvis was trapped in a large crowd. I struggled to get through to him, hoping he would recognize me, but I couldn't reach him.

And, each time I awoke, I missed him more.

The tragedy of Elvis's death brought my father back into the family circle. He saw what we were dealing with, and in his way wanted to help with all that was going on.

In late September, my father offered to drive us to Los Angeles to help us escape Memphis and the haunting events that had taken place at

Graceland, which hung over us like a dark cloud. Terry and my brother were unable to take off work, but my mom, dad, Rosemary, and I headed west in the Lincoln Continental Elvis had given them.

It felt good to be away. In Los Angeles, my family and I just drove around for a few days, seeing the sights. *Star Wars* had just been released, and as we passed a few theaters, I was amazed by the number of people standing in line to see a movie.

Ed Parker had continued to reach out to us and took me under his wing. I told him we were coming to L.A. and he invited us to his home. Another evening, he took us to dinner and a taping of *The Tonight Show*. Ed even managed to have one of the show's aides get us backstage before the show started.

As we stood in a hallway, the aide disappeared into a nearby room and then returned. Shortly, Johnny Carson suddenly stepped out of the room, dressed in a white T-shirt with tissue around his neck, obviously in the middle of having makeup applied. As if just looking to see who we were, he smiled, winked at us, and walked back inside. The aide later told us that he'd never seen Johnny do that while in the middle of getting ready.

We went to watch the show, which I really enjoyed, and for a moment it took my mind off things.

On our return trip to Memphis, we decided to stop in Palm Springs so my parents could see Elvis's home, since Rosemary and I still had such indelible memories of being there with him. We drove up Chino Canyon Drive to the house, pulled to the side of the road, and got out of the car to look at it for a few moments.

A security car slowly drove past us, then stopped. A guard got out. When I told him who I was, the guard kindly offered to open the locked gate in the front yard. I felt like Elvis was smiling down on us at that moment. What were the odds that a guard would show up at this exact time?

As the guard opened the gate, he told me and my family that he was sorry he didn't have the keys to the house. That would have been wonderful, but just being able to walk around the outside of the house, I felt happy to revisit a place I had shared with Elvis.

The guard walked with us to the pool in the backyard. It felt eerily dreamlike as I looked out over the landscape. Taking in the serene surroundings was relaxing, as it had been the first time I saw this place, but I felt sad, too, thinking about the changes Elvis had wanted us to make to this house, like the king and queen chairs in his screening room. Now we'd never have the fun of making a home together here or at Graceland. There was an awful finality to that realization.

I thanked the guard as we returned to our car. I knew I had to continue my life without Elvis and that he would want me to be happy. For his sake, as well as for my own, I was going to have to be strong. I needed to find a way to live with my heartache and leave the past behind.

On October 2, I was happy to hear that Vernon's petition had been granted. The bodies of Elvis and his mother were moved to Graceland and placed in the meditation garden. "Elvis has come home," I thought—a sentiment shared by many.

The following evening, CBS televised the *Elvis in Concert* special they'd been filming while Elvis and I were touring together. Elvis looked heavier on camera, as I'd sensed he would, but overall he had done a fine job. The special showcased his unique voice and it sounded as strong and rich as ever. As I watched the special, the excitement and concern I'd always felt during Elvis's shows, as I hoped everything would go well for him, came rushing back.

Elvis in Concert included film footage of Elvis introducing his father and me. Then, in the middle of Elvis singing the song "Hurt," an image of my face appeared on-screen beside Elvis. For a few moments, through the magic of editing, Elvis and I were connected again.

It was very emotional seeing our images linked in that way, but I was grateful knowing that our relationship had been acknowledged, and even documented, in such a public way.

I was learning that the death of someone you love is so final, and so terrible, that you try to grasp and hold on to the ghost of the person you lost. You hold on tighter and tighter to whatever you had together, because you don't want any of it to disappear. Yet, the harder you try to hold on, the more reality takes it away from you.

I didn't want to let that happen, and so, as the weeks went by, I began devoting my time to writing down my memories of Elvis. I tried to capture the way he sounded, right down to his exact words; the way he felt; the events we'd experienced together; and much of what he'd tried to teach or share with my family and me.

Things remained difficult for a long time, but I gradually began to heal, thanks to the loving support from family and friends. I also received numerous condolence letters from Elvis's fans. The letters brought me great comfort, and I answered every one I could. Even when the electricity went out in our home once, I got a flashlight and continued to answer those letters of sympathy. Knowing that so many cared about me gave me the strength I needed to get through the first terrible months without Elvis.

I turned twenty-one on November 13. Not long after that, Vernon decided to allow fans to visit the grave sites of Elvis and his mother. I'd read earlier that the divorce between Vernon and Dee Presley had been finalized; remembering Elvis once mentioning Dee, I hoped everything had gone smoothly for his father.

The day before the meditation garden was opened to the public, Vernon kindly called me at home, asking if I would like to visit Elvis's grave first. It meant a great deal to me that he did. I invited my mother to accompany me.

Driving through the gates of Graceland felt so strange. It was almost as if nothing had changed. For a moment, I could imagine I was just driving to Graceland to see Elvis, the way I had done almost daily for nine months.

My mother and I drove around back, parked, and began walking toward the meditation garden. I saw a large marble statue of Jesus standing off to the side; later, I learned it had been erected to mark Gladys Presley's former burial site.

Elvis and his mother had been buried near the fountain. Their resting places were covered with bronze and granite grave markers with inscriptions I would later learn Vernon had written. On the marker for Elvis, were the words:

> HE WAS A PRECIOUS GIFT FROM GOD
> WE CHERISHED AND LOVED DEARLY.
> HE HAD A GOD-GIVEN TALENT THAT HE SHARED
> WITH THE WORLD. AND WITHOUT A DOUBT,
> HE BECAME MOST WIDELY ACCLAIMED;
> CAPTURING THE HEARTS OF YOUNG AND OLD ALIKE.
> HE WAS ADMIRED NOT ONLY AS AN ENTERTAINER,
> BUT AS THE GREAT HUMANITARIAN THAT HE WAS;
> FOR HIS GENEROSITY, AND HIS KIND FEELINGS
> FOR HIS FELLOW MAN.
> HE REVOLUTIONIZED THE FIELD OF MUSIC AND
> RECEIVED ITS HIGHEST AWARDS.
> HE BECAME A LIVING LEGEND IN HIS OWN TIME,
> EARNING THE RESPECT AND LOVE OF MILLIONS.
> GOD SAW THAT HE NEEDED SOME REST AND

CALLED HIM HOME TO BE WITH HIM.
WE MISS YOU, SON AND DADDY. I THANK GOD
THAT HE GAVE US YOU AS OUR SON.

My mother and I stood at the grave for a while. I couldn't help but feel an energy, as if Elvis were near us.

It was hard to believe that just a little over a year ago, I had gone with my sisters to Graceland for the first time to meet Elvis. That night, my life was transformed, my world forever changed.

Over the past months, I had been trying to convince myself that God must have needed Elvis in heaven more than here on earth. Whether that was true or not, I was grateful to have been able to share a part of my life and love with Elvis, and to be loved by him. I had no idea what the future would hold for me. I could only take things one day at a time. However, now that I'd known and loved Elvis, my mind was open to new experiences. I would be forever grateful to him for that.

My mother had dealt with some health issues before. They now caught up with her again, forcing her to quit her job. With some severance pay she would be able to pay the bills for a little while, but I knew that wouldn't last long. Rosemary and Terry had gotten jobs and we all chipped in to help.

I was speaking with Ed Parker one day when he told me that he had once worked on some independent films in North Carolina. Ed mentioned a movie he was going to be in called *The Concert* about a country western singer. The producer was looking for a woman to play a part, and Ed asked if I was interested in acting.

This was soon for me to think about what steps I should take next after Elvis was gone, but Ed was probably thinking as I was: What should I do with my life now? I told Ed that I'd been in one commercial when I was younger, but had never really thought about acting. Before hanging up, I told him I just needed time to think about it.

My family and I were sitting at home one afternoon close to Christmas when our doorbell rang. Sandy Miller was standing on our doorstep.

I invited her inside, surprised but pleased to see that she had brought a gift for me from her and Vernon. I hadn't expected anything and apologized for having nothing for them.

"Thank you," I said as I opened the present.

Inside the wrapping paper lay a hat and a pair of gloves. Sandy didn't stay long, but I deeply appreciated her gesture.

When Christmas Day came, I tried not to think about it being the day Elvis and I had planned to get married. It hurt too much.

I made it through Christmas and New Year's with my family, hoping that the New Year would start on a more peaceful, joyful note. I was feeling a little stronger and finally getting out of the house a bit more.

The year did start on a better note. In January 1978, Ed called again, and said that the producer of the movie he was going to be in was still looking for a girl to be in his film. Acting would be a whole other world for me, but I was aware that I definitely needed to start earning a living, not only for myself, but also to help my mother. I didn't want to just return to the dress shop; in fact, I thought it might be better if I started a completely new life. The movie producer seemed like a nice man. He had two sons, one named Rhett and the other Elvis. I took this as a good sign: I had loved *Gone with the Wind*, and I certainly loved Elvis. The film's name had been changed to *Living Legend* and Roy Orbison would even be doing the soundtrack. As I understood the script, it would be a backstage view of life on the road with a country singer and some things that went on behind the scenes. I was even going to get to sing!

The script was still being written, so I read something else and got the part of a model/girlfriend to the country singer. The producer said he would also develop parts for my sisters. Filming was supposed to begin later in the year. Finally, I felt like my new life was beginning.

As sure as things in my life were looking up, however, I momentarily got pulled back down again. A short while after being back in Memphis, on February 18, I was handed a subpoena to appear for a session of a grand jury investigation into Elvis's doctor, George Nichopoulos. The grand jury had been convened to find out whether he had acted responsibly in caring for Elvis according to the codes and ethics of his profession. After all, why did a forty-two-year-old man die? The bottom line: Dr. Nichopoulos was being investigated for overprescribing medication to Elvis.

Being served the subpoena only reminded me that I'd had the same concerns about Elvis and his sleep packets. Doctors, nurses, and dentists had consistently cared for Elvis, and I was a twenty-year-old girl who'd experienced only normal interactions with the medical community, like checkups. I had looked up to the health professionals caring for Elvis as responsible healers and had no reason to think otherwise.

When I entered Elvis's amazing world, where he could have the best of everything, I had certainly thought that his doctors must be the best. They had to know what they were doing; this was Elvis they were caring for, after all. I had assumed he was receiving the best medical care money could buy.

Now that I'm older and somewhat wiser, I have many lingering questions about Elvis's medical treatments. However, at the time, Elvis and those around him had never raised any questions about his healthcare or impugned Dr. Nichopoulos's capabilities.

The grand jury was convened on the third floor at 211 Poplar Avenue. My mother accompanied me and the two of us saw the Graceland maid, Nancy Rooks, in the ladies' bathroom. We hugged each other and she told me Aunt Delta was afraid because she had given Elvis a third packet of medication the morning he died. I was so stunned, I didn't even know how to respond. This was a major thing if it were true! I was too focused on the grand jury investigation to start asking questions as I had never been in anything like this before. My mother and I went out the door, wondering, Had Nancy told this to anyone else? Did Vernon know? This was his sister. I was aware that right after Elvis's death, Vernon had stated in our local paper that his sister had just taken water and a paper up to Elvis that morning. Had she also brought a third packet up, while I was sleeping? If so, what was in it? Could this have contributed to Elvis's death?

Nobody asked me about this during the grand jury questioning. I would go on to hear rumors about this third packet over the years but I don't know whether it was ever determined that one was actually brought up to Elvis.

Dr. Nichopoulos was eventually acquitted on all counts, but many years later he would ultimately lose his license to practice medicine in the state of Tennessee.

February didn't turn out to be a very good month at all, as my mother was now backed into a financial corner. When she had agreed to her divorce, she didn't ask for any alimony from my father because Elvis told her that her mortgage was being paid off. With her funds now at a low point, she sought legal counsel and was told that she was entitled to the full payment of her mortgage, the gift Elvis had promised her and thought had been taken care of before he passed away. As difficult as it was for her emotionally, she decided to follow the advice of an attorney and file a lawsuit against the estate for the full payment of her mortgage in an attempt to keep her home. At one point, Elvis's stepbrother David Stanley offered to help, which was very appreciated, but my mother's attorney decided that he wasn't needed.

Some people incorrectly saw this as my mother attacking the estate, and thereby attacking Elvis. They were wrong. My mother—my entire family—loved Elvis dearly and would never do anything to besmirch his memory.

Of course, my mother's lawsuit rapidly became fodder for the tabloids and news shows. Around the same time, I also began seeing bits and pieces of interviews with some of the people who'd known Elvis saying that I was no longer welcome at Graceland. This was painful, as I knew none of them had a clue about the truth of what had happened regarding the lawsuit.

On March 24, I was astonished to get a call from Vernon Presley. As Terry handed me the phone, I was even more nervous speaking to him because of the lawsuit.

"Hello," I said.

It was immediately apparent that Vernon had also heard some of the negative comments in the press, because he said, "Ginger, you're always welcome at Graceland. Just let me know when you're coming and I'll mention it to the guard at the gates."

Vernon's words were extremely comforting. "Thank you, Mr. Presley," I said. Out of respect, I had never called him Vernon.

We didn't speak long and as I hung up, I believed this call came as a result of Vernon knowing what his son had wanted to do for my family, no matter how things turned out legally.

Life moves forward no matter what kind of emotional state you're in. I could feel myself slowly continuing to heal, and I was finally up to visiting Elvis's grave again. I called Vernon to arrange it, and on July 10, I took Rosemary with me after Graceland was closed to the public for the afternoon.

It was an overcast day. Rosemary and I walked down to the meditation garden and I placed a potted plant beside Elvis's grave. As the sun momentarily peeked through the clouds, Rosemary and I glanced at each other and smiled, remembering how Elvis had raised his hands to part the clouds in Palm Springs during our visit there.

Just then, I saw Vernon's truck pull up to the front of Graceland. A few minutes later he joined us. It was good to see him and I gave Vernon a hug.

He walked around with Rosemary and me, pointing out some improvements that had been made to the area by the graves. Before long, Rosemary and I prepared to say good-bye.

As he started to walk away, Vernon glanced toward the pastures and said, "Lisa's around here somewhere." It had been almost a year since I'd seen her. It would be nice to see her again.

Rosemary and I headed toward our car. In the distance I saw Lisa on her golf cart, watching us. I waved to her and yelled, "Hi, Lisa!"

Smiling, she called, "Hi!" back at me.

Rosemary shouted, "Just what are you doing?" in a teasing voice.

Lisa laughed, took off on her golf cart, looped back around, and stopped again, looking at us.

Rosemary yelled, "Come over here."

"I can't!" Lisa said.

In unison, Rosemary and I shouted, "Why not?"

Lisa replied, "I was told not to talk with anyone."

It was a strange moment. I understood the fear for Lisa's safety when she visited Graceland, but this was crazy. On the other hand, nobody was around to ask if we could approach her, and I didn't want to go banging on any doors looking for Vernon.

In the end, we called good-bye to Lisa.

A sad feeling came over me again. I wished I had gotten to know her better, I thought wistfully. Driving out the back way, I looked in my rearview mirror and saw Lisa as she raced along in the distance. She stopped the golf cart for a moment to watch us drive out the back gate.

I knew Elvis was watching over her. Lisa looked happy, and I was glad. I hoped life would be good to her and keep her that way.

This would be the last time I would ever go back to Graceland.

CHAPTER 29

My mother's lawsuit was turned on a legality known as promissory estoppel, and she lost because there was no written contract. We were disappointed, but my mother's lawyers said they would take it to the court of appeals.

When I signed a contract to do the film *Living Legend*, I did so naively without having it reviewed by an agent or entertainment attorney. There was no script approval clause, and no other protections for me that people usually think of as standard in the industry. I only knew the script was still in development.

I was excited to finally be doing something on my own. When the producer had mentioned developing parts for my sisters as well, they had thought it would be fun, and I was looking forward to having a chance to work with them on a project.

At one point, the screenwriter and producer visited my sisters and me in Memphis to get ideas for character development. With the script still in the works, I traveled to North Carolina and staying at the producer's studio complex during preproduction, I went into wardrobe and saw a jumpsuit similar to one that Elvis had worn.

My mouth went dry. What was this? A country singer wouldn't wear this outfit! I felt terrible and then suddenly understood: The singer in the movie was going to be loosely based on Elvis. Had I known originally, I would have declined the part.

I went back to my motel room, which was part of the studio complex, and cried. I had signed a contract; I felt locked in and didn't know what to do. I panicked, hoping that, at the very least, they wouldn't have the main character pass away in the movie.

When the script was completed, the main character would live, but oddly enough, Ed Parker wasn't in the film, nor would my sisters be written in. I wondered if Ed had become aware of the changes in the story and bowed out gracefully. If so, he hadn't thought to warn me. I met a great group of brothers, though, who were members of Roy Orbison's band, and we became friends.

In the end, the film certainly wasn't Elvis's life story, but there were too many similarities for me to ever feel comfortable with it. I never did ask Ed about it and eventually lost contact with him.

Was I taken advantage of? Yes, but I did feel that the producer was a nice man. Now, reflecting back on things, I think he just got caught up in his admiration for Elvis and never realized that, by placing me in a film with a character even remotely like Elvis, it could hurt me. We remained friendly, and I would go on to honor the obligation in my contract to do another film with him.

Unfortunately, not long after working on the film, a tabloid would come out saying that I was banned from Graceland with a negative interview from Elvis's uncle Vester, a man I never got to know.

I was completely stunned. I called Vernon Presley at home, telling him about the article. "Mr. Presley, am I banned from Graceland?" I asked. He instructed, "Ginger, don't believe anything unless you hear it from me," and then referring to his own brother's comments, he said, "Vester, that redneck, I told him not to do that." Once again, I found strength in Vernon's words.

Vernon Presley went into the hospital later in the year. I sent a card to wish him well and received a nice response from Sandy.

In 1979, I worked for a couple of months on my next film, *Lady Grey*, which called for me to play the role of a young girl who becomes a country singer. I was getting to sing again and learning not to be as frightened about it. Country music entertainer David Allen Coe was also cast. We filmed some concert scenes for the movie, and my friends from Roy Orbison's band played the roles of my backup band. An up-and-coming band named Alabama also performed in the movie.

Alabama went on to become a huge success in the country music field. My singing wasn't bad—one of my songs even became a *Billboard* pick of the week—but my acting clearly had a long way to go. I was learning the old-fashioned way, by simply jumping into the entertainment business with both feet and doing it.

In the spring of 1979, Vernon was hospitalized again. This time I sent flowers and received another nice reply from Sandy.

Then, on June 26, 1979, I was in the middle of driving to Florida with my friend Teri for a vacation, when we heard on the radio that Vernon Presley had passed away. I hadn't spoken to Vernon in a while. He was only sixty-three years old, but his weak heart had finally failed him. As saddened as I was by this news, I took comfort in knowing that at least now Elvis, his mother, and father could be together again.

The following year, I decided to go to New York to pursue a modeling career and make it on my own. I didn't want to use Elvis's name or contacts. New York was a vastly different world from Los Angeles, and from Memphis, too, and hardly anyone recognized my name. I was just one more young woman trying to make a start. No paparazzi followed me, and I was not in any of the papers.

I signed with the Ford Modeling Agency and, when my agent asked why I was getting such a late start, I finally told her about Elvis. I was quite successful in commercials and also did print bookings daily. I began taking vocal lessons in New York and landed a Canada Dry ginger ale spot, in which I got the opportunity to sing again.

In May of that same year, a grand jury indicted Dr. Nichopoulos for overprescribing drugs to many patients. That same year, the Tennessee Board of Medical Examiners found him guilty. Dr. Nichopoulos had his medical license suspended for three months and was on probation for three years.

Fifteen years later, Dr. Nichopoulos's license to practice medicine in the state of Tennessee would be permanently revoked by the state Board of Medical Examiners. I would always question whether he could have done more to help Elvis.

My mother's lawyer had taken her lawsuit to the court of appeals. The court decided she had foregone remedies available to her in her divorce, in reliance on a promise made by Elvis, and moved that the estate should be stopped from dishonoring Elvis's promise. My mother won that battle.

Ultimately, however, Elvis's estate then took it to the supreme trial court. The judgment was reversed when the court ruled that Elvis had not made, in its eyes, a "legal gift" of the money (a signed agreement with the mortgage holder). A verbal promise was not enough.

I was saddened that things hadn't gone my mother's way legally, but in my own life, I had come a long way physically, emotionally, and spiritually. I was strong and independent. I had begun a new career and was successful at it. I took acting classes at the Actor's Studio in New York, studying with Lee Strasberg and then with his wife, Anna. My work in commercials led to agents who suggested that I also audition for jobs in Los Angeles, so from 1986 to 1991 I shuttled between New York and L.A., doing print campaigns, commercials, and guest spots on shows like *Hollywood Beat* and *Life Goes On*. I also spent six months on the soap opera *Capitol*.

I met my husband in New York City. We married in 1991 and had our son three years later. I happily quit my career to devote myself to motherhood, and although it may be a cliché to say this, my son is one of my proudest achievements. He is a passionate athlete as well as a serious student, and biased as I might be, a wonderful young man. Throughout his childhood, I went to his soccer, baseball, and basketball games as an ardent supporter, fan, and proud mother. I didn't want anything to diminish the attention I could give him or my experience of fully sharing in his childhood. I have no regrets about this choice, as it brought me immense joy.

When my son went off to college, there was a huge space in my daily life, so I decided now was the time to embark on the journey of finally writing this memoir. I knew that it would take every ounce of my energy, focus, and ability.

I am not a writer, but I wanted to do this myself, have it be in my voice and not that of a story told to a ghostwriter. I had written down so many of my experiences after Elvis died to preserve my memory of him for myself. I had to mine the deep recesses of my memory and bring myself back to those nine months, to relive the unique experiences and the powerful emotions of that time. It was not easy and the process was sometimes very painful. But I gave great thought and time to the effort of being as accurate as possible in sharing what I experienced.

Writing this book was a long and arduous task. No one can explain love, but I had an amazing story to tell about one of history's most influential performers and a complex and wonderful man. Just as you can't capture lightning in a bottle and just as a photo is only a two-dimensional representation of a multidimensional moment, I knew it would be almost impossible to portray what it was like to be in love with, and loved by, Elvis Presley, for him and myself and for history. Whatever I wrote would surely fall short of the mark. Yet, I felt I owed it to him, to myself, and to his fans to try.

In writing this book, I have given it my very best effort, and in life that is all one can do. In this book, I surely did that for me and, with all humility, for Elvis, too, as a way of honoring him and the love we shared.